D1590050

RELIGION, LANGUAGE, AND NATIONALITY IN WALES

IN WALES

Historical essays

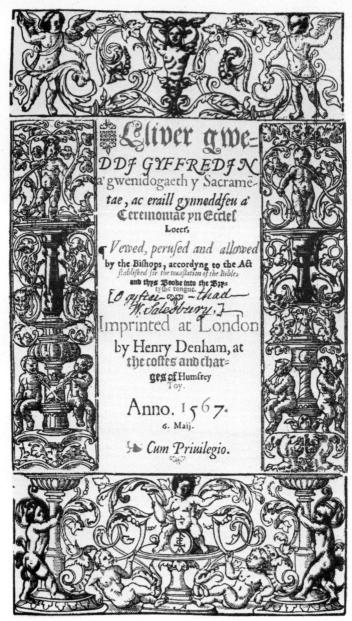

Frontispiece. Title-page of the First Welsh Book of Common Prayer,
1567 (*Roger Davies, Esq.*)

RELIGION, LANGUAGE, AND NATIONALITY IN WALES

Historical Essays

by

Glanmor Williams

Cardiff
University of Wales Press
1979

063044

110757

© Glanmor Williams, 1979

British Library Cataloguing in Publication Data

Williams, Glanmor
  Religion, language and nationality in Wales.
  1. Wales – Civilization – Collected works
  I. Title
  942.9'008   DA711.5

  ISBN 0–7083–0702–7

All rights reserved. No part of this book may be reproduced, stored in a retrieval system, or transmitted, in any form or by any means, electronic, mechanical, photocopying, recording or otherwise, without clearance from the University of Wales Press.

Printed by A. McLay & Co. Ltd., Cardiff

To
Ieuan and Maisie Gwynedd Jones,
kindest of friends

PREFACE

Though I have never embarked upon a systematic study of the interplay of religion, language, and nationality in Wales and among the Welsh in exile, I have long been fascinated by the subject. From time to time over the past ten or fifteen years I have written on a number of different aspects of the theme which have specially interested me. I have brought those pieces together within this volume, and I trust that its readers will think that I was justified in doing so. The first essay was specifically written for this volume to provide a general framework within which the others might be fitted. The remainder were written as *pièces d'occasion*, and all except one (no. III) were written for a non-specialist audience, most of them having been first delivered as public lectures. As a result they take in broader sweeps of history and make more venturesome generalizations than is usual in articles written for the historian's 'trade journals'; possibly they are none the worse for that. I should like to think that they might find a non-specialist readership while providing something of interest to more professional students of history as well.

Six of the essays (nos. II, III, V, VI, IX and X) have appeared in print before, and I am grateful to the following friends for so readily allowing me to reproduce them in this book: Dr. Michael Thompson of the Ancient Monuments Division (Wales) of the Department of the Environment (no. II), Professors H. Hearder and H. R. Loyn of University College, Cardiff (no. III), Dr. David Walker, University College of Swansea (no. V), Professor R. H. C. Davis, Birmingham University (no. VI), Professor David Pritchard, University College of Swansea (no. IX), and Messrs. Owen Edwards, Controller Wales of the BBC, and Haulfryn Williams, Hon. Sec. of the Cymmrodorion Society, (no. X). I should also like to thank Mrs. Patricia Moore, of the Glamorgan Archives Service, Mr. Peter Smith, Secretary of the RCHM (Wales), and Mr. Roger Davies, of the University College of Swansea, for helping me with the illustrations. The secretaries of the Department of History at the University College of Swansea, Mrs. P. M. Thomas, Mrs. E. Nicholas and Mrs. A. Frey, to whom I am always greatly indebted, were their customary cheerful and obliging selves in helping with illustrations, photocopying, and other chores. My friend, Mr. John Rhys, Director of the University of Wales Press, and his colleagues, took a keen personal interest in the book for which I am grateful. My wife's help and encouragement were, as they have been for more than thirty years, beyond praise.

Swansea,   Glanmor Williams

1 September 1977.

CONTENTS   Page No.

Preface   vii

List of Illustrations   xi

I.   Religion, Language, and Nationality in Wales   1

II.   Monuments of Conquest: Castle and Cloister   34

III.   Prophecy, Poetry, and Politics in Medieval and   71
       Tudor Wales

IV.   Religion and Education in Wales: an Historical   87
       Survey

V.   The Tradition of Saint David in Wales   109

VI.   Language, Literacy, and Nationality in Wales   127

VII.   The Gentry in Wales   148

VIII. The Welsh in Tudor England   171

IX.   Religion, Language, and the Circulating Schools   200

X.   A Prospect of Paradise?

       Wales and the United States, 1776–1914   217

Bibliographical Notes   237

Index   245

1*

LIST OF ILLUSTRATIONS

Frontispiece. Title-page of the First Welsh Book
of Common Prayer, 1567

I. Chepstow Castle

II. Dolbadarn Castle

III. Caernarfon Castle

IV. Raglan Castle

V. Strata Florida Abbey

VI. Tintern Abbey

VII. Saint David's Shrine, Saint David's Cathedral

VIII. Memorial Stone to Llywelyn ap Gruffydd ('The Last'),
Cilmeri near Builth

IX. Singleton Abbey, University College of Swansea

X. Poster Advertising Emigration to the U.S.A.

xi

I. Religion, Language, and Nationality in Wales

Our first glimmering of how the Welsh, or at least their immediate ancestors, saw themselves comes from a sixth-century author. The *De Excidio Britanniae* ('Concerning the Destruction of Britain') by Gildas is the only sixth-century literary source for the history of early Britain written by a native British author. It gives a most emphatic statement and, as it turned out, a lastingly influential one, of what the place of religion was, or should have been, in the early British people's sense of identity. Himself a Christian priest, intensely conscious of the duties of his calling, Gildas thought that their religious beliefs should have indisputably the highest claim on his countrymen's loyalty. Steeped in holy writ, he viewed past and present through the eyes of an Old Testament prophet. He saw the long record of Christian belief and learning among the Britons as having been a signal mark of God's favour, which chiefly distinguished them from their pagan and barbarian enemies among the Picts and Saxons. He recalled with gratitude their early conversion and their subsequent steadfastness in face of imperial persecution and, later, the spread of heretical beliefs. Like the ancient Hebrews, as long as the Britons had remained faithful to God's commands, they had prospered, but by the fifth and sixth centuries, the wickedness of rulers, people, even priests, had brought down upon them divine wrath. For their sins they had been punished by the victories of enemies who had overrun much of their former territory. Gildas's writings were to have an unusually long-lasting impact; partly because of the extreme scarcity of early written sources, partly because of his own colourful and declamatory scriptural style, and partly because for so many centuries after his time history was in the main the province of clerics, to whom his approach was especially congenial.

This Christian connection is also reflected in two other very early sources – the inscriptions on the stone monuments in Wales dating from the fifth to the tenth centuries, and some of the oldest parish placenames. The stone monuments commemorate the burial-place and the allegiance to Christianity of rulers of the little kingdoms which emerged in Britain after the end of Roman rule. One such ruler, Vortepor of Dyfed, was a contemporary of Gildas and is

actually named by the latter in his text. The Latin inscription on
Vortepor's gravestone describes him as 'Protector', a title of classical
origin, revealing his pride in being associated, however tenuously,
with Rome as well as with Christian belief. Not that he seems to have
been an ornament of the Christian religion, any more than some of
his fellow-rulers, if we accept Gildas's condemnation of him as being
'from top to bottom defiled by various murders and adulteries',
among other depravities.

The oldest Welsh parish-names commemorate those devoted
monk-missionaries, the Celtic saints, who were responsible for
converting large parts of Wales to Christianity in the fifth and sixth
centuries. They mark the *llannau* ('enclosures' or 'churches') of
Dewi, Dyfrig, Illtud, Cadog, Teilo, Beuno, Padarn and many
other more obscure native saints whose names still identify the
majority of the parishes of rural Wales. By no means all of the
dedications, even of the earliest saints, go back to their own period,
yet those placenames have been ubiquitous and ever-present reminders of the Welshness of the country's Christian origins for many
centuries, in some instances for as long as fourteen or fifteen hundred
years.

In his writings Gildas gives some inkling of other loyalties which
existed among the Britons of his time. Out of the gloom of the post-
Roman era some native heroes had emerged, notably Ambrosius
Aurelianus (later known to the Welsh as 'Emrys Wledig'). A worthy
representative of the integrity and courage associated with the best
Roman traditions, Gildas thought him, and one who had successfully
defied and defeated the pagan invaders. Even some of the sinful
'tyrants', the native kings so savagely and scripturally flayed by
Gildas, reveal themselves, despite his strictures, as men of force and
determination who enjoyed the fidelity of their subjects. There are
glimpses, as well, of the cultural milieu of these rulers, who were
praised, exhorted, and immortalized by bards, already heirs to
a well-established poetic tradition, it would appear. If, as seems
probable, some of Taliesin's poetry and the Gododdin of Aneirin
go back to the sixth century itself, then we have surviving examples of
the kind of verse addressed to Gildas's 'tyrants'. The poets were a
group who would, for centuries, be crucial to the preservation not
only of the glories of princely descent and achievement but also of the

language and the literature in which they were enshrined. They may have been still too near to the non-Christian Celtic world for the moralist Gildas; 'a rascally crew yelling forth, like Bacchanalian revellers, full of lies and foaming phlegm, so as to besmear everyone near them', was his sternly disapproving estimate of them.

Not until the early part of the ninth century do we have a group of sources which yield us a somewhat broader view of how the contemporary inhabitants of Wales saw themselves. They include the *Historia Brittonum* ('History of the Britons'), traditionally ascribed to the priest Nennius – though grave doubts have recently been cast on the authenticity of such an attribution; the chronicles known as the *Annales Cambriae* ('Annals of Wales'), a rather misleading title given them in the nineteenth century; and some early royal genealogies. The compilers of these documents were almost certainly clerics and were in the tradition of Gildas and Bede. They reemphasized the early connexion with Christianity, and had much to add concerning the contribution to early British Christianity of St. Germanus of Auxerre and St. Patrick. The British hero, Arthur, unknown to Gildas, or at least unmentioned by him, was claimed to have 'carried the image of Saint Mary, ever virgin, on his shoulders' and won his battles 'through the power of our Lord Jesus Christ and through the power of Saint Mary' *(Historia Brittonum)*. Though it was accepted that British defeats were the result of divine retribution for disobedience, the *Historia Brittonum* introduced a new and very influential notion that the downfall had also been partly brought about by treachery, by the base betrayal of his own people by Vortigern and the perfidy of the Saxons, in particular the savage massacre 'of the long knives'. It was an explanation more soothing to national pride that left an immensely long-lived imprint on the Welsh consciousness. (It has a modern parallel in the interpretation of the role of the gentry and the Act of Union (see pp. 160-3). Another source of consolation, which may well have been known at this time, though the *Historia Brittonum* makes no mention of it, was the prophetic theme of a future victory for the Britons over the Saxons, which was certainly known in Wales by the tenth century (see pp. 71-3).

In the age in which the *Historia Brittonum* was brought together, the Welsh had been cut off from any direct land communication with

other descendants of the Britons in the north and the south-west for
two centuries as the result of Anglo-Saxon victories. They were now
confined within boundaries defined by the sea and by Offa's Dyke,
itself a creation of the latter half of the eighth century; they spoke
Old Welsh, a language which had evolved from the earlier Bryth-
onic; and they may perhaps have already begun to refer to themselves as Cymry. Yet our sources leave us in no doubt that the
inhabitants of Wales conceived of themselves as part of a people
with a wider identity, the descendants of the ancient occupiers and
lawful possessors of the whole island of Britain. There survived among
them a particularly intimate interest in, and identification with,
the men of the North, the denizens of the old kingdoms of Strath-
clyde, Rheged, and Elfed. Central to it was the seductive myth of
the illustrious common origins of all the old Britons as the progeny
of the Trojan Brutus and his companions. A similar myth had been
current among the Franks since the seventh century, and both
peoples derived immense satisfaction from the conviction that they
were sprung from the self-same stock as the most famous race known
to world history, the Romans. Not content with that, they believed
that the line of descent could be pushed back as far as Japhet, son
of Noah. In this early society, and for a long time subsequently, as
long as power depended on a mechanism of hereditary succession,
the claim to noble origins – of a people as well as of individuals and
families – was an almost unmatchable source of pride.

If affinities such as those just discussed embraced people and places
wider than Wales there were other loyalties directed to much
narrower territorial units and institutions, and these were the ties
most likely to have come home closest to individuals. Such would
be the allegiance they owed to one or other of the numerous kingdoms and dynasties established in Britain following the eclipse of
Roman rule. Hence the interest in the royal genealogies, which
traced the king's descent back to the founder of the dynasty, real or
alleged, oftentimes an illustrious figure associated in some way with
Roman rule, like Magnus Maximus or Cunedda. The royal genealogy
was the king's charter of rights to territory and jurisdiction; the
whole domain ruled over by him expressed itself through the
medium of his kingship, and his dynastic history was the history
of his people. Their livelihood, their lives even, depended on him; he

was expected to defend and protect them, and they in turn, or at least the able-bodied freemen among them, had a duty to fight for him, against rival British rulers no less than against Anglo-Saxons. Surprisingly enough, these local Welsh dynasties were maintained with remarkable stability for many centuries, which led Mrs. Nora Chadwick and others to argue that early society in Wales was more peaceful than has often been thought. Nonetheless, all the early heroes were, above all else, winners of battles, and the ideals of kingship proclaimed in the surviving Welsh poetry (the earliest examples of it coming from North Britain) and in the oldest prose sagas are those of a heroic warrior age, in which resolution and courage in battle were the cardinal virtues. The entry in a Welsh chronicle on the death of Gruffydd ap Llywelyn as late as 1063, though expressed in the terse workaday prose of the chronicler, nevertheless sums up what a bard might have commemorated in more eloquent verse: 'Gruffydd ap Llywelyn, golden-torqued king of the Welsh and their defender, died after many plunderings and victorious battles against his foes, after many feasts and delights, and great gifts of gold and silver and costly raiment; he was sword and shield over the face of all Wales.' The two concepts of being affiliated to a people of ancient British, ultimately Trojan, stock and of belonging more nearly and more concretely to a *gwlad* ('region' or 'locality') and its ruling house would long persist in the minds of the free population. The idea of owing loyalty to a country thought of as Wales would come very slowly and relatively late.

These early kingdoms were sustained by a society in which family descent and the bonds of kindred were paramount. Relationships were regulated by a relatively highly-developed, flexible, and sophisticated body of law. Readily capable of expansion and adaptation to meet new circumstances, it was common to the whole country, apart from minor variations, and took little account of local boundaries. In the first half of the tenth century it seems to have been clarified and systematized as the result of the initiative of Hywel Dda (died *c.* 950), ruler of the greater part of Wales, according to a tradition which modern scholars still accept to be probably valid. It speaks volumes for the maturity and subtlety of the Welsh language and the Welsh lawyers that they were capable of giving such admirable expression to a body of law, at one and the same

time a 'mirror and a mould' (Goronwy Edwards) of the institutions
which formed so integral, distinctive, and unifying a feature of
Welsh life. True, no written recensions of the laws have survived
from this period, but later lawbooks in Latin and Welsh leave no
doubt that the laws were originally conceived, administered, and
preserved in the native tongue, even if they are not found in manuscripts going back earlier than the twelfth century.

From the end of the eleventh century onwards two developments
combine to give us a better understanding of the Welsh sense of
nationhood in the Middle Ages: the invasions of Wales by the
Normans; and the increased volume of sources available to us.
Dangerous as the attacks from the Old English kingdom and the
Viking marauders had been, the Normans put the Welsh under
greater pressure than ever before. For two hundred years the latter
were obliged as never previously to exert themselves in defence
of their own country, an obligation which reinforced their earlier
sense of being the appointed sentinels of their mountain strongholds.
Much of the low-lying south and east was quickly overrun, and in
the end, by 1283, the whole country had been obliged to succumb
to superior force (see pp. 34–45). At many points before then, the
threat to independent existence, even of complete annihilation,
had seemed painfully real. In 1114 the chronicler of *Brenhinedd y
Saesson* ('The Kings of the English'), identifying the Normans with
an older enemy, could record: 'And then the Saxons gathered a
host from the extreme point of Cornwall . . . to the extreme point
of Scotland . . . and they swore together that no living person would
be left in Wales'. The events of these two centuries undoubtedly put
a sharper edge on both the sense of Welsh identity and the hatred
of a common enemy. We need, however, to be wary of overstressing
either aspect, since it may well be the fuller sources open to us which,
in measure, create this impression. From the twelfth century a
growing corpus of material survives in the shape of chronicles, lawbooks, saints' lives, Welsh prose and poetry and, above all perhaps,
the work of two of the most gifted and influential writers of the
Middle Ages, Geoffrey of Monmouth and Gerald the Welshman.

One of the outstanding features of the era of conquest is the degree
of continuity preserved from the pre-Norman period. That awareness
of a wider British identity, already commented upon, was in many

ways reinvigorated, and by none more than Geoffrey of Monmouth. He did not write his *History of the Kings of Britain* for a Welsh audience; on the contrary, the inhabitants of Wales came out poorly as compared with their kinsmen, the Bretons, from whom Geoffrey himself sprang. But his work was nowhere more popular than among the Welsh, into whose language it was quickly translated and frequently copied, and among whom its main themes circulated widely and were rapturously received. Happily, we are not here called upon to examine the vexed, and possibly insoluble, question of Geoffrey's sources and the 'very ancient book written in the British language' from which he claimed to have obtained his material; but it is quite evident that he borrowed heavily at some points from Gildas and the *Historia Brittonum*. Thanks to his own endlessly resourceful and fertile imagination, however, he infused into the themes of the Trojan descent, the glorious pre-Roman British history, the matchless British heroes (Arthur pre-eminently, of course), and Saxon perfidy a detailed vividness and a thrilling drama, the like of which they had not remotely had before. Nor had the mystery of Merlin or the prophetic theme of the recovery of lost British glories ever been accorded such sensational prominence as in Geoffrey's work. He had given the descendants of the old Britons a vision of past and future, a history and a hope, that would sustain them for centuries. Inspiration from a heroic British past was also a constant theme in the verse of contemporary Welsh poets, though it was not so much the Galfridian heroes as the indomitable warriors of the epic sixth century in North Britain – Urien, Owain, Rhun and others like them – whom the bards held up as the models of valour and pride to be emulated. The poets, like Geoffrey, directed their hearers to horizons of the future by keeping evergreen the prophetic themes and adapting them to changing circumstances (see pp. 71–80).

In Gerald's unique and brilliantly perceptive sketch of the characteristics common to all the Welsh the traits upon which he seized show a striking similarity to those already familiar from an earlier age. Much impressed by the long and distinguished genealogies of the princes, from some of whom he was himself descended through his Welsh grandmother, he told how they were preserved by bards, 'written in the Welsh language, in their ancient and authentic books'. What was more unusual was the ardent interest in descent and lineage of even the common people. He recalled their Trojan origins and had much to say of their deepseated respect for the gift of prophecy among the *awenyddion* ('those inspired by the muse'), though he did not conceal his scepticism of that 'angelic voice' prophesying future Welsh victory, which Geoffrey described as conveying its awesome secret to Cadwaladr the Blessed, the last of the recognized native kings of Britain. The willingness of the people to defend their inheritance with courage and tenacity and their refusal to accept the rule of foreigners moved him to admiration, as did their delight in eloquence, poetry and music. In Gildasian vein he was not slow to criticize their inconstancy, their moral shortcomings, and their internecine feuds. Their essential characteristics, however, bore a strikingly close likeness to those ideals and *mores* of their predecessors already made familiar to us.

Two clerical authors like Geoffrey and Gerald could hardly fail to comment on attitudes to religion. Making considerable use of Gildas's evidence, Geoffrey gave a prominent place not only to the long-established themes of the early conversion of the British under King Lucius and their steadfastness under persecution but also to the depravity which had brought about their downfall. Gerald confessed himself to be the staunchest admirer of Gildas's view of religion and history, declaring in his preface that 'of all the British writers, Gildas alone appears to me ... worthy of imitation ... Gerald therefore follows Gildas, whom he wishes he could copy in his life and manners.' It comes as no surprise, consequently, to find Gerald attributing to the Welsh as their highest virtue 'the antiquity of their faith, their love of Christianity, and their devotion'.

But there were urgent preoccupations nearer in time and place for contemporary rulers and their subjects which thrust more local loyalties to the forefront. The princes of Gwynedd, Powys and Deheubarth were the main foci of Welsh adherence and resistance. It was not a question of the Welsh conceiving of themselves as a people fighting in unison against a common enemy; even such coalitions of princes as were achieved from time to time were short-lived and entered into for tactical advantage. The Welsh chronicles present a sad story in which Welsh princes were as often fighting against one another, with royal kinsman pitted against kinsman in an atmosphere of rivalry, intrigue, treachery and bloodthirstiness, as they were against outsiders. Nevertheless, within an unmistakably medieval context, paralleled in other European countries, of a kaleidoscope of jostlings for power and advantage between English kings, Marcher lords, and Welsh princelings, there emerged in thirteenth-century Gwynedd a concerted effort to achieve a wider unity and a more concentrated ruling authority. Supported by the resourcefulness of lawyers, the administrative talents of churchmen, and the propaganda of bards, the two Llywelyns came near to consolidating a feudal principality over a large area of Wales well beyond the original boundaries of Gwynedd (see pp. 42-4). Universal acceptance for it was far from being won in Wales; quite apart from the resentment it evoked on the part of king and baron, it encountered stubborn resistance amid the Welsh population itself. Allegiance to local *gwlad* and dynasty, and belief in the equal rights of sons of ruling houses, were not easily overcome; within the princely house of Gwynedd some of its cadet members were themselves among the worst enemies of the two Llywelyns.

The struggle within the political and military sphere had links with the parallel effort to maintain ecclesiastical independence. The autonomous heritage of the Church from Celtic times was subject to drastic encroachment by the king, barons, archbishop of Canterbury, and the new Latin-style monasteries (see pp. 39-41). In reaction there was an indignant Welsh backlash, which found expression in upholding the virtues and privileges of the Celtic Church and its saints, especially those of Saint David, his church, and his diocese (see pp. 111-6). Champions of Welsh aspirations were also found amid those Cistercian houses founded as the result of Cistercian activity in *pura Wallia* ('Welsh Wales'). The wide-ranging links of their order may have stimulated some Cistercians to take a more than local or regional perspective and encouraged them to engage in chronicling history, fostering learning, language and literature, and actively participating in politics and government. So, to a lesser extent, did some of the Welsh friars. A significant number of Welsh churchmen, secular and regular, were associated with the enterprises of the house of Gwynedd, and it was not surprising that immediately after his political settlement of 1284 Edward I should have wasted no time in journeying through Wales to assert his authority over the Church as well as the laity.

The defeat of 1282–3, to all outward appearances, might have been thought to constitute a cataclysmic setback for what had hitherto been the most virile and distinctive ingredients of the Welsh sense of identity. It was the final step in extinguishing the independent ruling dynasties, whose roots went right back to the fifth century, and the subordination of their territory to alien rule. The very existence of such rulers had, up until this point, been also the *raison d'être* of the bards, the recognized custodians of genealogy, language and culture. Native law, too, had been upheld by the princes, however much they had found it necessary to bend its provisions to serve their own interests. Non-Welsh rulers could be expected to introduce a greater admixture of their own law, with all which that might mean for the erosion of social as well as legal institutions. Contemporaries had good reason to lament bitterly the loss of their princes and to dread the destructive consequences of what might ensue. When Llywelyn the Last was killed, the *Brut y Tywysogyon* ('Chronicle of Princes') recorded that 'all Wales was cast to the ground'. The poet, Bleddyn Fardd, saw it as the unforeseen sequel to the loss of ancient Troy come to shatter the Welsh descendants of the Trojan race. His fellow-bard, Gruffydd ab yr Ynad Goch, in what became the best-known and most poignant elegy in the language, uttered the distraught and anguished cry of despair:

O God! that the sea might engulf the land,
Why are we left to long-drawn weariness?

In practice many of the long-standing lineaments of Welsh life proved to be more sturdily durable than might have been supposed. The key to their continuance was the fact that the conquerors' power to effect change was limited largely to the thin layer of the topmost levels of governance. Below these there survived a ruling class of Welshmen with prerogatives derived from pre-conquest sources of authority, whose practical influence remained mostly intact. Their belief in the inherited account of early British history and the rights which they deemed to spring from it remained undiminished; and they still clung secretly to dreams of future recovery. The author of the fourteenth-century *Life of Edward II* had no doubts about their attitude nor any sympathy for it:

The Welsh habit of revolt against the English is an old-standing madness . . . And this is the reason. The Welsh, formerly called Britons, were once noble crowned over the whole realm of England; but they were expelled by the Saxons and lost both the name and the kingdom. The fertile plains went to the Saxons; but the sterile and mountainous districts to the Welsh. But from the sayings of the prophet Merlin they still hope to recover England. Hence it is that the Welsh frequently rebel, hoping to give effect to the prophecy. (See also pp. 72–80).

Welsh families who could look back to age-old noble, or even princely, origins continued to cherish their birthright and found ways of accommodating their ambitions within the framework of royal or marcher overlordship. Without them neither king nor barons could have controlled their Welsh subjects. Men of this status may well have supported bards before, but after the conquest they quickly perceived the enhanced potential value to themselves of the bardic functions of history, genealogy, praise, and propaganda previously carried out for the benefit of the princes. These were now diverted to applaud the *uchelwyr* ('noblemen'), who took upon themselves the patronage of the bards. It paid off handsomely; the bardic order entered upon the two most prolific and illustrious centuries in its history. Poets found an additional source of support among some of the higher clergy and Cistercian abbots, drawn from the same social background as lay patrons. Not only did they foster literature and learning, they also maintained their fidelity to the native political tradition. On more than one occasion in the fourteenth and fifteenth centuries, Cistercian monks and secular clergy were taxed with being responsible for encouraging their compatriots' *levitas capitis* ('lightheadedness'), the unflattering phrase used by English officials to describe the prone-ness of the Welsh to assert native rights and to rebel against outside authority. The Welsh laws, though harder hit than Welsh literature, retained much of their vitality and their inherent capacity for development, in the Principality and in the Marches, despite growing competition from English law.

No matter what adjustments the Welsh might make to protect themselves as best they could, the fact remained that during the period after 1284 they lived in what has appropriately and justly been described as a 'colonial' situation. Under such a régime there was always the risk of an upheaval; a risk made all the greater by the acute disruption being caused by the malign effects of plagues, depopulation, prolonged outbreaks of warfare between England and her enemies, and serious economic decline. Rumblings of discontent and danger were heard on a number of occasions in the fourteenth century, the gravest being the threat from Owain Lawgoch ('Owain of the Red Hand'), a scion of the house of Gwynedd in service with the king of France. He declared himself to be the lawful prince of Wales and proclaimed his intention of returning to claim the inheritance rightfully his by virtue of his descent from the ancient ruling family, but was killed before he could do so. Not until the first years of the new century did the cauldron actually boil over in the rebellion of Owain Glyn Dŵr. The rebellion and its leader remain a subject too complex and enigmatic to be discussed in anything but broad outline; but some conclusions do emerge fairly clearly. Owain himself and, presumably, many of his followers were firm believers in the traditional British history and the prophecies associated with it. He based his claim to rule on his descent from the royal houses of North and South Wales and sought to revive the title and jurisdiction of a native prince of Wales. He also resuscitated the claims of St. David's to be the see of a metropolitan archbishop independent of Canterbury. He appealed to, and overwhelmingly relied upon, a hard core of support from a class of notabilities of patrician descent, closely tied to one another by kinship and marriage, though this did not preclude his winning followers from among men of lesser status. Important to him also was the favour he won in the eyes of poets, native churchmen, Cistercians, and Franciscans, all of whom might have been expected to sympathize with his resurrection of old aspirations, ecclesiastical and secular.

The attractiveness of Owain's personality and programme has struck deep into the mind and imagination of nineteenth- and twentieth-century historians and patriots. His policies could easily be interpreted as having about them an aura of enlightenment and modernity which fitted in uncannily well with the glowing hopes of Victorian liberals and present-day nationalists. The planks of his 'platform' – 'home rule' for Wales, its own parliamentary assembly, an autonomous church, independent universities, and a 'democratic' appeal to all ranks of Welshmen – read almost like a charter of the 'Young Wales' movement of the 1880s (pp. 27–9) and made him look like a man born preternaturally before his time. The greatest of Welsh historians, Sir John Lloyd, saw him as the 'father of modern Welsh nationalism', and a brilliant contemporary historian, Professor Gwyn A. Williams, considers that if 'there is doubt about Welsh consciousness, even Welsh nationalism, before the revolt, there can be none after it . . . Modern Wales, in short, really begins in 1410.'

While there can be no gainsaying the extraordinary magnetism of the man or the perennial fascination of his rebellion, both are best understood by reference to their own age and not a later one. Owain looked back rather than forward for his inspiration, which he drew from his predecessors' understanding of history, legitimism and destiny. He was aiming to revive an earlier concept of the principality within the context of early-fifteenth-century politics and society. If he won, he needed to match his own power-base against that of the Percy in the north and the Mortimer in the south and the east, and if he could include within it, as he once seemed confidently to hope, large stretches of English territory and a sizeable English population, he would not have regarded it as weaker or less justifiable for that reason. His main sinews of strength were his fellow-patricians not a popular following, and his designs for parliament, church and education were not those of an advanced liberal reformer but a down-to-earth practical politician of his own day and generation. As such he is a sufficiently attractive and extraordinary personality; he needs no investing with the anachronistic ideals of a later age. He came to grief not because he was born out of season but because the balance of power in his own era was too heavily loaded against him; what is surprising is not his ultimate failure but the length of time he was able to continue his resistance against overwhelming odds. Failure was followed by a disastrous aftermath of material devastation, stringent penal legislation by Parliament – 'more heathen than Christian' the Tudor historian, David Powel, called it – greatly intensified racial hatred between Welsh and English, and bitter feuds among the Welsh themselves. So melancholy an outcome led some chroniclers and a poet like Siôn Cent to revive an old theme that the latest downfall had been another divine punishment on the Welsh for their wickedness. But the majority of his country-men seem to have viewed Owain's efforts in a different light. For them he had injected a fresh vitality into Welsh patriotism. If the Hundred Years' War had breathed added life into the national awareness of both England and France, Owain's rebellion had done the same for Wales. What Bruce gave to the Scottish con-sciousness or Joan of Arc to the French, Owain had given to Wales. Perhaps it was not surprising that the English saw in him a sinister practitioner of the arts of black magic, just as Joan of Arc appeared to them to be a witch. Harsh as the consequences of his uprising had been for Wales, none of the poets reproached him for it. On the contrary, a number of them saw in him the very pattern of their hopes and desires. 'The poets in their eulogies of prospective leaders always saw with the inward eye the shape of Owain Glyn Dŵr' (E. D. Jones). The emotions which he had aroused did much to account for later Welsh support for Henry Tudor, whose victory some of the Welsh saw as Owain's belated triumph. The establish-ment of the Tudor dynasty held the satisfaction of vengeance, at least as much as of conciliation, for the Welsh.

The century in which the Tudors ruled proved to be for Wales, like many other European countries, a major turning-point. Four new currents flowed strongly in contemporary life. First, the monarchy in England, as elsewhere, if not 'new' was certainly rejuvenated. Ideologically, a much augmented emphasis was laid on the person of the monarch as the focus of unity, authority and loyalty, and as the main bulwark against fission and disorder, from within and without. The scope of its jurisdiction was enlarged at the centre and in the localities, and in the process many customary jurisdictions, laws, and franchises were extinguished. Second, its enlarged authority was not confined to secular life. Within the sphere of religion, the rule of the pope was rejected in exchange for royal supremacy, and Roman doctrine was replaced by moderate Protestant episcopalianism. Third, cultural life, intellectual com-munication, and propaganda were transformed by the spread of printing and the diffusion of Renaissance values. Last, but certainly not least in importance, the backdrop against which these dramas were played out was one of considerable economic growth accompanied by a rapid rise in population and a sharp inflation of prices. This combination of changes provoked major upheavals in more than one European country, and there were observers who predicted or expected serious trouble in Wales. In Henry VIII's reign the imperial ambassador, Eustace Chapuys, reported to his master concerning the Welsh: 'The king hath taken away their national laws, customs and privileges, which is the very thing they can endure least patiently.' Other observers, domestic and foreign, expressed similar opinions concerning the likelihood of uprisings in Wales during the century. Viewed in the light of earlier Welsh history, forecasts like those of Chapuys were not unjustified. In the past, enlarging the power of any English king had normally had the effect of putting the Welsh under much severer pressure, as had been evidenced in the reigns of the second and fourth of the Henrys or the first and third Edward. In addition such rulers had usually imposed alien officials or agents, who had taken advantage of their authority to feather their own nests. The result, as a rule, had been to provoke bitter, even desperate, Welsh resistance. Again, the Welsh attitude towards religion had tended to be conservative and back-ward-looking, with an emphasis on their early conversion and their steady loyalty to the faith in the teeth of persecution and heresy. Despite their profound attachment to the tradition of their own Celtic Church they were notably less xenophobic in their attitude towards the papacy than were the English, and, moreover, they had been far less exposed to those influences that might otherwise have prepared the way for Protestant change – the forces of anti-clericalism, Lollardy, humanism, or Lutheranism. Their culture, too, had always been tenacious of the past and slow to innovate. Their historical awareness looked back to a glorious, if mythical, past; their literature and littérateurs were tied closely to a society in which family lineage and the links of kindred had been paramount; their men-of-letters espoused ancient values and were wedded to oral means of communication. Finally, the economy and society of Wales had sustained an unusually large element of small freemen, immensely proud of their birth and status. The emergence of a greater degree of individualism had already exerted a considerable pull during the fourteenth and fifteenth centuries. Could the new economic forces be markedly intensified during the Tudor period without provoking intolerable disruption?

Throughout the Middle Ages the preservation of the Welsh identity had depended very largely on a precarious equilibrium, often severely upset but never completely overturned, between three factors: the settlement of the Welsh in mountainous and relatively remote country, in which thinly-dispersed pastoral communities were able to cling to their own ways despite constant external threats and, from time to time, brutal military incursions; the deep attachment among the free population to their own claims to a separate identity and their stubborn determination to maintain it; and the pressure from a larger, richer, and more powerful neighbouring state, bent on effective control if not complete assimilation. Even so, not one of these factors was incapable of being modified in the way in which it operated in practice. Wales was not so mountainous and remote as to be completely isolated; there had always been personal and trading contacts between Welsh and English; they had grown in frequency and importance in the fourteenth and fifteenth centuries and would become much closer in the sixteenth century (see pp. 171ff.). Furthermore, it was only when the Welsh ruling élite were *in extremis*, when it looked as if there were no way of maintaining their position except by open resistance, that they had been unwilling to arrive at some kind of *modus vivendi* with English kings and Marcher lords which had been more or less acceptable to both sides. On the eve of the Act of Union they had petitioned the king 'to be received and adopted into the same laws and privileges which your other subjects enjoy: neither shall it hinder us (we hope) that we have lived so long under our own'; and they added in suitably flattering and supplicatory tone, 'we have always attended an occasion to unite ourselves to the greater and better parts of the island'. English kings and overlords, on their side, though determined to exert as much authority as they could, had usually recognized the impracticability of exercising much control on the ground in Wales except through the employment of leading local families as their agents. Once more, in implementing far-reaching Tudor changes in administration, law, and justice it would be these practical considerations, rather than any preconceived notion of sympathetic national treatment for the Welsh, which would lead to the entrusting of local responsibility to Welsh gentry families.

Thus, despite the apparent dangers which some observers saw of a violent confrontation between the Tudors and their Welsh subjects, there was, in reality, a great deal of common ground to provide the basis for a close working agreement. Politically, in an age when so much more insistence was placed on fidelity to the monarch, it was a substantial advantage that Henry Tudor and his descendants could be claimed as Welsh and, doubtless, it was a source of gratification to many of the Welsh to see them triumph as the representatives of the restored *British* monarchy. But when it came down to brass tacks that was of far less significance than that the Tudor arrangements for Wales aligned and satisfied so agreeably the interests of both the Crown and the ruling class (see pp. 156–8). Economically and socially, too, leading Welsh families and individuals, whether at home in Wales or across Offa's Dyke, had good reason to be pleased with the outcome of the alliance between themselves and the Crown (see pp. 152–6, 174 ff.). Culturally, the effects were more mixed. On the one hand, the strong historical strand in the fabric of Welshness – the saga of Trojan origins, the exploits of the pre-Roman British kingdom, the grandeur of Arthur's achievement, and a revived and more glorious British monarchy – seemed to have found a new strength and validity. Small wonder that Welsh authors like Sir John Price, Arthur Kelton, Humphrey Llwyd, David Powel, John Dee, John Lewis, and others should have been among some of its most enthusiastic and ingenious defenders, though they found equally ardent supporters among English authors such as Leland, Drayton or Spenser. 'For Welsh readers it was the paramount charter of their country's greatness; Englishmen, who were often extremely unwilling to acknowledge the barbaric Saxons as their ancestors, saw in the heroes and conquests of the Brut an obvious source of their country's present pride and valiant heart,' (T. D. Kendrick). Welsh protagonists of the need to graft the new stems of Renaissance ideas into the old stock of Welsh literature had cause for modest satisfaction (see pp. 132–5). On the other hand, those who had always been the protectors of the indigenous culture – the bards – were becoming increasingly aware of a social and intellectual order that was less receptive of all that they had stood for (see pp. 83–5). But it was in their dealings with religion that the Tudors skated on thinnest ice and came nearest to sinking into potential disaster. In most European countries it was when other sources of friction were aggravated and inflamed by the most irreconcilable conflict of all, that of dogma, that the most fissile situation was created. Predictably, perhaps, it was opposition to religious change which induced the severest strains between the proverbially loyal Welsh and their Tudor sovereigns (see pp. 190–2). Fortunately for both parties, the insight and determination of a small group of Welsh humanists, allied to the sympathy for things Welsh of statesmen as strategically placed as William Cecil and Archbishop Parker, brought about a remarkable *volte-face* in the policies of the monarchy to allow the propagation of the Reformation amid the Welsh in their own language. Coupled with this was the most amazing reinterpretation of early Christian history in Britain. All the most revered precursors, Gildas, the *Historia Brittonum,* Geoffrey, Gerald, and others, in recalling the antiquity of the conversion of the British to Christianity had attributed it chiefly to the mission sent by Pope Eleutherius to King Lucius. Following Gildas, too, they had sternly censured the British for that falling from grace which had led to divine punishment and Saxon victory. Welsh Protestant reformers, however, gave pride of place to the 'scriptural' conversion said to have been undertaken by Joseph of Arimathea and heavily played down Eleutherius's contribution. What was more, they praised the 'scriptural' purity of the Celtic Church in contradistinction to the corruptions of the 'Roman' faith brought to the Anglo-Saxons, which the latter in due course forced the Britons to accept at the point of the sword. If anyone had sinned against the light it was the minions of the papacy, not the unfortunate Britons, who had been compelled to abandon the truth. These Welsh reformers had, in short, succeeded in wedding the Reformation to some of the basic and primordial instincts in the Welsh attitude towards language, history and patriotism (see pp. 119, 134).

That last sentence prompts a comparison between the sixteenth-century experience of the Welsh and that of the Irish. Whereas the Welsh became less rebellious than at any time in the Middle Ages the Irish became irrecoverably intransigent in their opposition to the English. In 1582 Lord Burghley, writing to Sir Henry Wallop in Ireland, made the somewhat startling but justified admission that the 'Flemings had not such cause to rebel against the oppression of the Spaniards' as the Irish against the English. In reply Wallop agreed that the main cause of the rebellion of the Irish was the 'great affection that they generally bear to the popish religion'. He went on to make a shrewd observation, with which most modern historians would agree, that the three reasons for Irish hostility were 'partly through the general mislike or disdain one nation hath to be governed by another; partly that we are contrary to them in religion; and lastly they seek to have the government among themselves'. Wallop's three points would, indeed, have largely covered the causes of rebellious opposition in a number of sixteenth-century countries; England itself in Mary I's reign would have been a good example. His first point would have had considerable relevance in fifteenth-century Wales, when there was no shortage of anti-English outbursts; but by Elizabeth's reign the Welsh were convinced, or at least had allowed themselves to be persuaded, that they were ruled by a Welsh dynasty which, out of its beneficence, had transformed earlier oppression into a situation where the loyal subjects of Wales were accepted as equals with those of England in law and status. Wallop's third point was closely related to his first. But Wales, unlike Ireland, had experienced no policy of suppression or of plantations installed by armed force; and the wisdom of handing over local government and justice to Welsh gentry, despite the vehement opposition to the original plan by Thomas Cromwell's agent in Wales, Rowland Lee, had been increasingly vindicated. Religion, Wallop's second point, had carried the greatest risks, as we have seen. Even in that respect the Welsh, if not fully won over, had at least not been fatally alienated. The seventeenth-century Welsh Puritan, Charles Edwards, could venture as far as to argue that, looking back to the time of the translation of the scriptures into Welsh, the 'Saxons who were once ravening beasts have since become our protecting shepherds'. There could scarcely have been a wider gap between such an outlook and the way in which Irish Roman Catholics viewed successive English régimes. The contrast highlights the almost universal assumption of contemporaries that religious beliefs held in common were the best recipe for possible harmony within an individual country and between peoples of different nationalities, and that, conversely, a clash of religious confessions, especially between Papists and Protestants, almost inevitably destroyed any hope of unity. Differences in religion were seen as being much more divisive than those of nationality, language, or historical tradition.

There remains a further question as difficult to answer as it is important to ask. How widely shared among the population of medieval and early modern Wales was the sense of identity we have been hitherto discussing? Was it confined to the dominant and articulate groups – the gentry, bards, lawyers, and clergy? And was it hazy and indeterminate among many of them? Had it seeped lower down the social scale, and if so, how far? These are questions which at present defy any precise answer and may well continue to do so in the future. A few straws there are in the wind, though, and however tentative may be the indications they give us, they are worth seizing upon. First, there is the generally accepted proposition that the population of medieval and early modern Wales included an unusually large, if not exactly quantifiable, proportion of freemen. In his account of the Welsh, Gerald implied that the freemen associated themselves wholeheartedly with their princes, and that in time of war or danger the 'husbandman rushes as eagerly from his plough as the courtier from his court'. He added that all of them, down even to the common people, 'esteemed noble birth and generous descent above all things', and all the signs seem to be that his description of the Welsh was intended to embrace all the free population. There is also that striking observation on the people at large made by Archbishop Peckham to Edward I (see p. 80), which further attested that the humbler freemen were imbued with the same kind of devotion to their own autonomous institutions as their leaders. We have already noted the widespread support among the free population for Owain Glyn Dŵr, who was also recorded as having won the allegiance of some Welsh labourers. There are similar comments from the sixteenth century of continuing popular interest in history, genealogy, poetry, and music among 'the multitude of all sorts' (see p. 82). When the first Welsh books came to be printed in the sixteenth century their authors seem to have hoped for a wider public than simply the gentry, clergy and lawyers; they appeared to be looking to freeholders, yeomen, and substantial heads of households to read their work. The most arresting evidence of all, perhaps, is drawn from the impact which the Welsh made on the English in the sixteenth and seventeenth centuries. The literature of that period portrays the Welsh as possessing just those attitudes which had typified them in the Middle Ages (see pp. 194–5), even if the mirror held up to them often has the effect of exaggerating and satirizing. Admittedly many, possibly most, of the Welsh which those English authors encountered may have been drawn from the higher social strata, but they do not ever seem to find it necessary to draw a distinction between gentleman and commoner, rich or poor, educated or uneducated. The traits depicted were those found in all and any Welshmen. All this is not to argue that every Welshman was a highly self-conscious patriot. There were some who were condemned out of hand as being only too ready to disavow their nationality (see p. 193); and there must have been many among poorer farmers and labourers who had little or no consciousness of it. Moreover, during the seventeenth century strong influences adverse to the maintenance of the earlier kind of consciousness were at work, and in Restoration Wales there were unmistakable symptoms of its lowered vitality and decline (see p. 135).

For all that, the eighteenth century witnessed an astonishing up-surge in the realms of education (pp. 202 ff.), religion (pp. 100–4) and culture (pp. 22 ff., 137 ff.), not to mention the impact of the agrarian revolution and the industrial revolution. Our particular concern at this point is with the cultural renaissance of the century. Dismal as some of the portents had been during the previous half-century, they did not prevent the unfolding of a novel and lively concern for history, antiquities, folk-music, language and literature. In the process some clearly-defined shifts of emphasis became apparent. The most serious casualty of the preceding century had been the virtual extinction of the bardic order, with all the loss which that entailed in view of its nurture of language, poetry and collective memory from time immemorial. Welsh poetry did not disappear along with the bardic order, but it was depressingly reduced in volume and even more in quality and professionalism. Verse in the free metres flourished on a modest scale, and the strict-metre poetry itself, of which the old bards had been the supreme masters, survived among small, scattered groups of gentry, clergymen, freeholders and craftsmen in places as far apart as the Isle of Anglesey and Upland Glamorgan. Far downhill as it had gone, that verse could be and was revived, but only at the cost of a serious break in continuity and deplorable ignorance of earlier poetic achievement.

Another damaging blow had been the partial anglicization of most of the county gentry. They continued, it is true, to find some heart-warming enjoyment in some facets of their Welsh past. Daniel Defoe applauded their hospitality and their eagerness to inform him about their country: 'they value themselves much on their antiquity, the ancient race of their houses, families, and the like, and above all, on their ancient heroes, their King Caractacus, Owen ap Tudor, Prince Llewellin, and the like noblemen and princes of British extraction.' They evinced some willingness to extend their patronage to antiquities, archaeology, and harp-music and folk-song, but their concern for language and literature had largely evaporated.

The initiative in the cultural revival came mainly from men of middling status. Some were drawn from the lesser gentry, like Edward Lhuyd, much the most gifted and far-seeing of them all (see pp. 137–8), or Rhys Jones, editor of *Gorchestion Beirdd Cymru* ('Masterpieces of the Welsh Bards', 1773), an important collection of works by major medieval poets. Others were professional men, like the highly influential Morris brothers – Lewis, an agent of the Crown in Wales, Richard, a clerk in the Navy Office in London, and William, a customs officer in Holyhead. The finest poet of the century, Goronwy Owen, and the zealous scholar, Moses Williams, and others were clergymen. Two of the most remarkable, Iolo Morganwg and William Owen-Pughe (see pp. 139–40), were craftsmen. Unable to participate in the cosmopolitan aristocratic culture of the century, they clung all the more affectionately to their mother-tongue and their native associations. Not that they were cut off from all other external intellectual influences; they were, indeed, in close touch with scholars, critics, and men-of-letters in London, and to lesser extent, in Dublin. For instance, one of the ablest among them, the poet and scholar, Evan Evans, at Bishop Thomas Percy's prompting, published his *Some Specimens of the Poetry of the Ancient Welsh Bards* (1764) in the year before Percy's own *Reliques* appeared. Evans, a serious and honest writer, proved to be the most effective critic of the imposture of the Scot, James Macpherson, whose claim to have discovered and translated the verse of the ancient Gaelic poet, Ossian, deceived so many of his contemporaries.

Most of this group of Welsh savants and littérateurs were powerfully attracted to the current intellectual and literary trends. The neo-classicism of the Augustans fired them with an urge to seek out examples of earlier Welsh poetry, now only dimly known, for classical models drawn from Welsh verse that might be worthy to set alongside the work of great Latin and Greek authors. In such poetry they found paradigms for their own verse in the strict metres. The folk-music associated with the old poetry was another source of delight and admiration. Edward Jones, himself a harpist, published two widely-influential works, *Musical and Poetical Relics of the Welsh Bards* (1784) and *The Bardic Museum of Primitive British Literature* (1802). By Edward Jones's time we have reached the flood-tide of Romantic influences, which filled so many of those associated with the cultural revival with a dizzy euphoria. Jones, like many others before and during his time, shared in the prevailing eighteenth-century mania for the Celts, and especially for their Druids, who loomed so large in the Romantic imagination as the primeval repositories of religion, wisdom, poetry and culture. Alas! all too often, 'dedication, learning self-delusion, mischief, and error characterized this phase of Welsh studies' (A. L. Owen) – and not only Welsh studies, either! (see also pp. 137–9).

As might have been anticipated, the eighteenth-century revival was characterized by a keen interest in the relationship of the Welsh to religion. Paradoxically enough, the most influential book on the subject of the history of religion in Wales was one which did not set out specifically to chronicle the fate of religion but purported to give a general account of early British history. Theophilus Evans's *Drych y Prif Oesoedd* is one of the major classics of Welsh prose; a classic on account of its robust and engaging style not its content! First published in 1716, with a second edition in 1740, its attractive style gave it wide currency in Wales and it was reprinted many times subsequently. Evans was a devoted Anglican clergyman and his work contained much that was conventional. He accepted much of Geoffrey of Monmouth, the 'treachery of the long knives', Arthur's dazzling feats, and the idea of the Celtic Church as a kind of a proto-Protestant Church. The striking novelty was that he gave the first popular account in Welsh of the association of the old Britons with the Celts, as the latter were portrayed by the Breton, Abbé Pezron (see pp. 137–8). In addition he stressed that Gomer, son of Japhet, was the forefather of the Celts, thus giving them an impeccable Old Testament origin even more impressive than the old Brutus legend. And if that were not enough, their Welsh language was shown to be more closely akin to the language of the Hebrew people than any other, which conferred upon it unrivalled linguistic purity and distinction. Such a claim furnished an irrefutable argument for preserving and teaching the language. The organizer *par excellence* of Welsh-language schools, Griffith Jones, asked his supporters with due solemnity to consider, 'May we not therefore justly fear, when we attempt to abolish a language . . . that we fight against the decrees of Heaven, and seek to undermine the disposals of divine providence?' (see also pp. 137, 209). Rev. Thomas Richards, writing in comparable vein in the preface to his *British or Welsh Dictionary* (1751), reasoned that 'as this language has continued for such a long series of ages past, so we have no reason to doubt but that the Divine Will is that it be preserved to the end of time, as we have the Word of God most elegantly and faithfully translated into it'.

These eighteenth-century authors were voicing anew an old theme that divine providence had a particular purpose in preserving the Welsh language and those who spoke it. Gerald of Wales as far back as the twelfth century had recorded the famous utterance of the old Welshman of Pencader, reputedly made to Henry II, that the Welsh could 'never be totally subdued through the wrath of man, unless the wrath of God shall concur'. 'Nor do I think', he went on, 'that any other nation than this of Wales, or any other language . . . shall in the day of severe examination before the Supreme Judge, answer for this corner of the earth.' At the end of the fourteenth century Walter Brut advanced the idea that the Welsh had a special destiny to overthrow Anti-Christ. Sixteenth-century authors like Arthur Kelton and Edward Kyffin, or again, John Lewis and Charles Edwards in the seventeenth century, had pressed the theme that in preserving the Welsh and their language God had some historic mission in store for them. Such earlier motifs

6 944

were powerfully reinforced in Theophilus Evans's mind by the close affinities which he saw between the old Celts and the chosen people of the Old Testament. It led him to give a renewed and more graphic emphasis to the parallel between the Welsh and the Hebrews as an elect people, who had flourished as long as they remained faithful to the divine commands but who had been subjected to condign punishment when they followed their own sinful and wayward paths. These concepts of the Welsh people and their language as the objects of special concern on the part of the Deity were to be more than ordinarily congenial in the intensely religious climate of the nineteenth century.

The enthusiasms generated were transmitted from the eighteenth century to the nineteenth by means of patriotic societies, eisteddfodau, and, most potently and effectively of all, by the rapid development of printed literature in Welsh (see pp. 141-3). The experience of a Galician peasant, which was published as late as 1941, that neither he nor many of his fellows had fully realized they were Poles until they started reading books and newspapers, could equally well have been true of many Welsh people at an earlier stage. Certainly the nineteenth century gave rise to an efflorescence of Welshness that was astonishingly prolific and varied in its expression. The result was a vastly-increased density in the texture of life in Victorian Wales and a bewildering confusion and complexity of sources, which make it difficult to do anything but offer a few broad generalizations concerning the development of national consciousness during the last century.

Religion, it hardly needs to be said, was a uniquely compelling force in Victorian Wales, where the proportion of active membership and attendance at Christian churches, especially among the poorer classes, was very appreciably higher than in England. Religious incentives were intimately involved with the use and preservation of the Welsh language, not only in Wales itself but also among communities of Welsh exiles in England, the U.S.A., and elsewhere. The safeguarding of the language was regarded by many of them as synonymous with upholding religion; to abandon the former was to run the risk of losing the latter (see pp. 227-8). The Welsh language was thought to have the added advantage of inoculating those who spoke it against the hazards of the god-

lessness, vanities, and political sedition that found expression in
the English language. Nonetheless, there was a large segment of
the middle-class Nonconformists that was ambivalent in its attitude
towards Welshness. David Rees of Llanelli, for instance, probably
the foremost radical Nonconformist editor of a Welsh-language
journal in early and mid-Victorian Wales, thought the language
was doomed to fairly near extinction and that the future lay with
English. He believed firmly that his fellow-Nonconformists, sad
though it might be for them to lose their mother tongue, must
accept its fate and be prepared to cherish their politico-religious
principles, which he held to be more important than language,
through the medium of English.

A second characteristic of nineteenth-century national consciousness was its democratization. It became widely current not only
among the petty bourgeoisie, among whom it was most in evidence
early in the nineteenth century, but also among many of the tenant-
farmers and among the swiftly-growing ranks of industrial workers.
Professor Ieuan Gwynedd Jones argues with force and imagination
that 'the Welsh language was a precious and singular possession of
the masses of workers at a time when the inhuman, dehumanizing
and brutalizing forces of industrialism were alienating them from
nature and from society'. Admittedly there were appreciable
changes in the course of the century. Among some of the more
successful middle classes, in this respect as well as in relation to
religion, serious doubts about the usefulness of championing Welsh
nationality came to the surface. The attitude was expressed neatly
enough in a cartoon in *The Welsh Punch*, where nationality was
depicted as an old lady dressed in traditional Welsh costume vainly
waving an umbrella in an attempt to hold back a railway engine,
which represented the onward rush of technology and commerce.
The allegiance of the workers, too, by the last two decades of the
century, was being wooed by strong and successful rivals to the older
religious and nationalist ideals (see pp. 145–6).

Perhaps the most telling consideration, however, is that it was
from about the middle of the century onwards that Welsh patriotism
turned into something recognizably like Welsh nationalism. The
late Professor R. T. Jenkins drew the distinction with his customary
percipience and lucidity, when he wrote,

Nationalism involves more . . . than an awareness of nationality, for it is a *deliberate assertion* thereof, and a *conscious direction of effort* towards some *external* manifestation which is conceived, rightly or wrongly, to be essential to the well-being of nationality. Granted these definitions it will be found that nationalism in Wales is a very modern thing, little older . . . than the second half of the nineteenth century.

Before the rapid build-up in the economic resources of the community, the spread of media for the dissemination of news, opinion and awareness on a country-wide basis, and, not least, immensely-improved ease of travel by railways, the creation of those 'external manifestations' mentioned by Professor Jenkins would hardly have been conceivable or feasible.

The first expression of the new spirit took the form of cultural nationalism, and manifested itself in developments like the founding of the Cambrian Archaeological Association (1846), a national anthem (composed in 1856), and the National Eisteddfod (dating effectively from 1858). It also spurred on an energetic campaign for better education, though this was mounted on utilitarian grounds at least as much as for nationalist reasons. Still, it led to the founding of Training Colleges for teachers at Bangor (1862) and Swansea (1849), University Colleges at Aberystwyth (1872), Cardiff (1883), Bangor (1883), and the University of Wales (1893). There was successful pressure for the teaching of Welsh as a school subject, the Welsh Intermediate Act of 1889 authorized the establishment of secondary schools, and the Central Welsh Board for Education was founded in 1896. In 1907 came the establishment of a National Library and a National Museum. Side by side with all this in the last quarter of the nineteenth century had blossomed a remarkable renaissance of Welsh learning and literature. It consisted, briefly, of the rediscovery of the earlier classics of Welsh literature, which had practically been lost sight of in the nineteenth century. The most important starting-point, if it is possible to single out an isolated event in this way, was the appointment of John Rhys as professor of Celtic at Oxford in 1877 and the publication in the same year of his *Lectures in Celtic Philology*, the first attempt at a systematic and scientific study of the Welsh language by a Welshman since the time of Edward Lhuyd. Rhys himself had no great sensitivity to literature, but he gathered round himself an outstandingly talented group of young students who made good that deficiency. It is not too much to say that they revolutionized the linguistic, literary, and historical standards of Wales.

Such political nationalism as there was, evoked many more doubts and divisions. It emerged out of the sweeping ascendancy which the Liberals enjoyed in Wales after 1868. Encouraged by the victories of nationalism on the Continent, still more by the parallels with Irish nationalism, and most of all by the growth of cultural nationalism in Wales itself, it culminated in the 'Young Wales' movement of the 1880s and 1890s. Its four-point manifesto marked the most far-reaching declaration of nationalist intentions ever enunciated in Wales: the maintenance of the identity of the Welsh nation; the safeguarding of the language, culture, and traditions of Wales; the advancement of its political, social, industrial, and educational interests; and home rule for Wales. Home rule was the key to it all, and for a short time there were euphoric expectations. Tom Ellis thought it would provide 'the highest embodiment of the national unity and the main instrument for fulfilling the national will and purpose', while Lloyd George believed that it could make Wales 'a nation that exiled oppression from its midst and . . . gave birth to a glorious period of freedom and justice and truth.'

Behind the ambitious facade there were paralysing differences of opinion. The most serious was that between the Liberals of the countryside and those of the industrial areas. In rural Wales, where the cleavage of interest was between a Welsh tenantry and an anglicized gentry, where the main issues were disestablishment and land reform, it might have been possible to equate political and economic conflict with nationality. But not in the industrial areas, where the interests of Welsh and non-Welsh industrialists and businessmen were manifestly the same; all the more so at a time when the industrial proletariat was more and more inclined to listen to the voices of trade unionism and socialism. And in the last resort it is doubtful whether any of the Liberal leaders were prepared to press the claims of home rule to the exclusion of all else. Home rule was essentially a matter of tactics, useful for bringing pressure to bear on the Liberal party, but something which was quickly dropped in face of a hostile Tory majority in the Commons. Long before 1914 home rule was dead, though the campaign for dis-establishment marched bravely on.

The half-century or so since the end of the First World War has been a time of dramatic and often painful metamorphoses for the kind of national consciousness which came to fruition in the nineteenth century. In the 1920s and '30s economic adversity cruelly dismantled much of the economic prosperity of industry and agriculture and the social optimism of the Victorian age. Some of the strongest bulwarks of the older sense of identity either decayed or were devastated, seemingly beyond repair. The romantic views of language and history which had exercised so seductive a sway over Welsh emotions were shattered. Gone were the Celts of the Old Testament and the Trojan forefathers, and even heroes like the matchless Arthur had either been exorcized or reduced to pale wraiths. The new history may have been sounder but it was much less exciting. Banished to the outer darkness, also, were the language of Gomer son of Japhet and the colourful Druidic myths (except the *Gorsedd* of the National Eisteddfod). The hold of organized religion, for centuries a linchpin of the language, the linguistic community, and the sense of a special relationship between the Welsh and the Deity, became much feebler. Not unrelated to the decline in religion was the marked falling-away in the activity of local patriotic and literary societies. But probably the most crucial change of all was the breaking-down, on an unprecedented scale, of the relative isolation of the population. It was this physical, linguistic, and cultural seclusion which, over the greater part of the history of the country, had insulated whole communities against extraneous influences and ensured the transmission of an individual way of life, largely intact, from one generation to another. Broad, dismembering wedges had been driven into it in the nineteenth century, but not to anything like the same extent as in the twentieth. On the one hand the physical movement of people into and out of the country and within it was made easier and more frequent; economic change and decline led to large-scale migration out of rural and older industrial communities alike, either to the more cosmopolitan coastal belts or out of Wales altogether; while into many previously strongly-Welsh areas moved a sizeable influx of non-Welsh people for employment, retirement, second homes, study, or tourism. On the other hand, the growth of modern means of communication enabled the media of mass entertainment and information, usually employing the English language, to penetrate to the remotest hamlets and dwellings. These trends have all contributed to bringing about a sharp drop in the numbers of those able to speak Welsh from about 54 per cent in 1891 to 20.8 per cent in the census of 1971. Along the route, adult monoglot Welsh speakers have virtually become an extinct race, though it is necessary always to remember that there are still a number of extensive, if thinly-populated, areas in the north and west where Welsh is still the normal medium of day-to-day communication on the part of the population.

Changes of the kind already noted have, of course, awakened an intensified response among many Welsh people. Much of it has been directed towards what may loosely be categorized as cultural activities: the unpolitical and unmilitaristic youth movement, *Urdd Gobaith Cymru*; the National Eisteddfod, all of whose proceedings have for many years been conducted completely in Welsh; and the movement for Welsh nursery, primary and secondary schools, which have spread widely and scored signal success.

The sharpest reaction has been that of political nationalism. In the nineteenth century, despite the explosive upsurge of Welshness, the dominant concepts of European nationalism made only a limited impact on Wales. Deriving originally from Herder, they conceived of a nation as a natural division of the human race endowed by God with its own unique character, which developed in a historic continuity of organic cultural growth. The nation and its culture were founded primarily on language, which was the fundamental distinguishing feature of nationality. This sacred patrimony of language, literature, custom, and culture must, as an inescapable duty, be preserved and transmitted pure and inviolable by those who shared in it. The most effective way of doing so was by means of an independent sovereign state based on the culture-community of the nation – the only valid and justifiable form of political authority. The implications of these ideas were accepted by a few individuals like Michael D. Jones and Emrys ap Iwan, but they were voices crying in the wilderness. Largely unheeded in their own time, they were greatly respected as neglected prophets by the nationalists who founded the Welsh Nationalist Party, the first completely independent Welsh political party, in 1925. Founded mainly by intellectuals and writers who viewed with horror and despair the decline of the Welsh language and the disintegration of the culture based on it, the party's overwhelming reason for demanding self-government for Wales was that only thus could the historic identity and the unique cultural inheritance be preserved. Its appeal was for many years confined to ministers of religion, teachers, writers, and other intellectuals, though its influence on cultural activities as a 'ginger group' was far greater than its relatively small membership would have suggested. Up to the outbreak of the Second World War it found no mass-following and achieved no success at the ballot-box.

Yet if the party was ever to win effective power it must find ways of appealing to an electorate, the large majority of whom were not Welsh-speaking and unlikely to respond *en masse* to a programme centring on the needs of Welsh language and culture. In the 1950s and '6os the party became less of a cultural pressure group and much more recognizably a political party, with a clearly-defined social and economic platform as well as its cultural objectives. Yet it may be doubted whether it was the party's programme and its youthful enthusiasm which accounted for its success nearly as much as the run-down of old industries, the persistent economic malaise, the widespread disillusionment with all three major British political parties, and the general emergence of 'protest' groups and parties. Whatever the reasons, the party has undeniably achieved a considerable measure of electoral success: three members of parliament in 1974, a number of close-run by-elections in industrial constituencies, and some hundreds of local government representatives. Clearly, politics in Wales and elsewhere in the British Isles have become more volatile and unpredictable; but party leaders' conviction that Plaid Cymru is now poised to become the majority party in Wales, as the Liberals were in the last century and Labour was earlier in this, seems to be based more on hope than realism. It is still too early to tell with any certainty in what direction the future for the party lies.

Plaid Cymru's own more broadly-based political programme and its efforts to win over a large section of the non-Welsh electorate have created a certain amount of strain and tension within the nationalist movement. Those who hold that it is the claims of nationality which chiefly validate political activity and that language is the decisive ingredient and distinguishing token of nationality must always be fearful of the risk that in an effort to win mass support, the language issues will be demoted from the position of primacy they ought to enjoy. The fabian tactics of a protracted political campaign may come to be seen as too dilatory to do much to arrest the disintegration of a language. Dilemmas of this kind gave the strongest impetus and urgency to the Welsh language movement of the 1960s and '70s, the adherents of which contended that the most critical issue was the fate of the language, to which the attainment of political aims must take second place. Following a remarkable broadcast of 1962 by Mr. Saunders Lewis on the fate of the Welsh language, in which he argued that the safeguarding of Welsh must take clear priority over any campaign for self-government, the Welsh Language Society was formed. It concentrated its protest, agitation, and propaganda exclusively on such linguistic issues as the increased use of Welsh in local government, education, broadcasting, roadsigns, official forms, etc. – sometimes to the embarrassment of Plaid Cymru. The avowed object of the movement was to make it possible for Welsh speakers to live their lives wholly in Welsh. Recognizing that such an objective could hardly be attainable outside *Y Fro Gymraeg* ('The Welsh heartland'), i.e. those parts of north and west Wales where Welsh remains the language of the majority, the most ardent spirits of the movement appear to have been coming more and more to the point of view that a 'Quebecstyle' autonomy, giving Welsh unquestioned supremacy in official and public usage within *Y Fro Gymraeg*, is the target at which to aim. An unprecedented crisis, it is asserted, requires unprecedented solutions. It is, as yet, too soon to be able to tell how likely they are to be adopted. But measures along those lines would seem to involve the extreme and unheard-of step of dividing Wales into two parts that might drift farther apart in mutual incomprehension. Language could be nearly as divisive in the twentieth century as religion was in the sixteenth.

Yet it need not be, if genuine attempts were made by Welshspeakers and non-Welsh speakers to understand each other's aspirations and to remove each other's fears. There are elements on both sides who are in danger of becoming a prey to their own fantasies. On the one side are those who conjure up a gigantic state conspiracy hell-bent on committing the murder of the language. Opposed to them are those who detect what they believe to be a clique of extremist fanatics determined to impose themselves and their language on an unwilling majority. Neither linguistic group has the moral right to coerce the other, nor should it claim such a prerogative. What is called for from the non-Welsh-speaking majority, especially, is a positive act of imaginative sympathy to try to understand the near-desperation of the minority at the dire prospects for the language and the culture based on it. The Welsh-speaking minority need to recognize more readily than some of them always do that there are a great many of their countrymen who find deeply hurtful the suggestion that those who do not speak the Welsh language are to be regarded as being either not Welsh at all or at best second-class Welsh people. Language is not the only component in nationality and until recent times it has not been regarded as the all-important one. There are a number of nations in the world who manage to cohere happily enough despite linguistic differences between their members. There have been other factors besides language which have gone to the making of the sense of Welsh identity, as this brief survey has shown. They are shared by all the Welsh regardless of their language. They deserve to be more widely known and more fully appreciated. There is a strong case in the twentieth century for emphasizing what the Welsh have in common rather than the differences between them. They are too small a people to indulge in the masochistic luxury of self-inflicted wounds.

II. Monuments of Conquest: Castle and Cloister*

Historical survey

The early Welsh had an unhappy propensity for quarrelling violently among themselves. As Gerald of Wales, that astute commentator on their national characteristics, observed: 'From this cause continual fratricides take place . . . and whence arise murders, conflagrations and almost a total destruction of the country.' This was never more true of any period than of the century or so between 949 and 1066, when no fewer than 35 Welsh rulers are known to have met a violent death, four more were blinded, and another four imprisoned. Any measure of unity brought about by a powerful ruler like Hywel Dda ('the Good') who ruled *c*. 920–950, or Gruffydd ap Llywelyn (1039–63) was too fragile to outlive the reign in which it was achieved. The effects of Welsh feuds, aggravated by Anglo-Saxon interventions and Viking raids, kept the country politically feeble and divided. Wales's independence was maintained precariously alive only by its difficult terrain and by the relative ineffectuality of its neighbour, the Old English kingdom, which was strong enough to threaten but too weak to extinguish Welsh autonomy. Even so, the remarkably resolute campaign successfully mounted by Harold, son of Godwin, in 1063 pointed clearly to the potential danger of the military subjugation of Wales by the Old English kingdom.

The danger that had been latent before 1066 became actual once the Norman kingdom was capable of exploiting the potential of the Old English polity to the point of making itself the most powerful state in western Europe. It was unlikely to tolerate unmoved the existence along its western flank of a group of turbulent independent Welsh kinglets. Furthermore, the Conqueror and his companions, schooled by the stern necessities of life in their Norman duchy, were a closely-knit military élite, an aristocracy organized for war. They numbered in their ranks some of the most hardened and efficient exponents of frontier defence to be found anywhere in Europe. This fact of Norman life Wales soon learnt to its cost. As early as 1067 William I planted at Hereford one of his ablest lieutenants, William Fitzosbern. Fitzosbern, having rapidly established himself in the border castles of Wigmore, Clifford and Ewyas Harold, soon overran the Welsh-speaking area of Herefordshire known as Archenfield. He then penetrated into Wales proper and, between 1067 and 1071, had

---

*First published in *Ancient Monuments of Wales* (HMSO., 1973), pp. 58-99.

built a number of forts along the river-line of the Dore-Monnow-Wye, from Clifford in the north through Monmouth to Chepstow in the south. Before his death in 1071 he had pressed deeper into Wales to seize a great part of the country westward to the Usk. His exploits had already set the pattern for the future Norman conquest of much of southern and eastern Wales: piecemeal initiative by an ambitious and vigorous frontier lord; rapid military penetration followed by quick consolidation with castles at strategic points; and seizure of the political and legal rights of Welsh rulers as well as their land in order to create new and largely independent Norman lordships.

In Mid and North Wales the keys to Norman expansion were the palatine earldoms of Shrewsbury and Chester where, in 1071, Roger of Montgomery and Hugh of Avranches were respectively installed. Earl Roger and his brood of warlike sons, thrusting up the valley of the Severn, established a main base for the conquest of Mid Wales at Montgomery, to which they gave their name. By 1086 they were already perched in the hilly wilds of the Plynlimmon region ready to descend into south-west Wales as soon as the opportunity offered. Farther north, Earl Hugh of Chester entrusted the task of breaking into North Wales to his energetic kinsman and lieutenant, Robert of Rhuddlan, so called after the castle he had built by 1073 on the bank of the River Clwyd, whose marshy unreclaimed estuary at this time formed a major natural barrier protecting the heart of North Wales. Rhuddlan, as the lowest fording-place on the river, was to prove a key point in the six-century-long struggle (c. 700–1300) between Welsh and English along this northern border. Another hardly less crucial point was Degannwy on the Conwy estuary where, by 1075, Robert of Rhuddlan had set up a castle as his forward base. Robert's dramatic success had within a few years led William I to recognize him as his lieutenant of all North Wales (potential rather than actual), holding it directly of the Crown. Following Robert's death in 1088, Earl Hugh himself took up the task of conquest. He pushed on deep into the heart of Gwynedd, building a castle at Aberlleiniog in Anglesey and another at Caernarvon, a primitive fore-runner of the huge Edwardian fortress now standing there.

Meantime, down in south-west Wales, a native Welsh ruler, Rhys ap Tewdwr, was recognized by William I as a vassal, a kind of Welsh southern counterpart to Robert of Rhuddlan. This shrewd stroke by the Welshman was instrumental in keeping the Normans at arm's length for some years. But Rhys's death in 1093 shattered the dam that had hitherto stemmed the tide of Norman encroachment into the south and west. From all sides now, the Normans poured through in such a way as to suggest a pre-concerted plan, though it may in fact represent no more than the unleashing of a number of eager individual ventures. The Montgomery family, led by Roger's son, Arnulf, swept swiftly through Ceredigion as far south as Pembroke. Near Carmarthen William Fitzbaldwin, sheriff of Devon, was actively planting a lordship on the king's behalf. The de Braose family moved into Radnor, and Bernard of Neufmarché completed his conquest of Brycheiniog (Brecknock). Most significant and long-lasting in its effects was the rapid overrunning of Morgannwg (Glamorgan) by Robert Fitzhamon from his base in Gloucester. The net effect of all these incursions by the middle of William II's reign was to make it appear likely that the whole of Wales would fall easily into Norman hands.

Appearances proved deceptive, however. If Wales was a country of hill, moor and mountain not easily united, it was, by the same token, a land not lightly conquered. The speed and suddenness of this first phase of conquest acted like shock-therapy on the Welsh. They had not at first realized how dangerous an adversary the Norman was likely to be, and his initial victory over the hated Saxon had not been entirely unwelcome to them. They had even supposed they could with impunity invite him in as an ally in their own endless feuds and rivalries. Now, however, fully aroused to the swiftness and brutality of the Norman threat, they countered with furious uprisings aimed at ejecting the invaders. Between 1094 and 1098 there were onslaughts against the Normans in most parts of Wales. Led mainly by the ruling families of Powys and Gwynedd they achieved considerable success, particularly in the remoter and more rugged areas of the north and west. But when the waves of revolt finally subsided, the strongest rocks of Norman power in the south and east reappeared largely intact. The intruders were still in undismayed possession of all their key bases and could resume heavy pressure on the Welsh. Behind his frontier lords stood the formidable Henry I (1100–35), seen by the Welsh chronicler as 'the man with whom none may strive, save God Himself, who hath given him the dominion'.

This 'divinely-ordained' power was felt by much of Wales. In Pembroke, Carmarthen (thereafter always a royal lordship), Cardigan, Kidwelly, and Gower, Henry's friends and vassals, including a large colony of Flemings in south Pembrokeshire, were firmly installed. The Welsh rulers of Deheubarth and Powys were particularly conscious of his iron hand pressing tightly upon them.

By the first quarter of the twelfth century, indeed, all the essentials of the pattern and rhythm of the relationships between the Welsh and the Normans for the next 150 years were already in existence. Between the kingdom of England and the independent Welsh lands of the north and west lay the Norman lordships of the March (from French 'marche' – frontier) carved out by the restless initiative of a couple of generations of tough and venturesome Norman lords. The March swung in a rough arc south from Chester to Chepstow and thence west to Pembroke. At some points, between Hereford and Llandovery, it widened to as much as 50 miles across, and at others, between Cardiff and the northern limits of Brecon lordship, it was some 50 miles deep. Most of it had been won by the sword. Small groups of armoured Norman knights and men-at-arms, often taking advantage of local vendettas among the Welsh, had pushed determinedly in to seize the latter's territory. Once the intruders had gained a foothold, almost their first reaction had been to throw up castles, usually of motte-and-bailey construction with earthworks and wooden defences (see below, pp. 50–1). Primitive as these castles were by later standards they offered their occupants strongpoints from which they were not easily dislodged. The castles were invaluable in subduing and holding what had already been won and as a springboard for further expansion. Even in those rare instances when a Norman lord took possession by means other than conquest as, for instance, when Henry de Newburgh, Earl of Warwick, obtained his lordship of Gower from Henry I *c.* 1105 seemingly without having to fight for it, castles were quickly constructed.

As a means for undermining Welsh resistance the new Norman lords seized not only the lands of Welsh rulers but also the sovereign rights that went with them. These rights had in pre-Norman Wales been based on the Welsh territorial division known as the commote (Welsh 'cwmwd'), which was the unit of political, judicial and administrative authority. It now became the unit of incursion and conquest, when the old commote was in many instances turned into the new lordship. Within its boundaries the lord ruled like a little king, enjoying such prerogatives as holding his own courts with rights of life and death, levying taxes, minting coins, creating boroughs, and even making war. Each lordship had its own 'caput' or capital, where its chief castle was built. This served not merely as a stronghold and barracks but also as a home for the lord and his family and servants, a financial and administrative headquarters, a prison and a court of justice. To provide for the needs of such a castle it was usually necessary to create a borough. Its burgesses, at first drawn strictly from a non-Welsh population, were given a charter of privileges normally embodying exclusive trading rights and limited rights of justice and self-government. In this, as in other respects, William Fitzosbern was the pioneer. He conferred upon Hereford a charter based on that of his borough of Breteuil in Normandy; and this, in turn, served as a model for most of the boroughs of the March. Many of the oldest towns of South Wales – Chepstow, Abergavenny, Monmouth, Cardiff, Brecon, Neath, Swansea, Kidwelly, Haverfordwest and Pembroke, to name but a few – owe their origin to such a development. Similar steps had been taken in parts of North Wales. As early as 1086 Domesday Book recorded that Rhuddlan had its borough rights, based on those of Hereford, and that it also boasted a mint, some of whose silver coins still survive in national collections.

Each Marcher lordship had its own autonomous organization; but the general pattern in each was very similar. Many lordships were divided into two parts; the Englishry and the Welshry. The former normally covered the more favoured low-lying areas below the 600 ft or even the 400 ft contour. It was usually divided up into knight's fees to be held by the lord's vassals on condition of loyal service. These vassals, in turn, constructed lesser castles or fortified houses for their own security. In the Englishry, manorial farming, with its customary features of open fields and unfree labour service, was often introduced. The Englishry was also separately administered with its own officials and courts of justice in which an amalgam of Anglo-Norman law and custom normally prevailed. By contrast, in the upland areas lay the Welshry. Here the old Welsh laws and customs still continued, and so, too, did traditional Welsh agricultural and pastoral practices. The inhabitants came very largely under the authority of their own native ruling families and owed only a shadowy allegiance to the Norman overlord. Passionately devoted still to their own language, culture, and *mores*, they lived with their Norman overlords on terms not far short of an armed neutrality which not infrequently broke out into open hostility and insurrection.

Another instrument for undermining Welsh resistance, at first sight improbable enough for the purpose but one which the Normans used with marked effect, was the Church. The piety of the Norman ruling classes as evinced in their native duchy before 1066 was real enough of its kind, but carried within it a broad streak of character- istically down-to-earth practicality. It was expressed in two highly typical ways. The first took the form of a rough conventional devo- tion which aimed at vicariously appeasing the Deity for many a bloody deed and carnal transgression by means of lavish endow- ments to a number of abbeys in Normandy which had come under the influence of Cluny or some other reform movement. The second was the creation of a close-knit body of aristocrat-bishops intimately linked with and dependent upon the duke and his leading barons. Both methods were successfully transported across the Channel to England and Wales.

Having arrived in Wales, the Normans had neither understanding of the institutions of the Celtic Church they found there, nor any sympathy with them. They consequently wasted no time in applying to the Church those familiar methods which had worked so well in Normandy. In the process they broke up many of the old 'clasau' of Wales and, promptly laying hands on the patrimony of these ancient institutions, they transferred it to favoured abbeys in France or England. The trendsetter here again was Fitzosbern. It was he who created at Chepstow a daughter priory to the abbey at Cormeilles which he himself had founded. Other Norman lords quickly followed suit. Goldcliff Priory was affiliated to the Norman abbey of Bec, Abergavenny to St. Vincent of Le Mans, Monmouth to St. Florent of Saumur, Llangenydd to St. Taurin of Evreux, and Pembroke to St. Martin at Séez. Brecon Priory, on the other hand, was a daughter of Battle, Kidwelly of Sherborne, and Ewenni of St. Peter's, Glou- cester, an abbey which, together with Tewkesbury, was richly and freely endowed in Glamorgan. In addition to so handsomely patronising the Benedictine Order the Normans were also responsible for introducing three of the new reformed monastic Orders into Wales – those associated with Tiron, Savigny and Cîteaux. The Tironian Order founded the abbey of St. Dogmael's far away in Pembrokeshire some time before 1120. The Savignacs gained a foothold at Neath in South Wales in 1130 and at Basingwerk in the north in the same year. Even the Cistercians, the Order most intimately and readily associated with the life of Wales, first came to the country under the Norman aegis when they were established at Tintern in 1131 and Margam in 1147. It was the Normans, also, who encouraged the founding of communities of Augustinian canons in South Wales – at Llanthony in 1103, and later at Carmarthen (before 1143) and Haverfordwest (before 1200). But while individual lords were free to dispense their bounty to abbeys as they saw fit, control of the episcopate brought weightier forces into play. This was a sphere in which the King and the Archbishop of Canterbury were to have the leading voice. In 1107 Henry I and Anselm obliged the new Bishop of Llandaff to make the first profession of obedience by a Welsh bishop to the see of Canterbury. By the middle of the twelfth century bishops of all four Welsh dioceses had been induced to do the same. The degree of subordination to which bishops were subjected varied widely. Though all the bishops were obliged to recognize the spiritual authority of Canterbury, the measure of freedom from lay control they enjoyed was markedly different. The Bishop of St. David's was a Marcher lord in his own right; but the Bishop of Llandaff came very much under the thumb of the lord of Glamorgan, while the Bishop of Bangor was hardly better than the domestic chaplain of the prince of Gwynedd. However, in all the Welsh dioceses there now took place a thorough reorganization. For the first time the dioceses became territorially defined, and within the new diocesan boundaries other new territorial units – archdeaconries, rural deaneries, and parishes – were instituted. They provided the machinery for the introduction of the stricter canons of Roman discipline.

Admirably though these changes in the Church served the turn of the Normans, it would be wrong to think of them simply as expedients for political subjugation. The conquest had far-reaching consequences for good. The isolation of the pre-Conquest church in Wales carried with it the peril of stagnation as the price of autonomy.

Breaking down this isolation, the Normans threw the Church open to fresh and invigorating streams of reform flowing strongly from that fountainhead of early medieval religious inspiration, the reformed papacy. Moreover, churchmen of Welsh origin, themselves given new zeal and inspiration by ecclesiastical reform, proved to be no less eager to defend some of the peculiarly Welsh characteristics of the Church than to adopt the more stringent standards of a reinvigorated papacy.

So, over large areas of the territorial, political and ecclesiastical life of Wales, King and baronage had combined to impose their will. Yet the relationship between suzerain and vassals was an ambivalent one. Some of these lords held extensive territories on both sides of the Channel and enjoyed such far-reaching prerogatives as lords of the March as to make them almost rival potentates to the King. Dangers from them emerged at an early stage; the son of William Fitzosbern was deprived of his lands for sedition in 1075, and the Montgomery family were in deep disgrace in 1102. But, in the last resort, King and lords had each too much need of the other to abandon one another for long. The lords, without the backing of royal armies, would often have been in desperate straits from Welsh insurrections; and the King, for his part, could not risk a permanently unsettled or weakened western frontier. If the King had to allow his Marcher vassals unusual privileges to encourage them to hold down or hold off the Welsh, the lords in turn had to accept him as a powerful overlord, with unmistakable jurisdiction over them.

Meantime, both King and Marcher lords had to adjust their relationships with the Welsh rulers of the north and west. The latter, though frequently still bitterly divided among themselves, were always watchful of an opportunity to press their advantage against the Norman invaders. England's difficulty could be their opportunity. Thus these Welsh rulers could turn to good account such sources of English weakness as the anarchy of Stephen's reign (1135–54), or the conflict between Henry II and Becket (1162–70), or Richard I's preoccupation with the Crusades (1189–99). Nevertheless, during the long reign of Henry II (1154–89) some kind of unstable equilibrium was coming into being. The rulers of Wales recognized the King as overlord; in return they were conceded virtual autonomy within their own lands. This was effectively exploited by the ablest among them: Owain Gwynedd (1137–70) and the Lord Rhys of Deheubarth (c. 1155–97). Not the least of their achievements was that they learnt many lessons from their enemies. They had always been considerable masters of guerrilla warfare. Now they came to appreciate the importance of having castles of their own and of learning the tactics needed to reduce their enemies' strongholds. They also learned to win and use the support of the Church. Their scope for initiative in the control of the bishops and the hierarchy was limited; but in the patronage of religious Orders they could and did achieve much more success. The Benedictines they always rejected because they were too closely associated with the Normans. However, they were willing to encourage the Order of Augustinian canons to take over the former Celtic houses of Penmon, Bardsey and Beddgelert. The Cistercians found even more favour in Welsh eyes (see p. 9). In return, the White Monks became more closely associated than any other clerics with the political aspirations of the princes and with the literary and patriotic associations of Wales.

The full scope of this Welsh renaissance was not achieved until the thirteenth century. Although in Deheubarth and Powys by this time the ruling families were reduced to fragmented groups of ineffectual rivals, Gwynedd was the scene of a remarkable essay in statebuilding. This was the achievement of its two most gifted rulers: Llywelyn ab Iorwerth ('the Great', 1194–1240) and his grandson, Llywelyn ap Gruffydd ('the Last', 1247–82). Each contrived to exploit to his own benefit those conflicts in which the English Crown from time to time found itself embroiled with France, or the Church, or a disaffected baronage. Both princes successfully applied to Welsh conditions the statecraft and military science of the thirteenth century. They tried to adapt and modernize Welsh institutions to strengthen the authority of the prince of Gwynedd. His vague claim to supremacy over other Welsh rulers was turned into a successful assertion of his feudal overlordship. Customary Welsh law was modified to restrict the influence of the kindred and to give keener edge to the jurisdiction of the prince. The growing population was encouraged to adopt a more closely-defined and intensive pattern of agricultural settlement, early native boroughs were established at places like Pwllheli and Caernarvon, and trade was fostered. Such expedients made in turn for more effective control and taxation to finance ambitious political policies and the military backing needed for them. A number of fairly highly-developed castles capable of withstanding improved methods of siege warfare, such as those at Castell y Bere, Dolbadarn and Dolforwyn, were constructed. Favoured followers were given lands on conditions of military tenure, and from among them came some of the prince's most trusted lieutenants. Able servants were also drawn from among the religious Orders favourable to the princes and generously supported by them, chief among them the already-established Cistercians and the new Orders of friars, who spread widely in thirteenth-century Wales with warm princely encouragement. The high-water mark of these state-building policies was reached at the Treaty of Montgomery of 1267. Concluded between Henry III and Llywelyn ap Gruffydd, it accorded Llywelyn the title of Prince of Wales and recognized him as overlord of a large part of the country. This was as near to a position of legal independence as he could hope to come.

Llywelyn's newly-won authority lasted no longer than ten years. In acquiring it he had awakened the suspicion of the King of England, the alarm of Marcher lords, and the resentment of some of his own countrymen. His position was, at best, one that needed careful nursing; yet after the accession of Edward I in 1272, Llywelyn seemed almost to go out of his way to court the King's anger. For four years he seemed unable or unwilling to recognize how powerful was this most formidable of medieval English kings. He refused the homage and the money payments owing under the treaty and arranged to marry the daughter of Edward's former arch-enemy, Simon de Montfort. The considerations which may have impelled the Welsh prince to so rash a course – over-confidence, mis-reading the political omens, under-estimating his enemies' strength – remain uncertain. What is not open to question is the grave retribution his miscalculation provoked. By 1276 Edward I, in his public postures giving the impression of a suzerain exasperated beyond endurance but secretly not wholly displeased, perhaps, that his own unrelenting pressure had encouraged the recalcitrance of the Welsh prince, resolved to settle his account with Llywelyn. Edward, a warrior-king who was his own commander-in-chief, using Chester, Montgomery and Carmarthen as bases, during the winter of 1276–77 exerted pressure on Llywelyn's outlying possessions so as to pen him in Gwynedd. By midsummer 1277 he was ready to send a fleet to Anglesey to cut the Welsh off from their corn supply, while his main army moved along the narrow coastal strip. Flint and Rhuddlan marked the stages in the advance to Degannwy at the mouth of the Conwy. Meantime his army in South Wales was pressing up the Towy Valley into Cardigan. Llywelyn, confronted with vastly superior odds, had no choice but to negotiate from a position of weakness. Humiliation predictably followed; the Treaty of Aberconway (1277) stripped him of his feudal overlordship and most of his territory outside Gwynedd, though it left him with the now almost empty title of Prince of Wales.

The events of 1276–77 seem to have been for Llywelyn a traumatic experience which destroyed all his earlier illusions. He was now painfully anxious to fulfil all his commitments to Edward. Nor did Edward give him much choice. From the outset in 1276 the King seems to have been set on constructing a series of powerful castles at Flint, Rhuddlan, Aberystwyth and Builth which would confine the lion of Gwynedd within his ancestral mountain lair. Edward now firmly installed his own men at these new castles as well as in older-established bases like Degannwy, Carmarthen, Cardigan, and Carreg Cennen. These English officials ruled the country with a mailed fist and provoked a deal of discontent among the Welsh. Edward also comforted Llywelyn's Welsh enemies and kept him waiting for legal redress of his complaints. Yet Llywelyn himself refused to be provoked. It was his brother Dafydd, Edward's ally in 1277 ironically enough, who, in March 1282, raised the flag of Welsh revolt. But once it had been hoisted, all Llywelyn's instincts and experience drove him inexorably into joining the insurrection. This time it was a fight to the finish and as such was more bitter and protracted than had been the campaign of 1276–77. Edward's strategy was much the same as it had been earlier: all-round pressure in West Wales and the Marches, and in the north a sea-borne occupation of Anglesey to coincide with a coastal advance to the Conwy.

In November 1282 a premature crossing from Anglesey to the mainland brought a serious disaster for the English army; but Edward remained undeterred. Even before the news reached him in the next month of Llywelyn's death in mysterious circumstances near Builth in December 1282, Edward had determined to fight a winter campaign whatever the difficulties. His tenacity was rewarded. In January 1283 he captured Dolwyddelan Castle, focal point of Snowdonia's communications, and so opened the road to all parts of Gwynedd. Two other major Welsh strongpoints, Dolbadarn and Castell y Bere, were overcome, and Prince Dafydd was reduced to skulking the countryside like a hunted animal. By the summer he, too, was captured and executed. The odds had been too great; Gwynedd had been militarily crushed and its princes killed. With them died the political independence of Wales.

Edward had won more complete success over the Welsh on the field of battle than any previous English ruler had done, but he was too much the realist not to appreciate that Welsh princes had been beaten before, only to reappear or be replaced disconcertingly quickly. This time he intended that the defeat should be final. No Welsh successor to Llywelyn, direct or indirect, would be recognized in Gwynedd; this heartland of Welsh political independence and aspiration would be brought under direct royal rule. The transference of jurisdiction from Welsh to English royalty was symbolized within a few years (1301) by conferring the title and status of Prince of Wales upon the King's eldest son, a practice which has since been traditional in the British royal family. Even before that, from 1284 onwards, Edward had embarked upon a thorough-going process of subjugating newly-conquered north-west Wales; militarily, administratively, and legally. Militarily, royal strategy was based on the construction of a series of magnificent castles – notably at Caernarvon, Conwy, Beaumaris and Harlech (see pp. 57–9). The logistics of supplying the castle garrisons were ensured by creating for each castle its own adjacent borough, planted with officials, traders and craftsmen. To encourage English and foreign burgesses to come there Edward offered them a guarantee against loss and banned trade in the major commodities of Wales (oxen, cows, horses and other wares) from all places except the boroughs. As a further attraction the King in some instances built fine town walls to protect his burgesses. These walls, still so memorably part of the townscape at Conwy and Caernarvon, were themselves an extension of the castle's defences. They illustrate the interlocking roles of castle and borough in the task of safeguarding security, commerce and conquest. Yet at

Caernarvon, outside the walls, Edward allowed the old Welsh township to continue side by side with his new borough, a symbol, no doubt, of his intention that the conquered Welsh population should also come to recognize the value of his boroughs as convenient markets and ports.

The castles and boroughs also had an administrative and legal function. They were to be the centres of the new administration by which Edward intended to extend into North Wales English methods which had for a long time proved their worth to the Crown in its government of the royal lordships of Carmarthen and Cardigan in the south. Gwynedd was now divided into the three new shires of Anglesey, Caernarvon and Merioneth, and these were further subdivided into hundreds based on the former commotes. In the north-east the new county of Flint was carved out and attached to the county palatine of Chester. Within these shires Edward established the usual shire officers of sheriff and coroner, but at the lower levels of the commote he kept the customary Welsh officers known as the 'rhingyll' and 'rhaglaw'. The shires were grouped together for the purposes of finance and justice, with an exchequer and chancery at Caernarvon, and two similar institutions for the south-west at Carmarthen. Legally, Edward introduced many of the provisions of English criminal law and also a number of English judicial procedures.

The King's settlement of Wales was a characteristically autocratic, thorough and practical blue-print for subordination. Yet it was not by any means wholly unacceptable to all the Welsh. Some of them had been becoming restive under the increasing weight of Prince Llywelyn's authority and were able to accept without much embarrassment the exchange of an English master for a Welsh one. Some leading Welsh families were prepared to co-operate with the English authorities by holding office at the level of the commote. A favoured few even aspired to higher things like the office of sheriff of a county or constable of a castle. Many other Welshmen looked for fame, fortune and adventure by fighting in the English armies in their many battles against the Scots and the French. The skill and ferocity of Welsh archers were much in demand. They fought with distinction in battles like Falkirk (1298), or later with the Black Prince at Creçy (1346) and Poitiers (1356). Meanwhile, in Wales itself,

English law and customs of land-holding were slowly becoming more widely adopted. Together with the spread of trade and a money economy they were gradually breaking down both the subsistence pastoral economy of Wales and the social and legal institutions based on the kindred groups. However, Edward, a ruler accustomed to governing a multi-lingual empire, saw no reason to try to proscribe the Welsh language or to suppress the literary culture of Wales, which now moved into its golden era. In these respects it might have appeared as if a slow peaceful assimilation of Wales into the English state was unhurriedly maturing.

There were, nevertheless, other darker aspects of the Welsh scene. Even if Edward asserted his authority over the lords of the March more bluntly and masterfully than any of his predecessors, he still left Wales divided between the royal lands of the Principality and the feudal lordships of the March, with the latter remaining as autonomous, fragmented and turbulent as before. If the Welsh population of both areas were to become reconciled to the loss of their independence much would depend on the spirit in which the régime in both Principality and March was administered. All too often, unfortunately, the attitude of officialdom in both areas was self-interested and oppressive, being in all essentials that of a colonial regime. Moreover, the fourteenth and fifteenth centuries were almost bound to be a difficult and unsettled period anyway. This was an age of war, heavy taxation, plague, depopulation and depression, when there was always an incipient risk of rebellion. All the more so among a people only very partially willing to accept the idea of conquest and still cherishing prophecies, assiduously kept evergreen by the bards, of an ultimate victory for the Welsh nation, led by a prince of destiny, over the alien usurpers. Within ten years of Edward's conquest there had been serious rebellions led by Rhys ap Maredudd (1287) and Madog ap Llywelyn (1294). The surprising thing perhaps is that there was not more trouble in Wales; especially when England was heavily involved in war with France and Scotland, both of which from time to time recognized the possibility of exploiting for their own advantage Welsh hostility to the English. Such dangers were thrown into sharp relief in 1370–72. At this time Owain Lawgoch ('Owain of the Red Hand'), a descendant of the princes of Gwynedd who had taken service in the armies of the King of France, threatened to return to Wales to claim his inheritance with French help. Much more formidable was the rebellion (1400–15) of Owain Glyn Dŵr. Intensely imbued with a consciousness of being the deliverer foretold by the prophecies, he appealed to Scotland, Ireland and France for help in setting up an independent Welsh state. For a time he achieved remarkable success; he virtually extinguished English authority over a large part of Wales, captured great castles like Harlech and Aberystwyth and closely besieged others, like Caernarvon. But, for all the bright hopes it had kindled, his rebellion ended in failure and bequeathed a disastrous aftermath of physical destruction, economic malaise, and sapped morale. Wales had far from recovered from these ills when the civil wars broke out between the rival factions of Lancaster and York. Both sides drew a good deal of military strength from the disturbed and warlike areas of Wales and the March. In the course of these internecine struggles some of the greater castles of Wales were strongpoints of considerable strategic importance and changed hands more than once.

In 1485, after a generation or more of inconclusive faction, feud and civil war, a long-suffering population might have been forgiven for seeing in the victory of Henry VII at Bosworth only the fleeting success of yet another transient and short-lived occupant of the English throne. As it turned out, however, his accession marked the end of the wars and the inauguration of the most successful ruling house in British history. The dynasty which Henry Tudor founded was one for which the Welsh had a particular place in their affections. In the accession of Henry VII, scion of an Anglesey stock claiming descent from the old Welsh ruling families and himself born in Pembroke Castle, many of his Welsh compatriots saw the triumphant vindication of all the ancient prophecies which had foretold the eventual restoration to a member of the ancient royal house of Wales a place of rightful rule over the whole island of Britain. As the prophesied 'man of destiny', Henry drew to himself the hearts of Welshmen 'as lodestone doth the iron', in the words of George Owen, the most famous of Welsh antiquaries of the Tudor period. This mystique of Welsh loyalty and affection was transmitted from Henry to his descendants. Nor did this more co-operative Welsh attitude towards the Crown of England go wholly unrequited. Henry

VII offered something of a 'new deal' to some of his Welsh subjects by entrusting leading figures among them with some of the highest offices in Wales and encouraging others to migrate to England in search of wealth and position.

His son Henry VIII went further. By the parliamentary 'Acts of Union' of 1536 and 1542–43 he merged the whole of Wales into England. For the first time he gave Wales a uniform system of law, justice and administration based on existing institutions in England. The March was at last finally swept away, and the whole of Wales was shired and given all the paraphernalia and personnel of shire administration, including assize courts and quarter sessions, parliamentary representatives, sheriffs and justices of the peace. The Welsh language was not proscribed but was relegated to an inferior position, and English was made the language of law, administration and record. The strong rule of the Tudors exercised through the Privy Council, Council of the Marches and the organs of local government brought a greater measure of peace, order and stability. There was still a considerable amount of sporadic violence and disorder but markedly less than there had been in the fifteenth century. Parallel with the improved state of public security had gone the growth of population and the economic recovery common to many parts of western Europe. Estates were expanded and consolidated, agricultural methods were improved, industrial resources began to be tentatively exploited, and commerce revived. These stabler and more prosperous conditions were reflected in the decay of medieval castles. They had outlived their purpose and many were allowed to fall into ruin. Others, like Raglan, Oxwich or Laugharne, were remodelled and turned into more peaceful and comfortable country houses, not unlike the new town and country mansions now being built for a quieter, wealthier and more law-abiding age. The day of the castles was over except for a short interlude during the civil wars of the seventeenth century (1642–46 and 1648–50) when they were once again put to warlike uses. For a few brief storm-laden years castles like Raglan, Montgomery and Pembroke once more became vital strongholds bitterly fought over.

The decline of the castles was slower and less dramatic than the end of another highly characteristic medieval institution, the monastery. Monasteries in England and Wales were swept away as the result of

Henry VIII's repudiation of papal authority in 1534. When once Henry and his chief adviser, Thomas Cromwell, had made the king Supreme Head of the English Church, almost their very next step was to transfer a large part of its property to the royal possession. Following a survey in 1535 of the material endowments and spiritual condition of the religious houses, an Act of 1536 dissolved all of them with a clear annual income of less than £200. All the Welsh monasteries except three disappeared under this Act. For those which survived – Whitland, Neath and Strata Florida – the respite was short-lived; they, too, had gone by 1539. In Wales the end of the medieval phase of government and law coincided remarkably closely with the end of the Middle Ages in religion.

Castles

MOTTE-AND-BAILEY CASTLES

Castles are the characteristic product of the feudal Europe that emerged in the ninth and tenth centuries AD amid the disintegration of the empire founded by Charlemagne in 800. Scholars are now divided in their views whether or not there were castles of some kind in Britain before the Norman Conquest, but it is quite certain that if the Normans did not actually introduce the castle into England and subsequently into Wales they made much more effective use of it than anyone else had previously done and turned it into the indispensable instrument of their conquest and consolidation. Some of the earliest and strongest of these castles were placed at the main centres of Norman power along the border with Wales: Chester, Shrewsbury, Hereford, Gloucester, and Bristol. From these bases Norman magnates pressed forward into Wales, consolidating their position with castles, which were not massive and elaborate stone buildings but earth-and-timber structures known as motte-and-bailey castles. These consisted of two parts. The first, the motte, was the stronghold and consisted of a mound usually some 20 to 30 ft in height (either a natural hillock scarped and shaped, or an artificially constructed mound of heaped earth) surmounted by wooden buildings within a palisade and defended all round by a moat, wet or dry, with its counterscarp. At Cardiff the original motte, now surmounted by a stone tower, can still be clearly seen, while at Rhuddlan the Norman motte, now known as '*The Twthill*', rises plainly visible a short distance to the south-east of the Edwardian castle. Adjoining the motte were one or more baileys. The bailey was an oval or right-angled enclosure with one gateway at the furthest point away from the motte. It, too, was defended by ditch and rampart and by a stockade which ran up the side of the motte to join the palisade at the top. Access from bailey to motte was gained only by means of a sloping bridge across the ditch between the two. The whole area might encompass about 1½ acres, increasing in some instances to a maximum of about 3 acres. This is the kind of castle which can be seen so graphically illustrated in the Bayeux Tapestry, where there are scenes of men at work constructing such fortifications.

In addition to the motte-and-bailey castle proper there is a variation of this type of defence-work usually described as a ring-motte. Where this occurs the circular area on which the wooden keep was built was not raised above the general level of its surroundings but was protected by steep banks of earth dug from the surrounding ditch.

Some motte-and-bailey castles were later rebuilt in stone, sometimes preserving the outlines of their motte-and-bailey origins. At Cilgerran the inner ward of the castle occupies the site of the motte and the outer ward that of the bailey. At Skenfrith, where the motte can still be seen, we know that as late as 1187–88 money was still being spent on the timber defences which surrounded it. Tretower preserves the remains of a motte that had to be revetted with a stone wall at an early date because of the softness of the soil from which it was made. The encircling ditch of the ring-motte at Llawhaden can still be seen, although the bank had subsequently been levelled and covered with later buildings.

EARLY STONE CASTLES

The earliest Norman stone building known in Wales was part of Chepstow Castle where, before 1071, William Fitzosbern erected an oblong tower of two storeys made of stone and also raised part of a stone curtain wall. This was exceptional, but from the twelfth century onwards more and more stonework began to appear. This did not, of course, mean that timber structures were replaced wholesale in a very short space. At Rhuddlan even in 1241–42 parts at least of the defences were still made of wood, as they may have been at Raglan as late as 1400. The process of replacement in stone was gradual, continuous and piecemeal, and since stone buildings called for greater skill and much more money than those of earth and timber only a minority of motte-and-bailey castles were so rebuilt and many of the lesser examples were abandoned. The first stone or partly-stone castles of the second half of the twelfth century and the early part of the thirteenth were thus the lineal descendants of the motte-and-bailey castles and 'grew' out of them. The process of strengthening in stone began, understandably, with what had formerly been the motte, replacing it usually by a powerful stone keep with the entrance at the first-floor level, which generally contained the lord's chief residence, although many of the smaller examples hardly seem to have been large enough to have served this purpose. The ruins of a number of keeps dating from the twelfth century can be seen in Wales. Ogmore has a rectangular keep of rather rough construction, though part of it is skilfully dressed with ashlar, going back to the early part of the twelfth century, possibly indeed to the period of its founder, William de Londres (died c. 1126). Two neighbouring castles, Coety and Newcastle (Bridgend, Glam.) have each a square keep and a curtain wall of late twelfth-century date. Even more striking, perhaps, is the thirteenth-century rectangular keep at Dolwyddelan, which was obviously once surrounded by a courtyard enclosed by a timber stockade, later rebuilt in stone. The particular interest of Dolwyddelan is that it was built by one of the Welsh princes, thus showing how the latter had learnt from their enemies something of the art of military architecture.

Square and rectangular keeps, because of their weight, were not usually built on the motte itself but on ground level near it. A more common form of refortifying the motte in stone, therefore, was the shell keep consisting of a circular or polygonal wall built round the top of the motte in place of the earlier palisade. Along with the building of a shell keep of this sort went very often the replacement of the palisade of the bailey by a stone wall which was carried up two sides of the motte to join the keep. An unusually good example of this technique can still be seen at Cardiff and another at Tretower Castle in Breconshire. A modified expedient of the same kind was adopted at Carmarthen, where the stone wall of the shell keep was built at the base of the motte and carried up as a revetment wall to the whole mound.

The thirteenth century brought further improvements in fortification. The twelfth-century square and rectangular keeps, formidable though they were, had serious shortcomings. Any right-angled tower was necessarily weak at its angles, which were susceptible to mining and created 'blind spots' which the defenders could not command except directly from above. This led to the building of free-standing circular keeps, still with the entrance at first-floor level as with the right-angled keeps. Instances of such towers exist in France, Germany and England in the twelfth century but most of the surviving examples in England and Wales date from the early part of the thirteenth century. Of the known Welsh examples of the latter, about half are situated in the south, being concentrated mainly in Pembrokeshire, Breconshire, Monmouthshire and on the Herefordshire border. Incomparably the finest specimen in Wales is the 75 ft high tower built about 1200 by William Marshall within Pembroke Castle, a stronghold of exceptional importance at the time because it was being used as a base for expeditions designed to conquer Ireland. Smaller but excellent examples of the same technique can be seen at Skenfrith, where the round keep (diameter 24 ft) was set on the top of the motte, and at Tretower, where its three-storeyed tower (diameter 21 ft) was raised within an earlier shell keep. Others exist at Bronllys (Brecs.), Caldicot (Mon.) and just over the border at Longtown (Herefs.). This concentration of round keeps in South Wales at this time is thought to have been the result of the rivalries of the Marcher lords among themselves and of their concern at the growing power of Welsh princes, especially that of Llywelyn ab Iorwerth of Gwynedd, who was building castles of his own. At Ewloe, an outpost of Welsh power in Flintshire, there stands an interesting D-shaped keep which was very probably built at Llywelyn's orders, and at Dolbadarn Castle, another of his or his grandson's strongholds, there is a round keep of about 20 ft in diameter rising to 40 ft in height, which leaves no doubt of the mastery of the art of castle-building now being achieved by the Welsh rulers.

THIRTEENTH-CENTURY CASTLES

The emphasis in thirteenth-century building, nevertheless, lay in the development not of the keep but of the bailey or curtain wall, together with the adoption of the rounded mural or flanking tower. These wall towers brought to a number of separate points along the curtain-wall all the advantages of the round keep. Each tower was one of a series of self-contained strongholds which enabled the defenders to cover the outer face and base of the wall while remaining protected; each at the same time commanded the summit of the wall and divided it into sections, thus preventing a single break-in from endangering the whole castle. Some of the earliest of such towers were semi-circular and solid in their construction; but the merits of building them hollow so as to give extra accommodation and more fighting platforms were soon appreciated.

At Chepstow, as at Pembroke, the great William Marshall applied himself *c.* 1190 to bringing the defences up to date. He built the curtain-wall between the middle and lower bailey together with gateway and towers, the particular interest of which is that it is one of the earliest instances in England and Wales of rounded wall towers and the provision of true shooting slits. Marshall's son at Cilgerran built two round towers astride the curtain wall, thus facilitating a more aggressive form of defence. But the best impression of early castles using rounded towers to strengthen the curtain wall can be derived from Grosmont and Skenfrith, both of which are thought to have been reconstructed along these lines, probably between 1228 and 1232, by the Justiciar Hubert de Burgh, who held these lordships from 1219 to 1239.

Such towers in themselves were not enough. It was also essential to ensure the security of the entrance, always potentially the weakest point of the defences. This was achieved by building an increasingly powerful gatehouse which, in its earliest form, consisted of twin towers, usually D-shaped, on either side of the entrance. Admission to it across the ditch was gained by means of a bridge which pivoted on an axle rather like a see-saw, the gate-passage being defended by a series of defences, including a gate and portcullis and 'murder holes' in the vault overhead. Furthermore, the defenders could fire arrows into the gate-passage through slits from the chambers on either side.

An early gatehouse still stands at White Castle, and another, partly ruined, at Montgomery, but a rather similar one at Cricieth, once thought to have been the work of Llywelyn ab Iorwerth, is now generally accepted to have been part of Edward I's reconstruction of that castle.

Later castle-building in thirteenth-century Wales reflects the fact that military and political power was being concentrated into fewer but more powerful hands. Thus, fewer Marcher lords ruled over a greater number of lordships. These lords were often locked in fierce rivalry with one another as well as with the King and the Welsh princes. Among the latter all others were eclipsed by the rise of Llywelyn ab Iorwerth (1194–1240) and Llywelyn ap Gruffydd (1247–82). By the era of the second Llywelyn's adroit interventions in the wars between Henry III and his barons during the years from 1255–67, it became evident that any royal or Marcher castles but the strongest could be in jeopardy from the Welsh. It is no coincidence that round about this time, or shortly afterwards, major works should have been begun on what were to be some of the most powerful castles in South Wales. White Castle was heavily refortified by the king's agents about the 1260s or 1270s; the inner ward at Kidwelly was built by Payn de Chaworth c. 1275; and, most significant of all, the castle at Caerphilly, one of the most superbly-conceived strongholds anywhere in medieval Europe, was begun by the strongest of the Marcher lords, Gilbert de Clare, possibly as early as 1268. Within the next decade Edward I had embarked on the programme of castle-building, unprecedented in scale and grandeur, which was intended finally to conquer Wales and to keep it conquered.

In terms of medieval military architecture the pinnacle of achievement was reached with the development of concentric castles in the last quarter of the thirteenth century. The concentric castle was provided with two sets of defences, one placed inside the other, and each complete in itself. On the inside was the four-sided inner ward, with its walls taken up to an immense height and protected at each corner by a drum tower and with its entrance or entrances sited between the towers and guarded by gatehouses and sometimes by barbicans as well. Surrounding this inner ward, only a matter of yards away, was the outer ward, also boasting a stout but lower

curtain wall protected by round towers. In some instances a fortified
town formed an integral part of the initial design, and its walls and
guard towers ran outwards from the castle walls in an unbroken
enclosure to form a single defended area.

Most of the concentric castles of Wales were built by the King, but
at Caerphilly and Kidwelly in South Wales there are two notable
examples built by the Marcher lords. Caerphilly is, next to Windsor,
the largest castle in England or Wales and covers no less than 25 acres.
At its heart is the inner ward, an irregular quadrangle of huge curtain
walls, its two entrances reinforced by prodigious gatehouses, and
its four corners protected by drum towers. Around this lies the
outer ward with its relatively low battlemented walls designed to
give a free field of fire from the inner ward. These two wards constitute the concentric castle proper but form only a part of the
fortifications as a whole, being further protected by a series of
intricate additional safeguards made up of inner and outer moats,
lakes, earthworks and other outer platforms. Kidwelly Castle, though
much smaller, is aesthetically one of the most striking and pleasing
of all Welsh castles in conception. Here, the inner ward, dramatically
crowning the steep ravine overlooking the River Gwendraeth, was
built first. It protected the hall, solar, chapel (an unusually arresting
feature in this castle) and other domestic buildings. So great was
the natural strength of the ravine behind the inner ward that when,
early in the fourteenth century, the outer ward with its formidable
gatehouse came to be built, it needed only to be a semi-circle,
rather like a bow in design, and did not need to be taken round
that part of the inner ward perched on the ravine.

The castle-building ambitions of the lords of the March, impressive
though some of their results were, are dwarfed by the immensity of
enterprise and planning represented in Edward I's castle-building
programme in Wales. Between 1276 and 1296 he built no fewer than
ten new castles of the first rank, remodelled three captured from the
Welsh, renovated a number of older border strongholds, and inspired the building of four new lordship castles along the lines of
those of his own creation.* So vast a scheme called for men,

---

*The ten new castles were Flint, Rhuddlan, Aberystwyth, Builth, Ruthin, Hope, Conwy,
Caernarvon, Harlech and Beaumaris; the Welsh ones were Dolwyddelan, Cricieth and
Bere; the border castles included Chester, Oswestry, Shrewsbury, Montgomery and
St. Briavel's; and the lordship castles were Hawarden, Denbigh, Holt and Chirk.

materials and money on a scale that taxed to the uttermost the abili-
ties of this most martial of English kings and the resources of his
prosperous kingdom, but in the end it secured permanent military
subordination of Wales. When Edward embarked upon it he was
already a seasoned warrior and strategist who had tasted war in
France and the Holy Land as well as in Britain. He was conversant
with the latest developments in the science of castle-building and
had had first-hand experience of the 'bastides', the planned fortress-
towns of southern France, and of their role in any design for conquest. Furthermore, he was able to take into his service Master
James of St. George, a man who had already made a name for himself by building castles for the King's cousin, Philip, Count of Savoy,
and who was able to incorporate in the castles of North Wales the
perfected refinements of medieval military architecture. Edward's
castle-building in Wales falls into two stages in phase with his two
main campaigns there. The earlier opened in 1277. The king realized
that the border bases traditionally used for controlling Wales were
not sufficiently far advanced for his purpose, so he planned four new
forward bases at key-points in Mid and North Wales – Builth,
Aberystwyth, Flint and Rhuddlan. To build them, his agents recruited in the summer months of 1277 from a wide area in the Midlands and the West Country a huge labour force – at least 1,845
diggers, 790 carpenters and 320 masons – who were put to work
immediately, being given bonus payments when necessary but also
being subjected to stoppages for absenteeism. The outstanding
legacy of their work at Flint Castle is the great round tower known
as the 'donjon' which may possibly have been intended as a residence
for the royal Justice of Chester. Alongside the new castle at Flint
they also built a new town, planned like a French 'bastide' along the
sands of Dee, and protected by earthworks and palisade – hence the
army of diggers. Rhuddlan, too, got a new castle of concentric design
and a new town girdled with earthworks. But here a uniquely ambitious engineering feat was also undertaken, the course of the River
Clwyd being diverted for some two or three miles in order to provide
access to the sea. It took an average of 77 men working six days a
week three years to complete, and the cost of castle, town and
channel together was, in modern money, well over £1 million. Work
on this first stage of Edward's building went on from 1277 to the eve

of the Welsh revolt of March 1282. Indeed, the very timing of that revolt is largely explicable in terms of Welsh alarm at the progress being made on the castles, for there seems little doubt that the Welsh struck when the intensive summer season of building was about to begin.

Faced with the rebellion of 1282 Edward reacted promptly and comprehensively. Within a month of its outbreak, orders were being despatched to every part of England, to Ireland and Edward's lands in France for men and supplies of every kind. The speed and scale of that operation leave little doubt that Edward had already determined on a final reckoning with the princes of North Wales. When the latter's resistance failed in March 1283, opening the road to the heart of Gwynedd, Edward lost no time in laying the foundations of those new fortresses that were intended to keep the Welsh permanently under control. Conwy was begun in March, Harlech in April and Caernarvon in July. Meanwhile, Edward was urging his vassals to build similar castles of their own, like those at Denbigh and Chirk. That such bastions were needed was convincingly demonstrated by the dangerous Welsh uprising of 1294–95, led by Madog ap Llywelyn, which inflicted serious damage on Caernarvon Castle and led Edward to begin work on a new castle at Beaumaris. By the time of his death in 1307 most of Edward's work was completed, although building continued at Caernarvon until 1330, while at Beaumaris the upper storeys of all the towers and the inner part of the southern gatehouses were never finished.

The Edwardian castles, still so largely intact, constitute as a whole one of the most remarkable groups of medieval monuments to be seen anywhere in Europe. Their grandeur is in proportion to the money that had to be raised to build them and which had to be forthcoming regularly or else the work stopped, as it did for a time at Builth in 1277. Some £95–100,000, it has been reliably calculated on the basis of the royal records, was spent on Edward's castles in Wales between 1277 and 1330 and more than 80 per cent of that total was spent before 1301. Caernarvon Castle, town walls and quay and other buildings alone cost £27,000, Conwy and Beaumaris cost some £14–15,000, Rhuddlan about £9,200. In so far as an equivalent in modern values can be given, the investment in these castles amounted to about £10–15 million and that at a time when the population of England and Wales was probably about one-twentieth of what it is now, and the gross national product infinitely smaller. The financial achievement was, therefore, as impressive as the feat of logistics achieved in recruiting the men and obtaining the supplies.

CASTLES IN THE LATER MIDDLE AGES

After the Edwardian Conquest the military need for castles became less acute. Diminished threats led to greater negligence in upkeep. At Conwy as early as 1321 several of the roof trusses had failed and in 1332 it and other castles in North Wales were ruinous, as was Cilgerran in South Wales in 1326. A detailed survey carried out for the Black Prince in 1343 of his castles in Wales showed that many of them, including Conwy and Beaumaris, were in poor shape. Yet Welsh castles were, in general, less neglected than those in England, except for the ones on the northern border. This was because there were still considerable military risks along the periphery of the kingdom. The fourteenth century was one of constant warfare against Scotland and France, and there were repeated reports and rumours of the dangers of invasion. Cricieth Castle, for instance, was to be fully garrisoned and provisioned against invasion in 1338; one of Edward III's last acts in 1377 was to order Cilgerran, Tenby and Pembroke to be repaired and refortified; and in 1384–85 Conwy was on the alert because of 'persistent rumours touching war, rapine, murder and arson and the Scottish enemies'. Behind all the alarms lurked the greater fear that the Welsh might rise in support of any invasion. They did not do so on any scale, however, until the rebellion of Owain Glyn Dŵr in the first decade of the fifteenth century. When this was at its height only the strength of some of the castles stood between the rebels and the complete overthrow of English power in Wales. Among those which proved too strong and too well prepared to be taken were Brecon, Chepstow, Rhuddlan, Conwy (except for one brief episode) and Caernarvon, which withstood a long and desperate siege by Glyn Dŵr supported by his French allies. But a number of other castles were captured or severely damaged. Extensive and costly repairs had subsequently to be undertaken at Ogmore, Kidwelly, Carmarthen and Carreg Cennen, described as 'lately completely destroyed and thrown down by rebels', while Cricieth was so badly damaged that it was abandoned. The rebels' greatest prizes were Harlech, which Glyn Dŵr for three years made his home and headquarters, and Aberystwyth. These two castles between them gave him control of large parts of western Wales.

Long after the rebellion had been suppressed, disturbed conditions persisted. They left an evocative monument in Raglan Castle, built by Sir William ap Thomas between about 1430 and 1445, and much extended by his son, William Herbert, the first Earl of Pembroke, from about 1450 to 1469. Its unique feature is its Great Tower, Twr Melyn Gwent ('Yellow Tower of Gwent'), which has no exact parallel anywhere else in Wales. Surrounded by water and cut off from the rest of the castle except for a drawbridge, it illustrates perfectly how the men of that age thought it necessary to have a self-contained fortified dwelling which could, if necessary, be held even against the owner's own retinue. Precautions of this sort were given added point by the rapid and brutal fluctuations of fortune and loyalty in the civil strife of the fifteenth century, in which contingents from Wales and the Marches played a considerable part. In such troubled times fears were expressed that a castle as strong as Carreg Cennen might become a bandits' lair to be exploited by 'all the misgoverned men' of the surrounding area who would live by 'robbery and spoiling of our people', and in 1462 they led to its being severely 'slighted' in order to avoid 'inconvenience of this kind happening there in the future'. In the north-west, Harlech Castle held out in Lancastrian hands for eight years and was the last castle to pass into the possession of the Yorkists.

In the sixteenth century stabler rule and a better ordered society were gradually established but the value of such castles as were used as centres of royal administration and justice increased rather than diminished after the Act of Union between England and Wales in 1536. It is not surprising to find in a survey of 1550 reporting on the state of Monmouth Castle a recommendation that repairs should be carried out on the grounds that the king had always had

> 'within the said Castle of Monmouth one place called the Exchequer where his auditors, receivers and other officers were wont to sit for hearing of matters, taking of his accounts and for receiving of his money; and now, by reason of . . . decays, they are driven to go into the town, which we think much unseemly.'

Other castles still inhabited by wealthy and powerful families were partially transformed into mansions where the accent was less on strength than ease, and more on luxury than security. Foremost among those who took advantage of the new possibilities in Wales were the Somerset family, Earls of Worcester and unquestionably the leading aristocratic family resident in the country. At their chief seat in Raglan, the third earl (1548–89) began work on the splendid hall, still the finest and least-decayed of the surviving apartments there, and on the long gallery. These projects were completed by his son, the fourth earl (1589–1628), who also added brick-built gazebos or summerhouses and a series of statue niches, 'a pleasant walk set forth with several figures of the Roman emperors in arches of diverse varieties of shell-works'. The same family was responsible for contemporary modifications at Chepstow, where they enlarged the windows and added a two-storey block of lodgings which has since largely disappeared. Oxwich Castle in Gower was almost wholly built by Sir Rhys Mansel (1487–1559), whose tall four-storey building with mullioned windows preserves fleeting shadows of its former grandeur even in its present ruinous state. Less ruined and even more magnificent is the work of Sir John Perrott (1530–92) at Carew in Pembrokeshire, whose 'long line of graceful and entirely civilian mullioned windows . . . is eloquent of the vanished military importance of the castle and its resultant transformation into a peaceful and palatial mansion' (R. A. Brown).

Yet, in spite of all appearances to the contrary, the military importance of the castle had not finally vanished. When the civil war broke out between King and Parliament in 1642, Wales was almost wholly royalist, with a number of Welsh castles being used as major bases in Charles I's cause. Conwy Castle was 'repaired, revictualled and supplied with ammunition' for the King by one of the borough's own sons, John Williams, Archbishop of York (1641–50). Caernarvon, three times closely besieged by the Parliamentarians, successfully withstood their onslaughts, as did Harlech. Fighting was even harder in south-east Wales, where, in the person of the Earl, later Marquis, of Worcester, the King enjoyed the support of one of his wealthiest and most loyal adherents. The Earl's castle at Chepstow was besieged twice and his headquarters at Raglan, the most formidable royalist stronghold in south-east Wales, endured in the summer of 1646 one of the most hotly-contested and best-recorded sieges of the war. By the end, the castle was being besieged by 3,500 men under the command of Sir Thomas Fairfax himself, and when it finally surrendered on 19th August 1646 the event was regarded by both sides as the virtual ending of the First Civil War. In the Second Civil War in 1648 Pembroke Castle, the one great base in Wales which had held out for Parliament throughout the First Civil War despite some very strong and sustained pressure was, paradoxically, being held by some of Cromwell's Presbyterian opponents. The great Oliver himself came to Pembrokeshire to conduct the siege that finally reduced this recalcitrant strongpoint. Neither here nor at Raglan had the use of gunpowder made a decisive difference, so powerfully constructed were the old stone defences. It was the subsequent 'slighting' which was ordered at both these castles and elsewhere, like Flint and Rhuddlan, that caused the real damage. Even then, at Caernarvon, where the inhabitants were entrusted with the responsibility for demolishing the defences, they found the task too laborious to justify the effort and expense involved.

Monastic buildings

Broadly speaking, there were four kinds of buildings found within the average monastery: (i) the church; (ii) the claustral buildings in which the monks lived; (iii) buildings in which they dispensed hospitality or charity; and (iv) buildings in which they exercised routine management of their estate and other administrative business.

THE CHURCH

This was the very heart of the monastery. It was here that the monks carried out their essential vocation of the service of God by means of prayer, praise and worship. Monastic churches were therefore designed to enable monks to carry out the 'Opus Dei' ('service of God'). They were nearly all cruciform in shape, and where they were not, as in Cymer Abbey, this was only because circumstances had prevented the carrying out of the original design. Many of the churches were very large: Margam, for instance, was 262 ft long and 63½ ft wide; Tintern was 228 ft long and Neath 223 ft. Some other churches were laid out on a grand scale which it was found impossible to complete; St. Dogmael's and Cymer because of the troubles caused by warfare, and Talley* because of a long and costly quarrel with Whitland.

The best surviving example of an early monastic church in Wales is at Ewenni. The nave, with its single north aisle, has the immense circular pillars and rounded arches of the early Norman style, which must presumably date from the original foundation of the priory early in the twelfth century. In monastic times it was used by the parishioners for worship. The crossing, presbytery, and transept, which were the monks' preserve, are of more elaborate Norman workmanship and were probably built in the late-twelfth century. Although there is some later rebuilding and though the north transept has virtually disappeared, Ewenni gives a more vivid impression of what a Norman church was like than any other in Wales. At St. Dogmael's, unlike Ewenni, Christian worship has not survived in the original monastic church, which has long been ruinous; and also unlike Ewenni, the church of St. Dogmael's underwent considerable modification in the thirteenth and fourteenth centuries. Even so, enough of the earliest work survives at St. Dogmael's to enable us to tell what the original church plan was like in the first half of the twelfth century. It, too, was cruciform, with an aisled nave, and it had a short presbytery, probably with an apse at the eastern end. Each of the transepts also had an apse at its eastern end, the outline of which can still be seen in the south transept.

The original twelfth-century Cistercian church was uncompromisingly simple in plan, as befitted an Order which laid such emphasis on austerity and the absence of ornament. A good example of such a design has been discovered by excavation at Tintern, slightly to the north of the site of the later church and overlapping it. Shorter, much narrower and simpler than its successor, this early church consisted of an aisle-less nave, short transepts with rectangular chapels on the east side, and a short, aisle-less, square-ended presbytery. The essentials of this early plan still survive at Valle Crucis even though it was not founded until 1201. Here, although the nave is aisled, the presbytery and both transepts are short and square-ended.

---

*A house of Premonstratensian canons.

The Cistercian church at Basingwerk, built early in the thirteenth century, shows the same 'family likeness' to Valle Crucis which tended to characterize Cistercian building. At Strata Florida, however, the great western door with its Celtic Romanesque design indicates a partial victory for the native instinct for ornamentation over the Cistercian insistence upon avoiding ostentation. The urge for more grandeur and display became even more pronounced in the thirteenth century, when the cumulative wealth, success and public recognition of the Order, coupled with the tendency for more monks to enter the priesthood and so to need more altars, led to a number of their churches being rebuilt on a grander and more elaborate scale. At Strata Florida the addition was relatively modest and involved no more than extending the presbytery eastward by about 20 ft. But at Neath and Tintern, in the late-thirteenth and fourteenth century, the church was re-built with an aisled presbytery having a series of chapels at the east end behind the high altar, aisled north and south transepts with chapels at the east end, and an aisled nave. Much of Tintern's magnificent church with its ambitious proportions, graceful vaulting and traceried windows still stands, and it illustrates clearly how far the White Monks had moved away from their founders' notions of simple and undemonstrative austerity.

The nave in the Cistercian churches was reserved for the use of the 'conversi' or lay-brothers. These were monks who took vows of poverty, obedience and chastity, but whose chief function was to cultivate estates, tend livestock and look after buildings belonging to the monastery. They often outnumbered the choir monks in the early days of Cistercian monasteries when the Order was developing hitherto uncultivated or deserted land. The aisles of the nave were shut off by solid stone screens to form the lay-brothers' quire, traces of which remain at Strata Florida and Tintern. The monks' quire covered the crossing and sometimes extended into the easternmost bay of the nave, where a stone screen known as a pulpitum marked the division. On Sundays and on certain holy days the abbot and his monks went in solemn procession visiting all the altars in the church and making a ceremonial round of all the claustral buildings. Later Cistercian churches like those at Neath and Tintern covered the west door with a small but elaborate porch known as a 'Galilee', so called because the abbot leading his monks in procession was thought to symbolize Christ leading His disciples into Galilee.

THE CLAUSTRAL BUILDINGS

The buildings in which the monks lived were grouped round three sides of a cloister, with the church itself forming the fourth side. The cloister was ordinarily placed on the south side of the church to catch the sun, but where other considerations, like those of drainage, dictated, it was sited on the north side of the church, as at Tintern. It was usually placed against the nave of the church, but there are examples – Penmon is one – of the cloister being set against the chancel of the church. The cloister consisted of four covered passage-ways or walks, with lean-to roofs, set round a square garth or court-yard. The walls had open arcades or, later, windows looking out on to the courtyard. Doors gave access from the cloisters to the range of buildings on each of its sides, thus providing a covered way between the church and all parts of the monastery. It was in the cloister, also, that a monk was expected to spend much of his time reading and meditating. This was generally done in the cloister walk next to the church; and halfway along this walk at Tintern can be seen the remains of the canopied seat occupied by the abbot during the Collation, the reading before Compline, while at Strata Florida the position of the lectern used in the Collation can still be traced.

In considering the claustral buildings of smaller Welsh abbeys and priories it must be remembered that many of these houses had never, at best, had more than the minimum provision. The eastern range usually consisted of a two-storey block, with the whole of the first floor forming the 'dorter' or dormitory of the monks, although at Llanthony it appears that they slept in the upper storey of the western range and at Penmon in the southern range. There was always direct communication between the dorter and the 'rere-dorter' or latrine block, the site of which was determined by the position of the main drain and the adequacy of the water supply needed to flush it. At Valle Crucis the rere-dorter lay immediately south of the dorter and in direct line with it; at Tintern it lay at right angles to the dorter; while at Neath it was placed parallel to the dorter and was connected to it with a bridge. Access from the dorter to the church was usually gained by means of night stairs which led into the south transept. A moulded handrail of such night stairs survives at Neath, and at Ewenni a newel staircase; but at Llanthony, perhaps because the dorter was in the western range, there appears to have been no direct communication between it and the church.

On the ground floor of the eastern range next to the transept there was, in early plans, a passage called a 'slype', which still exists at Llanthony. But in rather later Cistercian plans there was a narrow room serving as a sacristy where the vessels used in the church were stored. This was the arrangement at Basingwerk, Strata Florida, Valle Crucis and St. Dogmael's; but the same room might be used as a library and vestry, as at Neath and Tintern. The next room in this range was the chapter house, which came second only to the church in importance and was so called because it was there that the monks assembled each day after morning mass to hear a chapter of the Rule read and to discuss the business of the house. Early chapter houses were square or rectangular buildings with three bays, like the one at Valle Crucis, the west end of which was used as a library and contained a book closet. But because of its importance the chapter house was very often enlarged and made more ornate in later extensions. It was remodelled and extended at Basingwerk and Strata Florida; at Tintern it was rebuilt on much ampler lines with richly decorated doorways; and at Margam one of the loveliest and most elegant chapter houses anywhere in Britain was built in polygonal shape with intricate vaulting springing from a central pillar. Beyond the chapter house the ground floor of the eastern range might be used for a variety of purposes, including novices' lodgings (Basingwerk and Tintern), an inner parlour (Basingwerk and Tintern) or a warming-house (Basingwerk and Penmon) – the only place in the monastery, except the kitchen, in which a fire was permitted.

In the range opposite the church, which might be north or south depending on the position at which the cloister had been set, the chief room was the 'frater' or dining-hall of the monks. It usually had an entrance on the west side, near which was a lavatory where the monks washed their hands before meals. At meal-times one of the monks ascended to read a chapter from the scriptures from the frater pulpit, remains of which are still in evidence at Basingwerk and Tintern. The earliest frater ranges were built along the length of the cloister opposite the church, as can be seen at St. Dogmael's, Llanthony and Cymer. But this plan was markedly altered in later Cistercian arrangements whereby the frater was set at right angles to the cloister and projected well beyond the main walls of the range (Tintern, Valle Crucis and Basingwerk). This change made it possible to build a warming-house east of the frater and parallel with it. It also meant that the kitchen placed to the west of the frater could serve both its needs and those of the lay-brothers' frater which lay in the western range of buildings.

The western range of buildings in Benedictine houses contained the cellar or great storehouse of the monastery, so placed because the outer court, which was the outlet to the world, lay on the west side. The only other room that was invariably placed on the west side was the public parlour (Llanthony, St. Dogmael's and Tintern), which formed an entrance between outer court and cloister where conversation between monks and lay-people could take place. In Cistercian monasteries, however, the western range of buildings was given over to 'conversi' or lay-brothers for their frater and dorter (Neath and Tintern). This meant that the abbot's house and the guests' lodgings, which in Benedictine houses like St. Dogmael's were in the west range, had usually to be located elsewhere in Cistercian houses.

OTHER BUILDINGS

The 'farmery' or infirmary, where monks who were sick or very old were cared for, usually lay to the east of the cloister (Basingwerk, St. Dogmael's and Tintern). It had its own hall and chapel and often-times its own frater and kitchen as well. At Tintern they formed a sizeable block of buildings which shared a second cloister, the infirmary cloister, with the dorter and re-dorter range.

In the outer court to the west of the cloister buildings there might be a whole miscellany of structures. These could include the guests' lodgings where the abbot or prior, like any other great landowner, could entertain. The Prior of Carmarthen, for example, was reported as having had complimentary messages from the King of Portugal acknowledging his hospitality to Portuguese merchants. Also in the outer court, at appropriate points, there might be a variety of humbler buildings, many of them of wood, housing workshops, livestock or stores. In the same area, near the gateway, would stand the almonry, at which the poor and sick foregathered to receive charity dispensed by the almoner. The main gatehouse through which the monastery was entered was often a handsome two-storeyed affair, as can be seen at Llanthony or Neath. More than one gate-house was needed where the precinct was extensive, e.g. at Tintern, where the precinct wall enclosed 27 acres and was entered by a number of gates including a water-gate on the Wye. The outstanding precinct wall in Wales, however, is the one at Ewenni, complete with two impressive gates, stoutly-built towers, and a splendidly-preserved wall with battlements and a wall-walk in places. But it is not, as it is often said to be, an authentic example of a fortified ecclesiastical building since the battlements and towers are largely for display. On the vulnerable east side, where heavy defences would have been most needed, the simple precinct wall remained unfortified through-out the Middle Ages.

DISINTEGRATION AND DISSOLUTION OF THE MONASTERIES

The religious Orders had passed their peak by 1300 – no new houses were subsequently founded in Wales and those in existence had already begun to show signs of declining vitality. During the next two centuries they faced a succession of difficulties and crises. Long wars with France led to heavy taxation and to the cutting off of contacts with mother houses in France, including Cîteaux. The Black Death of 1348–49 and later visitations of plague caused a sharp reduction in the number of choir monks and made recruitment difficult afterwards; while the Cistercian lay-brothers virtually disappeared from the scene. Labour shortages and other economic troubles made it wellnigh impossible for the monks to cultivate their estates and they had no choice but to rent them out to laymen. To add to the monks' misfortune came the Glyn Dŵr rebellion, which caused havoc and devastation in many parts of Wales. In 1402, Strata Florida was occupied by royal troops, its monks expelled and its buildings desecrated. Talley by 1410 was said to have been 'despoiled, burned and almost destroyed', and Margam in 1412 to be in such a bad state that its abbot and monks were obliged to wander around like vagabonds. Ewenni and Llanthony also suffered grievous losses.

One small Welsh priory, the Benedictine cell at Cardiff, actually disappeared during the troubles, and a Cistercian house, Abbey Cwm-hir, was so badly affected that it was never more than a shadow of itself again.

It took a long time for the other Welsh monasteries to recover from this succession of adversities. In some respects they never really regained their former vitality. The complement of monks in practically every house remained persistently below strength; Tintern alone among Welsh houses seems to have had the thirteen monks regarded as the necessary minimum. The quality of monastic life tended to deteriorate – a monastery became less a community than a collection of individuals, and abbots, on whom the temper of life within the monastery chiefly depended, frequently built or adapted for themselves elaborate private lodgings in which they lived in comparative luxury. At Valle Crucis, for instance, there was a succession of three abbots of whom we know a fair amount: John ap Richard (*c.* 1450–80), Dafydd ab Ieuan (d. 1503) and John Lloyd (elected 1503). All three were liberal patrons of Welsh poets, who describe with admiration the energy and money which these abbots, and especially the first two, put into their building projects. But the main features of this fifteenth-century reconstruction do not speak very highly of the spirit prevailing in the monastery at the time. Only the eastern part of the church was being used, the nave being no longer required as there were now no lay-brothers. The eastern walk of the cloister was also abandoned and the northern part of the dorter and the room above the sacristy were adapted to provide a hall and chamber, complete with fireplace, for the abbot. New provisions for the abbot of the same general kind were made at Neath and Aberconway, less certainly at Basingwerk, and probably elsewhere as well.

Yet in the last resort it was not the decay of the monasteries which led to their final dissolution by Henry VIII between 1536 and 1539, so much as the political and financial needs of the Crown. But it was their decline which probably prevented any outcry against their closure, which was carried through in Wales without provoking any serious disturbance. Once the monasteries had been closed the fate of their buildings varied widely. Most of the churches belonging to the Benedictine Order or the Orders of canons, having previously been used for worship by layfolk continued in use as parish churches, and Brecon Priory church has in this century attained the status of a cathedral. However, at Talley in the eighteenth century and St. Dogmael's in the nineteenth, new parish churches were built to take the place of the old ones. The Cistercian churches, sited in lonelier and less populated places and not having served as parish churches, suffered heavily. The lead was soon removed from the roofs of many of them and melted down for the King's use; lead from Basingwerk was used at Holt Castle and even transported as far as Ireland to repair the royal castles at Dublin and elsewhere; but at Tintern a good deal of the lead was bought by the Earl of Worcester, to whom the site and many of the abbey's estates were granted. Stone and timber might also be removed for the King's benefit, as at Aberconway, whence they were transported to Caernarvon to repair the castle. Margam proved to be a rare exception among Cistercian churches; its church was truncated, and the nave only was afterwards used for parish worship as, indeed, it still is.

Conventual buildings, other than churches, in many instances disappeared completely or were incorporated into houses, farms or other buildings on or near the monastic site. This was especially true of the Benedictine and Austin canons' houses situated in busy towns. The same fate usually befell the friaries of the Dominicans and Franciscans although two of them, Brecon and Bangor, became adapted as schools, and a third, the Grey Friary, at Cardiff, which was modified to make a town house for a branch of the Herbert family, has disappeared only within the last few years. Ewenni's buildings were also incorporated into a private residence for a family of gentry and they have been continuously inhabited ever since. Part of St. Dogmael's western range became adapted as a rectory and was used for that purpose for a long time. A number of other monasteries were used as residences for lay folk – Strata Florida, Valle Crucis and Basingwerk – but have for centuries been uninhabited, while the site of Neath Abbey was occupied first by a Tudor mansion and subsequently by an iron foundry. Even now, in ruins, they retain much of their attraction. It is still possible to understand why John Leland described Neath as having been 'the fairest abbey in all Wales', or why the white-robed Cistercians of Valle Crucis once appeared to a medieval poet, Gutun Owain, as the very harbingers of Heaven itself.

III. Prophecy, Poetry, and Politics in Medieval and Tudor Wales*

At some point which cannot be more precisely dated than the second half of the fifteenth century the last of the great poets of Wales to commit himself almost exclusively to the composition of prophetic verse, Dafydd Llwyd o Fathafarn (*fl. c.* 1447–90), addressed himself to an imaginary conversation with a seagull. In this and many other poems he identified himself unhesitatingly with what he believed to be an unbroken continuity of close on one thousand years of prophetic poetry. He traced the origins of his own muse back through medieval poets all the way to the sixth-century fountainhead of Welsh prophetic verse, to 'Taliesin ddewin ddoeth' (Taliesin, wise soothsayer') and 'Myrddin burddysg mawrddoeth' ('Myrddin of pure learning and great wisdom'). Looking at the whole corpus of Dafydd Llwyd's verse we can readily discern that he was the heir to a good many other prophetic materials besides the indigenous Welsh ones. He could draw on the whole miscellaneous mass of medieval prophetic motifs: those of the Christian religion, the Sibylline oracles, Joachim of Fiore, Geoffrey of Monmouth, miscellaneous divinations widely current in England and Scotland, and the murky and esoteric science of astrology. Yet he was justified in his conviction that the hard core of it, to which all the rest could be expendable accretions, was the native tradition which he had inherited from the countless generations of his poet-predecessors. Admittedly, none of the Welsh prophetic poems which have come down to us can be traced back further than the ninth or tenth centuries, even though they may be spuriously fathered on the sixth-century poets, Taliesin or Myrddin. Yet there is no reason to suppose that those founding-fathers of Welsh literature were not prophets. It has been argued that Myrddin, none of whose poetry is known to have survived, as well as Taliesin was a sixth-century poet and that the chief claim of both to fame and remembrance among their bardic successors was precisely their pre-eminent reputation as prophetic poets. Nor need we doubt that the role of the poet as prophet goes back even further to the Celtic druids. One of the striking features of Celtic pagan religion was its addiction to those animal deities of dragons, boars, ravens, and the rest, which

---

*First published in H. Hearder and H. R. Loyn (eds.), *British Government and Administration: Essays Presented to S. B. Chrimes* (Cardiff, 1974), pp. 104–116.

were also among the most persistent and widely employed vaticina-
tory symbols in the poetry of early medieval Wales.

However, it would be very unwise to embark on highly speculative
excursions into the misty uncertainties of early Celtic religion in
order to uncover the roots of Welsh prophetic tradition. Let us
start at a clear and well-established *terminus a quo*, the Welsh prophetic poem *Armes Prydein* ('Prophecy of Britain'), which Sir Ifor
Williams conclusively dated to the early part of the tenth century.
For a period of some six centuries after that, down to the age of
Dafydd Llwyd o Fathafarn, it is quite evident that the prophetic
tradition remained virile and resilient among Welsh poets. It was
not the product of a rigid and unimaginative conservatism on the
part of poets too unintelligent or uninspired to find new themes;
rather was it the fruit of a powerful and necessary myth which
served a deep and enduring social need.

Having stressed the power and continuity of the prophetic tradition
over these six centuries, let us at once concede that within that period
there were marked differences of individual emphasis and approach. The *Armes Prydein* and other pre-Norman poetry obviously
reflect the political and military problems of the Welsh in the
Anglo-Saxon era. The poetry of the *Gogynfeirdd*, the court poets of
the twelfth and thirteenth centuries, is equally clearly closely geared
to the needs and policies of the native princes in the confused and
tumultuous centuries after the advent of the Normans. Geoffrey of
Monmouth injected a new and immensely potent stimulus into
prophecy in Wales and elsewhere. The disasters of 1282–3, when
Welsh political independence and the princely house of Gwynedd
were extinguished, were a traumatic experience for the poets, as the
heartbroken desolation of the elegies to Llywelyn ap Gruffydd
unmistakenly reveals; and yet, the prophetic theme, improbable as
it might have seemed, survived this débâcle. In the fourteenth
century it continued to place its hopes on a resurgent Welsh prince –
an Owain Lawgoch ('Owain of the Red Hand') or an Owain
Glyn Dŵr. After the failure of the Glyn Dŵr rebellion early in the
fifteenth century, visions of Welsh political independence seem to
have been abandoned by the Welsh poets in favour of capturing
power within the English political machine by means of a William
Herbert or a Jasper Tudor. Their prophetic appeals could be and

were ingeniously adapted to the exigencies of this kind of power politics. They were brought to what many Welshmen believed to be their consummation and fulfilment in the victory of Henry Tudor in 1485. Nor was their potential even now fully exhausted. When young Rhys ap Gruffydd, head of the house of Dynevor, became restive against his Tudor sovereign between 1529 and 1531, one of the accusations solemnly brought against him was his use of ancient prophecies to popularize his cause.

Numerous and diverse the emphases may have been, wide the variations in tactic and exploitation; and yet within and through them all there ran certain basic and unchanging motifs. The Welsh were held to be the heirs and descendants of an ancient and honourable race, the rightful owners and rulers of the island of Britain. They had been wrongfully and treacherously deprived of their patrimony by the Anglo-Saxons. However, the tables would be turned on the offspring of Hengist and Horsa by the return of a great British hero or heroes – Cynan and Cadwaladr, or Owain, or Arthur. His reappearance would presage great cataclysms, furious battles, and copious bloodshed. Finally, these tribulations would be surmounted and crowned with complete victory, in which the Welsh, reinforced perhaps by allies from Scotland, Ireland and Brittany, would be wholly and lastingly triumphant.

The consideration about these grandiose expectations that will immediately strike a modern observer is that they must have been disappointed with leaden and monotonous regularity again and again over the centuries. It is no wonder that from time to time there should be expressions of chagrin and resentment on the part of the disappointed poets. A fourteenth-century poet, keyed up to await the coming of Owain Lawgoch, expressed his bitter mortification that his hero had been killed before he could claim his inheritance;

> Er edrych am ŵyr Rhodri,
> Llyma och ym lle ni chawdd.
> Lleddid a diawl ai lladdawdd.

('Though I looked for the grandson of Rhodri, what grief it is to me not to have had him. He was killed and it was a devil who killed him.').

Nor is it surprising that for long periods the prophetic theme seems to have disappeared or at least to be dormant. There are other occasions when poets appeared only to be 'going through the motions' of voicing prophetic themes when their patrons were known to be holding office under the English Crown and fully co-operating with the English authorities. This led a historian as sensitive and percipient as the late Glyn Roberts to suggest that there might really have been no substance in the prophetic themes after 1282, that they were merely reflecting a kind of morbid or unthinking curiosity of the sort that leads people to read Old Moore's Almanack. Was the prophecy indeed just some fossilized vestige which had now become meaningless sentiment? It is difficult to accept it as such. Poetry of this kind was commissioned by patrons who were often 'hard cases'; experienced leaders who knew what o'clock it was in the political and military world of their time – Owain Glyn Dŵr, William Herbert, Jasper Tudor or Rhys ap Thomas. It is not easy to see them as men indulging in nothing better than sentimental commonplaces. Was it, then, cynical manipulation? Exploitation for selfish political ends by unscrupulous careerists of a genuine but uninformed loyalty on the part of the mass of the people? Henry Tudor has in recent times in Wales been cast in this role. It is impossible to deny that Henry was an astute political operator who knew how to capitalize his assets effectively. Professor Chrimes, his latest biographer, has also warned us against exaggerating the king's Welshness, and Dr. Anglo has reduced to its proper proportions the influence of the 'old British history' on the early Tudors. Yet it is difficult to escape the conclusion that these prophecies penetrated to some deep strata in Henry's complex and multi-layered personality. This is not the place to examine the issue in detail, but to take one single and seemingly crucial instance: the choice of the name Arthur for the king's eldest son. This must have appeared to many of his contemporaries as a bold and startling innovation. In so strongly dynastic an age, when so much depended on the heir to so fiercely contested an inheritance, this almost unprecedented choice of a royal name may perhaps be best explained in terms of a fascination which the prophetic theme exercised over Henry, who, as a king, was anything but a political gambler.

Whatever we may think of the influence of prophecy on Henry VII there seems little doubt that for many of his Welsh contemporaries the whole complex of prophetic hopes, longings, and predictions still retained its substance, that it was still capable of triggering off deep and powerful responses. Why had it been able to do this for many centuries and why could it still do so? The answer seems to be that it had been a great and necessary myth. It was the myth which for the Welsh made sense of their past history and their future destiny. Like many other peoples at an early stage of their development they found it necessary to render the past intelligible and the future meaningful by the selection of some focus or foci. That is precisely the function served by myth before much formal history exists. In Wales, as in other countries, myth received its literary expression mainly in poetry. It was the poets who were the conservators of the past and the heralds of the future. They had a vital role to fulfil for the society of which they were members. What M. I. Finley has written of the poets' function in ancient Greece can almost equally well be applied to Wales:

> Group memory, after all, is no more than the transmittal to many people of the memory of one man or a few men repeated many times over. The act of communication, and therefore of preservation, of memory is not spontaneous and unconscious, but deliberate, intended to serve a purpose. Unless such conscious, deliberate activity occurs in each generation the memory of any event will disappear for ever.

This kind of myth did not call for a detailed, accurate, and continuous narrative of the past; it would indeed have been encumbered by it. Very few early peoples enjoyed such knowledge. They knew far less about the past than we do, but they felt a much keener sense of continuity with it.

The essence of this Welsh myth was that it embodied a messianic hope. Recent studies by social psychologists and anthropologists, as well as historians, have brought out more strongly than ever how widespread and potent messianic hopes have been and still are. In all parts of the world in many different ages there has been an infinite variety of messianic expectations founded on traditional myths. Nearly all of them have a core of characteristics in common: belief in a Golden Age, the source to which a society must return in order to find fulfilment; expectation of a millenium which is to be

preceded by dire cataclysms and catastrophes; cofidence in the
appearance or return of a charismatic deliverer – a very common
motif in these beliefs is expectation of the return of the dead; and
conviction that the hero's emergence will be quickly followed by
final victory, the ejection or subjection of the erstwhile conquerors,
and the re-establishment of the Golden Age. The powerful aesthetic
as well as emotional attraction of such a myth, which appears so
harmoniously and organically to join past, present and future in
common unity, can hardly be overestimated. The situation in which
it most naturally arises is that in which acute anxiety is felt at the
prospect of disaster or threatened disaster, in which the autonomous
social and cultural values of the group concerned are threatened
with extinction. Among the Welsh it was pressure first from Anglo-
Saxon rulers and later from Norman kings and lords which naturally
enough evoked such fears. They persisted throughout the Middle
Ages. As late as the turn of the fourteenth century we have a note
on a Welsh manuscript prepared for Hopcyn ap Thomas, renowned
in his day as 'master of Brut', in which the copyist, having mentioned
earlier disasters experienced by the most eminent Welsh princes,
refers to the contemporary 'pain and want and alienage (or oppression)' ('poen ac achenoctit ac alltudedd') which made the
Welsh feel like exiles in their own land. The reference is all the more
significant because of the extreme rarity with which a littérateur
or manuscript-copier gives his own reaction to the contents of a
manuscript he was copying. In the face of this age-long fear of
destruction of identity, if not of physical extinction, it was the
strength of the myth which provided social cohesiveness and emotional compensation. This was not the product of morbid psychology,
or eccentricity, or collective derangement. It was a perfectly healthy
and normal reaction which could be intensified into unwonted
excitement in times of stress or crisis. It was not peculiar to Wales
in the Middle Ages but exercised a comparable fascination in other
Celtic lands, and there were similar motifs at work in other European
countries.

This kind of myth was widely associated with religion. Though
in Wales, on the face of it, it was wholly secular in content, there
were some subtle interrelationships with religion. Some of these
are far from clear, and much more detailed examination needs to be

undertaken before any confident assertions concerning them can be made. There is, for instance, the question of a possible connection between the old Celtic religion and the prophetic tradition. It is known quite certainly that there were well-marked prophetic elements in the old pagan religion and that the return of the hero and the revival of the dead were familiar to it. Christianity itself has a most powerful eschatological content, and one of the most striking repercussions in many pagan communities in the modern world into which Christianity has been introduced is that it has led to rediscovery of and re-emphasis upon traditional pagan prophetic myths earlier cherished. It is not out of the question that something of the same sort happened in early Britain. It may have been conflict between two rival sets of values, one of them having a 'tainted' pagan origin, which led Gildas to assail the bards so violently and later to the tension between priest and poet, which was always latent in medieval Wales and occasionally burst out into acrimonious controversy.

However, no myth of this kind could have continued to flourish in Wales throughout these centuries if it had been pagan or anti-christian; it had perforce to operate within the Christian framework. The intellectual and ideological content of that framework, never-theless, was not as monolithic as is sometimes supposed. It may be true that early British history was interpreted by Gildas and Bede in a characteristically Christian fashion, i.e. that the defeat of the early British and the alienation from them of much of their territory was a divine punishment laid upon them for their sins. But such an interpretation was not subscribed to by all British clerics, especially those of Wales. As long as the Roman and Celtic Churches remained separate it was natural that the Celtic Church should defend its national as well as its ecclesiastical tradition; nor could the one be separated from the other. It is this which may account for the persistence of one remarkable trait throughout the whole of the poetry – the close and frequent association of St. David with it. He was clearly the symbol for the autonomy of the Welsh Church and of the hope of its renewal in association with the victory of the national hero. He was invoked in the *Armes Prydein* and he was present in the prophecies at a number of critical points all the way down to Dafydd Llwyd o Fathafarn on the eve of the Tudor victory.

There were even prophecies attributed to his authorship. He finally came into his own at the time of the Reformation, when Welsh reformers tried to set the record straight after centuries of what they saw as spiritual calumny. They maintained that it was not the sins of the British that had been punished by Anglo-Saxon victory. On the contrary, the British had fallen into Roman idolatry and wickedness only when forced to do so at the point of Anglo-Saxon swords. The true vindication of the ancient prophecies, so the Welsh Protestant humanists argued by inference, was the spiritual renewal associated with the introduction of reformed doctrine.

Despite the existence of these religious associations and overtones, however, the myth remained an essentially secular one. When we ask ourselves what were its perennial sources of appeal and stimulation, we find that the first and deepest source of satisfaction that any myth could bring was that it helped to relieve the tension caused by the disparity between the actual and the ideal. Real life in medieval Wales brought pressures that were oftentimes well-nigh intolerable; the threat of defeat, enslavement, and even annihilation by external enemies. Perhaps the only way in which the disintegration of the people's morale could be prevented was by an appeal which transcended the anxieties of a disordered present by drawing sustenance from the supposed *mores* and achievements of a glorious past which were to be reinstated in the future. The sense of dignity of socially-repressed strata is most satisfyingly nourished, as Max Weber argued, on the belief that a special historic mission is entrusted to them. Moreover, one of the particular tribulations of the Welsh was their own fatal proneness to internecine feuds. It can hardly be an accident that an essential feature of the myth was its concentration upon a united past and a united future under a common deliverer. Again, the emphasis upon the awesome disasters and upheavals, bloodshed and battles that must precede final victory was stressed in Wales, no doubt as in other countries, in order to brace men to make those greater-than-normal efforts and sacrifices that would be needed 'to take arms against a sea of troubles'.

That the poets should shoulder the prime responsibility for conveying this message from one generation to another was to be expected. They were historians and genealogists, not just for the prince himself but for the whole community associated with him.

Descent and lineage were his and his subjects' claim to land and authority. The poets, too, were the ideologists, propagandists, and morale-builders, who were as conscious of their obligation to posterity as of their debt to ancestry. As such their influence was not confined to princes, noblemen and literary patrons; it ramified throughout the free population of Wales – an unusually large proportion of the populace – from whom the rulers and gentry hoped to recruit military and political support. The status and prestige of the poets were acknowledged by their own people in the honoured position they were accorded at court and in the laws. Their influence was recognized also by their adversaries, especially by some of the English kings, who identified the bards as the most dangerous organs of opinion and resistance in Wales (see also pp. 127–9).

At this point, two serious objections could well be raised: that the bards were, to a large extent, the creatures of their patrons; and that the latter could induce them to manipulate the aspirations enshrined in the prophecies to serve their patrons' immediate political ends. Both are valid. Very often the grandiloquent vaticinations of the poets wrap up the power politics of Welsh princes or gentry. Their fine phrases, stripped of bardic rhetoric, may mean nothing more than the assertion by one Welsh prince or gentleman of his own and/or his faction's right to land and authority in some part of Wales. Large-sounding prophecies were commonly used in the same way in other parts of Britain and Europe to advance relatively narrow ends, and contemporary politicians are no strangers to the art of identifying sectional advantage with the common good. However, the really interesting consideration remains that these Welsh poets and their patrons should nevertheless think it indispensable that they should go to the trouble of casting their ambitions in this particular prophetic mould; they believed it eminently worth their while presenting themselves as the true heirs to the myth. It would be easy, but foolish, to be cynical about them. Of course their motives were a mixture of personal ambition and patriotic pride; and the proportions of the amalgam varied widely from individual to individual. Could we expect it to be otherwise? Has there ever been an age when this was not so? Self-seeking and opportunism are constant ingredients in the chemistry of political activity; but if the myth and the ideology it encapsulated had been no more than the tool of private ambition it could never have lasted so long or exerted so profound an influence. Only as a response to a more broadly based and deeply felt social need could it have renewed itself repeatedly over so many generations. That is not to say that many, if any, of the medieval Welshmen expected the prophecy of the re-establishment of Welsh rule over the whole island and the permanent subjection of the English to be literally fulfilled. It did, however, embody for them two indispensable assumptions about their forebears, themselves, and their progeny; assumptions which they would never willingly or lightly relinquish. The one was that they were descended from one of the most ancient and honourable stocks in Europe, which gave them a separate identity as a people that they wanted to see preserved. The other was that their status as a people made them unwilling to submit to being treated as a race of conquered and untrustworthy barbarians; that whoever their theoretical overlords might be, the only men whose right they recognized to bear direct authority over them were men of their own race or those who had identified themselves with it. Again and again they could be induced to respond to the leadership of men who were able successfully to appeal to them on the basis of the vindication of these rights. In a glimpse we get from Archbishop Pecham of the attitude of the common people, as penetrating as it is rare, he warned Edward I that the 'people of Snowdon say that even if the prince would intend to hand them over to the king, that they had no intention to do homage to a foreigner *(alicui extraneo)* whose language, laws and customs are completely unknown to them'.

* * *

Interest in prophecy did not disappear in the sixteenth century. On the contrary, there is abundant evidence that it continued to grip popular imagination, especially in times of crisis. This was as true of England as Wales. There was a whole crop of prophecies circulating at the time of Henry VIII's breach with Rome, again in the shadow of the Armada, and once more during the course of the Civil War between King and Parliament and its aftermath. Dissident nobles like the Dukes of Buckingham and Norfolk, or the

Earls of Northumberland and Essex, encouraged the preservation and promulgation of prophecies favourable to their interest, as did the rebels associated with John Ket. 'Essentially it was the existence of rebellious feelings which led to the circulation of prophecies . . . It was no accident that the periods when prophecies were most prominent in English life were precisely those of rebellion, discontent and violent change' (Keith Thomas).

A similar pattern was observable in Wales. During the troubles in which the house of Dynevor became involved in the 1520s and 1530s, prophecy had its part to play. This family, with its highly evocative and emotionally charged arms of the three ravens, had long been associated with prophetic poetry. Among the charges brought against the young head of the house, Rhys ap Gruffydd, was one that he had encouraged seditious prophecies that the King of Scotland, together with the Red Hand ('Llawgoch') and the ravens would conquer all England. When Rhys himself was executed in 1531 his turbulent and ambitious kinsman, James ap Gruffydd ap Howell, went abroad unreconciled to the house of Tudor and bent on scheming against it. Some twenty years later, in the course of furious altercations between Robert Ferrar, a Yorkshireman who became Bishop of St. David's, and his leading clergy, one of the most serious accusations brought against him was that he had tried to curry favour with the Welsh in his diocese by stirring up old prophecies of Merlin that the Welsh were again to rule the whole island. Welsh Catholic exiles of Elizabeth's reign were much concerned to uphold Geoffrey of Monmouth's history and the possibility that prophecies propitious to their cause might still be fulfilled. As late as 1600, in a remarkable letter to Sir Robert Cecil, a disgruntled Welsh correspondent, Lod[ovic] Lloyd, claimed that 'the old Romans were not as addicted to their Sybils, the Egyptians to the priests of Memphis, nor the Frenchmen to their superstitious Druids', as many in his country were 'given to the prophecies of Merlin, or to the fond fables of Taliessin; . . . the Jewish Rabbins wrought not so much upon Moses' Pentateuch in their Talmuds, or the Turks upon their sacred Musaph in their Alcorans, as they which they call "Bardi Brytannorum" wrought of Merlin and Taliessin and others'. Were he sheriff that year in Cardigan he would bring 'such volumes of prophecies that after reading them

Cecil should make better fire of them in London than Duke Ogis made in Athens of all the writing tables of usurers'. In the following year another of Cecil's correspondents, John Garnons, wrote of his fears that the Earl of Essex and his confederates might derive support and confidence from the rather cloudy prophecies of a Welsh 'priest and soothsayer', Lewis Devett. In the disturbed days of the Commonwealth that Welsh prophetic original, Arise Evans, was urging the English to think of themselves as Britons so as to avoid the divinely-ordained punishment which the Saxons were destined to undergo; and in 1658 his fellow-countryman, Thomas Pugh, published his *British and Outlandish Prophesies: most of above a thousand years' antiquity* . . . in which he envisaged Oliver Cromwell, a descendant of Cadwaladr and of the princes of Powys, as the long-prophesied conqueror. Right down to the beginning of the nineteenth century the magic of Merlin's name and the enchantment of his prophecies continued to captivate some of the common folk of Wales. Printed in pamphlets and sold in fairs, the vaticinations continued to foretell the splendid, but bloody, victories in which the Welsh would 'wash their hands in the blood of Saxons'. (I owe this last point to the kindness of my friend and colleague, Dr. Prys Morgan).

There was no doubt, either, of the continuing popularity of the 'British history' and Geoffrey of Monmouth. Welsh scholars put up an ardent and spirited defence of the Galfridian version of history in reply to the 'calumnies' of Polydore Vergil and other critics. This did not necessarily mean that they thought the prophecies associated with it had been or were still to be fulfilled, but without belief in the traditional Welsh view of the past there could be no substance or meaning in the prophecies. The sixteenth century was, moreover, the age of the first great antiquary-collectors and copyists. Among the materials zealously sought after and preserved by them were the poetry and prose-writings associated with the history and prophecies. Such an interest was not confined to a select handful of littérateurs and scholars. It was reported of Wales that

> upon Sundays and holidays the multitude of all sorts of men, women and children of every parish do use to meet in sundry places . . . where their harpers and crowthers sing them songs of the doings of their ancestors, namely of their wars against the kings of this realm and the English nation, and then do

they rip up their pedigrees at length, how each of them is descended from those their old princes.

Despite this evidence of continuing interest in history and prophecy, a rapid and unmistakable decline came over Welsh prophetic poetry in the sixteenth century. Like other medieval forms of expression it found the soil and climate of Tudor Wales uncongenial. The living essence was drained out of it and no new growth took place. It found virtually no niche in contemporary verse, in either the customary fixed metres or in the new free verse now emerging. There was no longer any poet whose reputation was chiefly based on his knowledge of divination or his skill in expounding it. Prophetic themes had clearly ceased to have the same meaning and attraction for patrons that they had once enjoyed. Interest in them among the literary men of the age was largely confined to antiquarian curiosity, and prophetic poetry had almost no relevance as a weapon to be used in contemporary politics. Whatever difficulties there may be in trying to trace the dawn of Welsh prophetic poetry, there is no doubt that its sunset has to be placed in the sixteenth century.

No single reason will suffice to explain this sudden eclipse. Partly it was brought about by the decay from within of the bardic order itself. Though the circumstances which brought this about are as yet far from having been fully explained, it is clear that the medieval system became fatally weakened in the sixteenth century and by the end of it was in full decline. The whole function and status in society of the poets were placed in grave jeopardy during the period. This crisis in the fortunes of the bardic order, the originators, guardians, and mentors of the poetic prophecies, must grievously have impaired the continuing composition of them. Yet it can hardly provide the complete explanation, because the prophetic poetry withered much sooner and faster than other kinds of conventional verse and long before the general decline in Welsh poetry had reached crisis proportions.

The decay of the traditional poetry was paralleled by the rise of other cultural values and interests. This was the age of the Renaissance and the Reformation when Welshmen's eyes were turned to new horizons, which sometimes led to an adjustment of perspective that was sceptical and critical of customary Welsh literary criteria.

No doubt this helped to contribute to the enervation of some features of the old literary order. But too much stress should not be laid on this point. Everywhere in Europe Renaissance scholarship could be happily if incongruously married with some medieval conceptions. Wales was no exception; and Welsh Renaissance scholars were among the most ardent admirers of the earlier Welsh literary achievement and of the 'matter of Britain', whose cause they so warmly espoused. It is possible that particular Welsh views of the Reformation may have done more to deprive the older prophecies of their impact than the Renaissance did. Welsh Protestant humanists contended that the coming of the Reformation to Wales did not represent the imposition of anything new-fangled or foreign, but that it was the reinstatement of the pristine faith of the ancient British in their Golden Age, the restoration of the one cardinal virtue that, above all others, had made them great. Here indeed, it could be argued, was the true vindication, the supreme consummation, of the prophecies. Yet this exposition came relatively late, long after the prophetic poetry could be seen to be far gone in its decay and can hardly have been a primary reason in accounting for it.

Much more weighty than any of the considerations so far adduced was the belief of many of the Welsh that Henry Tudor's victory at Bosworth had fulfilled the Cymric destiny. The last front-rank stalwart of the poetic tradition of prophecy, Dafydd Llwyd o Fathafarn, certainly thought so. He sang of Henry:

Ag ef ni bu neb gyfuwch
Dan y nef nid â dyn uwch.

('No one reached as high as he; under heaven no man will go higher').

Many of his compatriots saw Henry's triumph in the same light. The Tudor had a very plausible case, particularly for those who wanted to believe it. Through his grandfather, Owain Tudor, he could claim to be sprung from illustrious Welsh lineage, and poets were prepared to acclaim his descent from the stock of Cadwaladr himself. In advance of his invasion his sympathizers had sedulously tried to whip up support for him in Wales as 'mab darogan' ('son of prophecy'). After his accession he had, on the whole, treated his Welsh subjects more favourably than earlier English rulers had done. To the general Tudor myth of the dynasty as the healers of the wounds of civil strife and the sole bulwark against another lapse into anarchy was added in Wales the image of Henry VII as the Moses who had led his people from bondage into freedom. Yet even here we have only part of the answer to our problem. The Tudors after Henry VII did nothing to identify themselves with the 'matter of Britain' and made no effort to encourage this notion of the fulfilment of the kind of prophecy associated with it. Not only did they not foster that prophecy but they showed considerable sensitivity on the subject of prophecy in general, and they went to great pains to suppress 'fond and fantastic prophecies' by all the paraphernalia of state control – statutes, proclamations, orders by the Privy Council, inquiries by justices of the peace, and episcopal visitations. The hostile attitude of local Welsh clerics to Ferrar's references to Merlin's prophecies and the views expressed by Cecil's correspondents suggest that people in Wales were well aware of the régime's disapproval of prophecies.

While we should be unwise to dismiss as of no consequence the genuine pleasure undeniably derived by many of the Tudors' Welsh subjects at the sight of what they believed to be a Welsh dynasty ruling on the English throne, it is hard to accept that this alone accounted for the extinction of the prophetic poetry. The critical factor was whether or not Welsh emotional satisfaction at the victory of the 'Welsh' Tudors was underpinned and perpetuated by the latter's willingness to meet the political, social and economic ambitions of the ruling class in Wales. This class wanted to preserve in the sixteenth century the two indestructible assumptions of their predecessors in early medieval Wales; that they were descended from one of the most distinguished peoples in Europe, and that the right to rule in their own localities ought to be reserved to Welshmen. It was to assert the former that they continued to cling so tenaciously to the old British history. But the prophecies had been invoked primarily to defend the latter, and were now no longer really necessary. What had decisively changed the situation was that the Welsh gentry's right to bear rule and authority in Wales had been made clear beyond all doubt and safeguarded by statute. The real key to the Tudors' success in Wales lay far less in their Welsh descent than in their willingness to align the interests of the

Crown and those of the Welsh landowners. That is the secret revealed by the panegyrics of George Owen, the most authentic and articulate surviving voice of the Welsh Tudor gentry. He drew the sharpest contrast between the pre-Tudor kings, 'who by open hostility and wars as by providing of extreme intolerable laws sought continually the subversion, ruin and impoverishing of Wales', and Henry VII and his son 'who came to redress those enormities and to establish good and wholesome laws among them and to give them *magistrates of their own nation*' (my italics). It had been the acceptance of this concept of the relationship between the Tudors and the Welsh which, more than anything else, had outmoded the prophetic poetry and rendered it superfluous.

IV. Religion and Education in Wales: an Historical Survey

If there is one man above all others whose name deserves to be honoured here today* it is Thomas Burgess, Bishop of St. David's from 1803 to 1825. His memory is particularly apposite to my theme because few churchmen have ever been more conscious than he of a historic bond between religion and education in Wales. In 1812, ten years before he laid the foundation stone of Saint David's College, Lampeter, he spoke with deep feeling of the seminary for young men intended for holy orders which he hoped to found. 'It is peculiarly incumbent on us to be zealous in the maintenance of the Gospel', he urged, 'and in the cultivation of every branch of knowledge most conducive to that end. The names of David and Asser, Sulien and Rhigyfarch, are sufficient to remind the natives of this part of the Principality' ... that 'their attainments and virtues afford models of piety, diligence, and erudition which will not be lost on the students of Saint David's College, whenever our wishes and endeavours shall be accomplished.' It was an inspiring vision which he offered his hearers. If his history was not at all times well-founded, his basic instinct was sound. There had, indeed, been more than a thousand years of close and fertile association between religion and education in their country to which the Welsh could look back with pride.

This close connexion between religion and education is not peculiar to Wales or to Christendom. Nearly all religions beyond the most primitive have found it necessary to maintain a priesthood which has served as the learned class in society. The specialization of the priestly role seems to have been one of the earliest and most widespread examples of the division of labour in human society. Even in archaic times a priest had to be educated to the extent of being able to master ritual and sacred texts, and also, in some instances, to keep records and work out a calendar. All the later world religions, including Christianity, have similarly attached great importance to the education of the priesthood. They did so even when education among the laity was of little or no consequence and

*This lecture was originally delivered at Saint David's University College, Lampeter, on 1 March 1977 as part of the celebration of the 150th anniversary of the opening of the College by Bishop Burgess. I have to thank the Principal of the College, Dr. B. R. Rees, for his kind invitation to deliver the lecture on that occasion and for readily consenting to allow me to publish it in this volume.

when such instruction as was imparted to the community at large was necessarily derived almost wholly from the religious teachers.

In Wales, indeed, over a very large span of the fourteen hundred years or so that come under review there was little or no demand for formal education among the mass of the population. Wales was, for much of that period, an agricultural country, and a remote and economically poor pastoral one at that. Its people, made up mainly of small farmers and labourers and their families, were thinly dispersed in isolated communities. There were few towns or concentrations of population, nor did there exist on any scale the kinds of trade or profession for which literacy was essential. The ruling élite itself had little need for or interest in book-learning before the end of the Middle Ages; and as for the mass of the people it was not until two centuries later that there was a concerted drive to bring even the minimal basis of literacy to them. Not that we should minimize the value of other kinds of training provided in such a society, especially the merits of fine craftsmanship and the long and rigorous period of apprenticeship needed to acquire it. But as far as education in the usual sense of the term was concerned, the driving-force came only and necessarily from the Church and its ministers.

Over the whole of the long era from the fifth century down to the nineteenth century, Wales was basically a Christian country, in which the teaching of the Church, or Churches, was accepted as the regulative norm of belief, worship, conduct and obligation – in theory, anyway. Throughout all these centuries it was this central fact which determined and coloured the impact of religion on education. There were three aspects in which its influence became particularly apparent: the education of the clergy; the instruction of the laity in religious belief and observance; and the maintenance of moral standards and social responsibilities. A brief preliminary discussion of the implications of each may be helpful.

First, there was the education of the clergy, which was inevitably shaped by the nature of Christian belief and the needs of public worship. Christianity is founded on what Christians hold to be the revelation of divine truth to men; originally through the agency of the religious genius of the Hebrew people and later through the life and teachings of the Son of God himself. The record of such revelation was enshrined in the texts of Scripture. It was essential that the Christian clergy should be able to read, expound and preserve these sacred books, and highly desirable that they should also have some acquaintance with the mass of exposition and commentary which had grown up around them. Furthermore, the ritual of public worship was also written down in service books which the clergy must master. Not only were there sacred books; there were also sacred languages – Latin in particular – with which the clergy ought to be familiar. For many centuries no other category of men in Wales had so compelling a need to be educated and literate, except the bards and the lawyers, and even they to a considerably lesser extent. Not surprisingly there was, for a very long time, a virtual monopoly of education by clerics. There was, however, an essential link between the education of the clergy and the use of the vernacular language. In the first place, the majority of the clergy had only a limited mastery of Latin. There was a ruling class among the clergy as well as the laity, and it was this ruling class only which underwent the long period of instruction in Latin. The majority of the clergy, the rank and file, often had not much more than a smattering of the language. Then secondly, however much or little the clergy themselves knew of the sacred languages, they had no choice but to instruct the lay people in their vernacular tongue. Nor were the clergy concerned only with the functional and utilitarian aspect of language; some of them also appreciated the fulfilment to be derived from being artists in the use of words. From very early times there has been a particularly close association of the clergy with Welsh literature, in poetry and prose, which has continued unbroken down to our own times.

As far as the instruction of the laity was in question, no matter how enthusiastic and diligent the clergy might be, in a largely illiterate society their capacity to instruct laymen was necessarily limited. It became potentially vastly more effective if those being taught were themselves literate. One of the key motifs of our theme in modern times is the prodigious effort made by some clerics, with the support of enlightened laymen, to extend literacy. This found expression not merely in teaching people to read but also in stimulating them to do so and in providing them with books on which they could exercise their newly-found skills. Beginning in the sixteenth century, the campaign gained enormously in strength in the seventeenth and eighteenth centuries, and reached its peak in the nineteenth. The object of such endeavour was to enrich religious belief and understanding and to strengthen Christian behaviour. That has always been recognized as the prime function of the clergy's role. Nevertheless, it has rarely been possible to divorce this from the inculcation of ideas of moral obligation and social responsibility, the third theme which calls for brief introductory comment.

While we may not need to accept in its entirety the view that the social function of religion is to support and conserve an ongoing society, it does seem difficult to deny that religion expresses group loyalties and sustains them. Its emphasis in practice has frequently been to accept, justify, and adjust to the existing order of things in government and society. But it is also true that there can often come into existence a state of creative tension between the values espoused by some Christians and those upheld by the existing institutions of secular and ecclesiastical authority. Of necessity this is less likely to happen in an established church than amid a reformed religious order, or a sect or denomination. An established church has to include all sorts and conditions of men and women; inevitably it lays stress on the sacraments, the priesthood, and the organization of teaching and practice to secure religious uniformity and social cohesion. Reforming movements or sects, on the other hand, are made up mainly of committed individuals, especially in their earliest phases. They emphasize the role and responsibility of believers and may challenge not only the religious and educational modes of the dominant church but also the political authority and social hegemony of the lay power which maintains the status of that church.

These three themes already touched upon – education of the clergy, instruction of the laity, and moral and social responsibilities – are inter-related constants throughout the whole of our period. But the forms they assumed and their impact on society varied markedly in the course of changing historical epochs. There are five of these major epochs in the history of Wales which we need to consider for our present purpose: (1) the era of the Celtic Church, from the end of Roman imperial rule in the fifth century to the advent of the Normans towards the end of the eleventh century; (2) the Middle Ages, from the Norman Conquest to *c.* 1500; (3) the epoch of the Renaissance and the Reformation from *c.* 1500 to 1642; (4) the age of fission from 1642 to *c.* 1800; and finally, the nineteenth century.

The Celtic era is much the most obscure of all. Mystery still surrounds the introduction of Christianity into Wales and the extent and nature of Christian worship and belief in the late imperial period. What we do know is that after the Roman legions left and Rome no longer exercised its sway the Celtic Church inherited a tradition of *romanitas* which it greatly treasured. *Romanitas* in this context meant two things: it implied upholding Christian values as opposed to paganism; and, what was almost synonymous, it involved maintaining civilization as against barbarism. The strongest early centres of Christian activity in post-Roman Wales lay precisely in those regions which had come most powerfully under the impress of the Roman Empire – Erging or Archenfield where Dyfrig laboured, or the Vale of Glamorgan where Illtud founded his great church and school. Throughout the centuries that followed, the Celtic Church was obliged to fight stubbornly to protect this original patrimony. It did so in face of all the threats of a turbulent and, at times, calamitous era in Welsh and European history. The pressures to which it was exposed were severe and protracted. When it had staved off the attacks of the Irish and the Anglo-Saxons it was, in later centuries, a favourite target for pillage and devastation by savage and pagan Scandinavian invaders. Nor did all the disruptive forces emanate from outside Wales. Within the country, the native ruling dynasties and powerful lay families, though converted to the Christian religion, were not above succumbing to a perennial temptation to divert the resources of the Church to their own mundane ends. The shortage of reliable sources of information makes it hazardous to pronounce too confidently on the state of Wales between the fifth and eleventh centuries, yet what evidence there is suggests positively that it was as true of Wales as of other European countries that what was retained of the religion and culture of Christian classical antiquity was preserved very largely by the Church. It did manage to keep the flame of belief and civilization alight even if there were occasions when under the force of barbarian winds it flickered perilously low and dim.

In this dedicated and tenacious succession one of the earliest and most illustrious names is that of Illtud, founder of the celebrated

school at Llanilltud Fawr (Llantwit Major). It was claimed for
Illtud that his knowledge of the Old and New Testament and of
other learning and the arts excelled that of all other Britons. To his
school came pupils from far afield; not only a cleric like Samson of
Brittany but also, possibly, even a prince like the rumbustious
Maelgwn, ruler of Gwynedd. The writings of Illtud's pupil, Gildas,
give us a striking insight into the quality of the education imparted
at Illtud's school. Although Gildas's complicated and rhetorical
effusions may not be to everyone's taste there can be no mistaking
the correctness or the vigour of his Latin prose nor his extraordinary
mastery of the Old Testament and the New. He was certainly no
half-educated barbarian mutilating a scriptural exegesis or degrading
a classical tongue. Indeed, there is some reason to think that the
Celtic Church of the generation of Illtud and Gildas set a standard
of cultural achievement that later generations, especially among
the saints of south-west and north-west Wales, found impossible to
maintain in full. Nonetheless, we know that the tradition was
respected and that the contacts were maintained with the Church
in other Celtic lands and on the Continent. Manuscripts like the
famous Gospels of St. Chad are reminders that if Wales was poorer
than either Ireland or Northumbria and less prolific in its output
of works of learning, it still continued to maintain scriptoria for the
production of manuscripts in some of its larger monasteries. Nor
should we forget that when the Anglo-Saxon King Alfred wanted
men who combined learning with piety to fructify the life of his
court and kingdom, among the most influential of those he summoned to his court was Asser, a man from the western diocese of
St. David's. Similarly, in the eleventh century, on the eve of the
Norman Conquest, the clerical family of Llancarfan in the diocese of
Llandaff and Bishop Sulien and his sons in St. David's leave us in no
doubt that the old Celtic Church, despite all its vicissitudes, could
still produce from among its ranks outstanding individuals and
dynasties among the clergy who were renowned for their administrative and intellectual competence as well as their spiritual
fervour.

Mention of Sulien and his sons brings us to the threshold of the Middle Ages proper. Those three centuries from the eleventh to the fourteenth were an impressively creative phase in European history. New and dynamic social energies coursed ebulliently through all the arteries of European life – demographic, economic, political, religious, educational, and cultural. In England and Wales the advent of the Normans may have injected some added stimulus, but even if they had never crossed the Channel it seems virtually certain that there would still have been a mighty upsurge of new vigour. The twelfth-century renaissance in religion and learning brought with it the founding of many new grammar schools, especially in the cathedrals and other major churches, where the clerical élite, the future bishops and higher clergy, were nurtured. Most of these were, predictably, drawn from among the ruling class in the laity; but one of the striking features of the medieval Church was that it offered some chance of social mobility that was much less readily available in lay society. A small minority of clerics of humble birth could climb high in the ecclesiastical hierarchy if they were sufficiently able and determined to make use of the ladder provided by education. The actual education provided for the clergy was, to all intents and purposes, much the same throughout western Christendom. It was rooted deep in the old world of Latin antiquity, consisting basically of a rigorous grounding in Latin grammar and a Latin literature partly pagan but chiefly Christian in content. In addition to the grammar schools associated with cathedrals there were also schools and centres of learning established in a number of the new-style monasteries of a Latin type now founded in Wales; not so much for the community in general but mainly in the interests of their own inmates. Within some of the monastic cloisters chronicles like *Brut y Tywysogyon* ('Chronicle of the Princes') were compiled, and in their scriptoria some of the most precious of Welsh literary manuscripts, like the Book of Taliesin or the Red Book of Hergest, were copied. By the thirteenth century the universities had come into being and were almost wholly monopolized by the clergy. Since the language of instruction was the international *lingua franca* of Latin it was not uncommon for the ablest young scholars of Welsh origin to venture to the most famous of medieval universities, especially to Paris. The most talented of their number – a John

4*

Wallensis, master of the Franciscans at Oxford and Paris, or a Thomas Waleys, also a celebrated graduate of Oxford and Paris – enjoyed a European reputation.

Because the clergy of this kind constituted by far the best-educated group in the medieval world it was not to be wondered at that their highly-trained and finely-tuned minds should be used in the management of lay affairs as well as in the service of the Church. Independent Welsh princes of the twelfth and thirteenth centuries, like other rulers of the age, used clerics extensively as advisers, administrators and diplomats. Just over a century after the extinction of these princes in 1282–3, when Owain Glyn Dŵr launched his bid early in the fifteenth century to re-create an independent state in Wales, significantly enough one of the boldest of his proposals was to establish two universities in Wales, one in the north and the other in the south. His intention in doing so almost certainly had far less to do with the need to reform religion or improve education than with the sternly practical necessity of having at his disposal an independent source to supply him with well-educated administrators.

So much for the minority élite among the medieval clergy; the Church also depended on a large body of rank-and-file clerics to minister to the day-to-day needs of the parishes. The academic attainments of the lower clergy were infinitely more modest than those of their superiors in the hierarchy and their knowledge of Latin distinctly more rudimentary. The splendid corpus of theological, philosophical and devotional literature in Latin was largely a closed book to them. Their needs had not been overlooked, however. A considerable volume of vernacular literature had been compiled with the object of grounding the parish priest in the essentials of Christian faith and practice to enable him in turn to pass on to his flock as much as he could of what he had learnt. There were Welsh translations of key passages from the Bible, Welsh versions of the creeds, popular hymns and prayers, manuals of instruction, sermons, saints' lives, and a variety of other religious prose texts. Alongside this major prose contribution to medieval Welsh literature, and often inspired by it, the poets created a wide range of religious verse, designed to convey religious and moral precepts and to voice men's awareness of the majesty and mystery of the Godhead. So all-pervasive was the influence of the Church on learning, literacy and literature that it thoroughly impregnated the education and attitudes of those who were members of what might have been thought of as being entirely secular professions – poets, littérateurs, lawyers and physicians. The Church was, moreover, the supreme patron and inspiration of music and of the visual arts of architecture, sculpture, painting, carving in wood and metal, and the like. All were permeated through and through by the themes and ethos of the Christian religion and most of their productions were dedicated to its service. The civilization of the Middle Ages was the child of two parents – the Church and the feudal aristocracy – but in that union it was the Church which was the more creative and fruitful partner.

Even so, in the century and a half before 1500 there were some clear signs that the clerical monopoly of piety and learning was not as complete as it had been. Partly this was due to the severe economic crises through which the Church passed between about 1340 and 1450, which sharply reduced the number of clerics being highly educated and damaged the prosperity of many monasteries. Furthermore, far more clerics now studied law than theology and were better fitted for careers as administrators than as pastors of souls. Quite apart from any shortcomings among the clergy, however, there was also emerging a positive trend towards more active participation in religious and intellectual life on the part of the more thoughtful among the laity. Much of the religious literature in Welsh was being commissioned by laymen for their own edification. A larger part of the most serious and meditative religious verse of the fifteenth century was composed by lay poets than by clerics. A sprinkling of layfolk was discerning the value of formal education, like Sir John Wynn's fifteenth-century ancestor who was sent to Caernarfon to learn English and Latin, 'a matter of great moment in those days'. A few were even venturing to the universities and even more to the inns of court. At least one of them, Walter Brut, returned from Oxford as a notorious Lollard heretic who could boldly debate theology and scripture in Latin in defiance of the bishop of Hereford and a formidable panel of high-ranking clerics brought to try him for heresy. Already in the fifteenth century the age of the Renaissance and the Reformation was casting some long and unmistakable shadows ahead of it. The monopoly of religious devotion, formal education, and intellectual initiative previously enjoyed by the clerisy had been perceptibly breached. More lay men and women understood the value of literacy, the private meditation of religious literature, and the consolation of individual piety. Lay governments had already extended their control over the Church at the expense of an enfeebled papacy. Great revolutions are often preceded by a period of gestation, which sometimes bears an air of deceptive calm, broken only by short-lived upheavals. Thus does the fifteenth century, viewed retrospectively, tend to appear in comparison with the tumults of the century which succeeded it.

When we survey the century and a half between *c.* 1500 and 1642 we can detect three sources of ferment, the effect of which on religion and education was nothing short of revolutionary. The three inordinately active viruses in the intellectual and spiritual bloodstream of Europe were the Renaissance, the Reformation, and the printed book. The significance of each of the three could form the basis of a study in itself; all that we can do here is to skate fleetingly over the surface of each.

The Renaissance brought a profoundly improved knowledge of the three sacred languages of the Christian tradition, and notably of Greek and Hebrew. This was matched by keenly refined critical techniques of establishing and editing ancient texts. In the light of the universal humanist emphasis on the need for a return *ad fontes*, to the fountain-head of the ancient world, what texts could be more worthy of the application of that greater mastery of language and critique than the very sources of the Christian religion itself – the Scriptures? Emphatically was this the frame of mind, seen at its most influential in Erasmus, of those earnest men of the Renaissance who saw it serve its true function only when it was the handmaiden of faith. Nor should we overlook the widely-diffused Renaissance insistence on the ideal of a classical education, which no man worthy of the name gentleman should lack. Such Renaissance inspiration was not restricted to the classical languages; it sparked off in many humanists a burning ambition to make their own vernacular languages and literatures worthy to compare in depth of content and felicity of expression with the three supreme languages of the ancient world.

Embraced by many who had already come under the allure of Renaissance humanism, the doctrines of the Reformation added a further emphasis of their own. The Reformers' insistence upon the exclusive authority of the Scriptures, taken in concert with their affirmation of the role and responsibility of the individual believer, placed an altogether new and enhanced value on the need to render the Bible available in the vulgar tongue and to make it as widely circulated, read, and understood as possible. It also envisaged an incalculably wider degree of intelligent literacy and participation on the part of the laity, as well as the clergy, than ever before.

For all their power and attraction the ideals of the Renaissance and the Reformation could not readily or fully have been consummated had it not been for the emergence of the printed book in the fifteenth century. It proved to be the essential key to the success and permanence of the cultural and religious revolutions of the age. Humanists and reformers, whether Catholic or Protestant, saw the printed book as being strategically indispensable for the dissemination of their doctrines. Printing was the medium which had revolutionized knowledge, education, and communication even more drastically, probably, than broadcasting has done in our own time.

How, then, did the combined influences of Renaissance, Reformation, and printing mould and modify religion and education in Wales? One remarkable paradox was that although the Reformation diminished the function of the clergy insofar as it proclaimed the priesthood of all believers, this led to a demand for a clergy that was more educated not less. The stronger insistence on the clergy's duty as preachers of the word required them to be more expert in their knowledge of the sacred texts and their exposition. More of them were encouraged to become graduates, though university-trained men remained a minority. Welsh papists also took cognizance of this need for better-educated clergy, and in their seminaries on the Continent sought to give their young missionary priests a more thorough training than ever most of the medieval priesthood had had. Reformers and Romanists were at one in their appreciation of the crucial need to extend the clergy's instruction of the lay people through the medium of the mother tongue. In Wales this was to be of immense significance. During the next two centuries the language and the literature of the country owed an enormous debt to the devoted labours of the clergy. They were the only literate and educated social group who had an inescapable need to use Welsh in the course of their professional duties. If the clerics among the great Welsh writers of prose and poetry over these two centuries were removed, the roll-call of Welsh authors of the front rank would be more than halved.

These developments also threw a spotlight on the place of the layman in religion and education. Humanists, reformers and statesmen all underlined the demand for a more learned laity. The outcome was a boom in formal education which attracted an unprecedented influx of laymen into schools and universities. Much of the impetus behind this was secular in origin; it sprang from the needs of the Crown for an augmented force of administrators in central and local government and from the ambitions of the upper classes to acquire greater power and influence as servants of the State. But a powerful religious driving-force also contributed. Sound learning was firmly believed to be the nurse of Christian belief, piety, morals and loyalty. Most of the teachers at all levels were still clerics; they were the tutors in private households or in the parishes, the masters in the grammar schools, whether endowed or private, and the fellows of colleges in the universities.

Though it was the sons of gentry and yeomen who benefited most from this spate of classical education, the needs of the monoglot masses were not wholly neglected. The campaign to teach them the new doctrines in their native tongue led to the translation of the Bible and the Book of Common Prayer. It was perhaps appropriately symbolic of the enhanced status of the educated layman and his increased participation that the two men first responsible for the translations were a layman and a bishop, William Salesbury and Richard Davies. Each was a dedicated humanist, a committed reformer, and an ardent protagonist of the absolute need to disseminate printed literature among the Welsh; and so were all their successors in the field. There were others, however, who perceived the limitations of the printed book in Wales while at the same time acknowledging the need for more instruction in the vernacular.

They continued to make use of the oral tradition, especially in the composition of popular religious verses, which circulated widely among the common people. Notable examples of the *genre* were the *cwndidau* of Glamorgan and Gwent, the *halsingod* of the Teifi valley, and, most influential of all, the immensely popular verses of Vicar Rhys Prichard, which were transmitted by word of mouth over a wide area of South Wales for a generation or two before being published in full in printed form for the first time in 1672.

The Reformation also had major repercussions on the relations between religion and politics, between Church and State. When the English monarchy broke with the papacy and fashioned its supreme headship of the Church of England, it became imperative that the new kind of sovereignty thus brought into being should be underpinned and buttressed by religious sanctions. Political and social theory taught that the prince derived his authority from God and knew no earthly superior. Obedience to him as head of State and head of the Church was, therefore, a religious duty as well as a political obligation. Disloyalty to him was tantamount to disobedience against God. It was religion which authorized all forms of governance within the realm; not only the rule of kings over subjects but the authority of magistrates over lawbreakers, masters over servants, landlords over tenants, husbands over wives and parents over children. Men and women of all social degrees were taught by ministers of religion to recognize and accept their place in society and the rights and duties attaching to their station. The outcome by the end of the sixteenth century in both Protestant and Catholic countries alike tended to be an erastian situation, in which kings and princes supervised ecclesiastical organization within their own countries. But in Protestant countries like England and Wales the Reformation had released energies which it would be difficult to contain within the bounds of a state church. Any challenge to that church on religious grounds must contain within it a threat to the established political structure and possibly also to the social order. Such a state of affairs had become apparent in the reign of Elizabeth when there emerged a powerful if unsuccessful Presbyterian opposition and even a tiny separatist enclave. James I recognized the implications clearly enough in his much-quoted aphorism, 'No bishop, no king'; they became still more unmistakable later in the seventeenth century as we move into what was earlier described as the age of fission, 1642–1800.

It would be impracticable to examine in any detail the nature of the conflict between Anglicans and Puritans which accompanied and intensified the political clash between Charles I and his adversaries. Suffice it to say that the term 'Puritan Revolution' has a very real meaning and that laymen and clerics on both sides of the divide took the issues extremely seriously. The gulf between them became more unbridgeable as the result of the conflicts of the Civil War and the Puritan régime which followed. That régime, though it lasted no more than a dozen years, left behind it harsh and permanent scars on the consciousness of Welsh Churchmen and Dissenters. The decade between 1650 and 1660 witnessed a concerted drive on the part of the Commonwealth State to eliminate the Anglican clergy's influence from church and school. Anglican incumbents were removed in large numbers from their benefices, to be replaced by ministers approved by the Puritan authorities. In tandem with the eviction of the clergy went the first large-scale experiment in state-provided education in Wales. The Propagation Act of 1650 set up in Welsh market-towns some sixty state-sponsored schools of a strongly Puritan complexion, the avowed aim of which was to wean the Welsh away from their adherence to Royalism and Anglicanism and to instil into them the ideals of the Puritan Commonwealth. It was a revolution which failed, but the impact of which was never obliterated. The split which it drove through Welsh religious loyalties has never yet been fully mended.

When in 1660 the King and the Church of England were brought back, that restoration could never be a complete return to the situation as it had been before 1642. During the years between, the Commonwealth régime had brought into being in Wales a hard core of Puritan Dissenters who could neither be compelled nor persuaded to conform to the worship and beliefs of the Established Church. Neither the persecution from 1660 to 1689, nor the toleration which ensued, could induce them to re-enter the fold. They remained a minority, it is true, but a significant minority. Henceforward, in religion and education we have to take account of a dual tradition.

This duality had far-reaching consequences. First of all there were to be two separate traditions of educating the clergy. Anglican clerics continued to be educated in the two universities, but for the next two centuries those institutions were closed to Dissenters. The latter were obliged to organize their own places of higher learning. The Nonconformist academies which came into being as a result were, in a number of instances, distinguished centres of scholarship; though within the sphere of the academies themselves there were further divergences between the denominations, each tending to make its own separate arrangements. Again, the dichotomy could be discerned in the instruction of the laity. It goes without saying that there could no longer exist a common view of the essentials of faith and worship. (This, strictly speaking, had been true since the sixteenth century, but the Catholic recusants had been far more successfully suppressed than ever it was possible to do with the Puritan Dissenters.) The differences between Church and Dissent were manifestly apparent in the output of Welsh books designed for devotion and edification. Many of them were controversial and polemical in content, intended to defend the author's particular standpoint and to attack rival Christian persuasions. Nor was the bombardment confined to skirmishes between Anglicans and Dissenters; there was equally fierce cross-fire between the Dissenters themselves. Such a dissipation of energies could ill be afforded by a small and poor country like Wales, where the total output of books was limited. But these various rivalries may not by any means have been a complete loss; their very acrimony was probably a stimulus to writers to publish more intensively than they might otherwise have done. Finally, there were serious clashes of opinion over the interpretation of religious obligations in the realm of political and social issues. Anglicans were naturally deeply suspicious of the radical views of the nature of politics and society which had surfaced during the Civil Wars. They harboured long-lasting fears of the subversive passions which they associated with Dissenting beliefs. Though Anglicans could hardly have been expected to realize it, many of their apprehensions were, in fact, ill-founded because Dissenters became increasingly more passive in their acceptance of existing institutions. They turned inward on themselves more and more, and assumed the nature of introversionist sects rather than conversionist ones. Nonetheless, they inevitably espoused ideas about politics and society noticeably less conservative than those of the establishment. The seeds of this difference, sown in the seventeenth century, germinating un-spectacularly in the eighteenth, ripened to an abundant but often unconstructive harvest in the nineteenth century.

It would be misleading, however, to overdraw the picture of con-trasts and divisions. A much wider degree of co-operation flourished among men of different persuasions than might have been supposed – for two reasons. First, all sincere Christians recognized what a mass of immorality, ignorance, superstition and apathy still survived, for which the sovereign antidotes must be systematic education and literacy. Second, there was profound and general unease among orthodox religious believers concerning the widespread dissemination of notions of deism, anti-trinitarianism, and even downright scepti-cism and unbelief, notably but by no means exclusively among the educated. If such notions percolated downwards in debased form to the poorer classes and circulated widely among them, then the very survival of accepted Christian doctrine might be in jeopardy. Given these dangers of the age it seemed incumbent on all earnest believers to act in concert to combat them. From such reactions sprang that series of philanthropic, moralistic and educational ventures in which Churchmen and Dissenters were often to be found working side by side from the seventeenth century onwards. They range from the Welsh Trust in the 1670s and '80s, the S.P.C.K. and S.P.G. in the early-eighteenth century, Griffith Jones's circulating schools of 1737–61, through to Thomas Charles and the Sunday schools and the Bible Society at the end of the eighteenth century (see also pp. 202ff.). The central aim of all these enterprises was to strengthen religion by teaching the common people to read and to provide them, either free or very cheaply, with suitable reading matter in the form of Bibles and other devotional books in Welsh. It has often been claimed for these Welsh charitable ventures that they were motivated almost exclusively by religious and moral incentives. Unlike other compara-ble activities in Great Britain, they are said to have shown little or no anxiety to condition the children of the poor, socially or politically. Such an interpretation is far from being entirely convincing. No one would for a moment deny the profound preoccupation of these enterprises with religion and morals, but any close reading of, say, the reports of much the most successful and ambitious of the educational organizations, Griffith Jones's schools, brings home at once their founder's equally burning desire that the success of his schools might serve to ward off the nightmarish possibilities of political subversion and social tumult. He warned, in a characteristic passage, that a 'general neglect of giving truly Christian instruction to the poor and common people . . . is the ready way to bring in confusion and slavery on the whole nation, in Church and State, to the utter ruin of both.' That passage is an important key not only to Jones's own approach but also that of most other contemporary philanthropists.

During the century and a half following 1660 the combined efforts of men of goodwill from all denominations wrought a massive improvement in the shape of an extraordinary diffusion of literacy and a vastly-increased publication of Welsh books, the large majority of them religious in content and intended to satisfy the voracious hunger that had been aroused by the spread of literacy. There was, indeed, a 'Great Awakening' in Wales in the eighteenth century. But it was not a phenomenon restricted to the Methodist Revival as is so often supposed; it extended much wider, across the whole spectrum of religious experience. The Established Church and the old Dissenters, as well as the Methodists, had all played a notable part in bringing it about. They had also shared in laying the foundations of that astounding religiosity and liveliness of Welsh educational and cultural life in the Victorian Age.

When we reach the unmistakable threshold of a new age with the end of the Napoleonic Wars the two most powerful forces which were largely going to dominate the life of Wales down to the First World War, at least, were clearly discernible: the rapid rise of Nonconformity and the impact of the Industrial Revolution. Ironically enough, although in the eighteenth century it was within the Anglican Church that the most dynamic energies in the revival of piety and the spread of education had been at work, it was Nonconformity which was to be the chief beneficiary. Especially was this true after

1811 when, after much heartsearching, the Calvinistic Methodists of Wales left the Church of England. During the first half of the nineteenth century all the Nonconformist denominations grew steadily and won over the majority of the population. Much of the reason for their success lay in the swift and dramatic nature of contemporary economic and social change. The steep increase in population in the rural areas and the even more explosive growth of numbers in the new industrial townships and villages put the Established Church at an immense disadvantage. It was the prisoner of its past: its endowment of tithe and glebe, its rigid territorial organization on the basis of parishes – especially the sprawling, old-fashioned upland parishes where industry was growing apace, its governance by a hierarchy that was often absentee and nearly always out-of-touch, and its dominance by the landowning classes, were the product of, and designed for, a static rural society. In the industrial communities, now so quickly multiplying, new Dissenting conventicles and churches could be founded with the minimum formality and the maximum ease. Needing no parish, building, endowment, or even minister of their own at first, meeting if need be in private dwelling-houses or any other convenient structure (including the 'long room' of a tavern), sustained by the voluntary contributions of their own members, and offering the conspicuous attraction of a much wider and freer opportunity for lay participation by men of middle- or working-class origins, Dissenting churches were very well adapted to exploit the sharp rise in population and drastic shifts in its location.

Industrial and commercial expansion on an unprecedented scale also had far-reaching implications for educational needs and opportunities. Economic development required many more people with a higher standard of education; it also provided more abundant means for meeting the growing demand for literacy and elementary numeracy. It created much the most spectacular extension down the social scale of a requirement for formal education which had hitherto been evoked in Wales. At no previous time had there been anything like such a call for book-learning for secular purposes as distinct from religio-social reasons. Not, of course, that that meant that education was as yet to be freed from the leading-strings of religious inspiration or church control. Far from it! The excesses and the irreligion of the French Revolution, on the one hand, and the speedy emergence of new and unparalleled social strains in the wake of industrial change, on the other, served to underline afresh all the old dangers which were to be apprehended from godless subversion and revolutionary upheaval. There might be a broad and even widening abyss between the principles of Churchmen and Nonconformists, between the upholders of the existing régime in Church and State and its radical critics; but on some issues they were in basic underlying agreement: that the Christian religion must still provide a basis for education; and that there was a continuing need for non-violence in politics and for moral restraint in social behaviour. It was the unanimity on these issues which chiefly prevented the religio-political differences of the age from following the same revolutionary paths as they did in a number of Continental countries.

In other respects, of course, an acute and intensifying rivalry was developing between Church and Chapel. Nowhere was this fiercer than in the field of education. Both sides recognized the pressing need for more elementary schools, but each went its separate way in trying to meet it. Each party feared that the other would proselytize pupils as well as educate them. So the Church founded its schools under the aegis of the National Schools Society, while the Nonconformists set up theirs under the British and Foreign Schools Society. The State, for its part, was willing to extend a measure of patronage to both. But many Nonconformists, morbidly mistrustful of a government made up largely of Anglicans and landowners, were loath to accept money from what they regarded as a tainted source and thereby, perhaps, to give hostages to its insidious influence. Their lurking suspicions were immeasurably enlarged and their anger inflamed to fever-heat by the Educational Blue Books of 1847 – the reports which became popularly known in Wales as 'Brad y Llyfrau Gleision' ('Treachery of the Blue Books' – on the analogy of the historic 'Treachery of the Long Knives', alleged to have been committed by the earliest Anglo-Saxon invaders). Though some of the wiser heads among the Nonconformists recognized that the Report had properly drawn attention to the desperate inadequacies of elementary schools in Wales, none of them could forgive what they saw as – and what indeed in many respects was – a grossly-prejudiced indictment of Nonconformity and the Welsh language as the twin founts of educational backwardness in Wales. It seemed that officialdom and the Anglican Church had conspired to put Nonconformist religion and its associated Welshness in the dock and had adjudged them guilty of condemning the people of Wales to ignorance, immorality and retardation. It is difficult to think of any other single factor which did so much to exacerbate Church/Chapel relations or to poison all hope of educational co-operation as the publication of the Report of 1847. This failure of Church and Chapel to agree substantially helped to bring about, in the long run, two major consequences for the educational system. It served in the first instance to highlight the inadequacy of schools founded by rival religious societies to cope with the demand, and so hastened the advent of a state-system of schools. Furthermore, the rivalries between the two camps made it almost inevitable that non-sectarian education, i.e. education from which religion was virtually excluded, would carry the day in state-supported education at all levels. In the hey-day of church- and chapel-going this did not appear to be too damaging in the eyes of believers. At that stage religious and moral education could, with some degree of confidence, be entrusted to the home and the place of worship. Only later did the significance of this severing of the traditional link between religion and education become apparent.

In another traditional theatre of instruction by religious bodies – that of the inculcation of political and social values – controversy and polemic were equally inflammatory. The steady extension of the suffrage eventually meant the diffusion of an interest in and respons-ibility for political and social issues among the whole populace. What had hitherto been almost the exclusive preserve of the upper classes now became the concern of all. Never since the momentous clashes of the seventeenth century had the political debate been so im-passioned, or so widely canvassed among all ranks, or so closely interwoven with religious differences. Never had so many looked to their religious leaders for political as well as spiritual guidance. Given the strength of Nonconformist ranks in Wales there was little likelihood of there being much basis for a common approach among all Christians to political solutions or social philosophy. On the contrary, sectarian differences contributed weightily to the shaping of diametrically opposed views on what constituted economic efficiency, political equity and social justice. There could be no question of a monolithic maintenance of a social consensus through the binding force of religion when religious believers were furiously split among themselves on the issues of which contemporary institutions should be discarded and what should take their place. The debates were conducted with bitterness and rage as well as conviction and idealism – in Welsh and English, newspaper and journal, pamphlet and book, in pulpit and on platform, as well as through hustings and ballot-box. Increasingly the argument became polarized in terms of religion. To be Anglican was virtually synonymous with being Tory; Nonconformity almost as inescapably became equated with Liberalism. Small wonder that disestablishment turned into the most rancorous and irreconcilable subject of political contention.

Looking back to the world before 1914 it seems hard to credit that the heat and fury of those educational and politico-religious vendettas of late-Victorian and Edwardian Wales should have evaporated so soon and so completely. In the course of the last fifty or sixty years the climate of opinion has altered dramatically and become very largely secularized. Not one of the three constants adumbrated at the outset – the education of the clergy, the religious instruction of the laity, and the inculcation of political loyalty and social responsibility on the basis of Christian doctrine – which for so long had a cardinal role to fulfil in the life of Wales now has much more than a marginal place in contemporary society. In contrast with the last century, when most of the ablest Welsh boys saw the Christian ministry as the most promising avenue of fulfilment, the number now entering it has dwindled to a mere handful, lost to sight amid the huge numbers receiving higher education; and even the theological colleges specifically devoted to their training are hard put to continue in existence. The ranks of practising or even professing believers, Anglicans and Dissenters alike, have been proportionately just as drastically thinned; and such religious instruction as the majority of the populace ever receive is given in school rather than a place of worship. Nor do most of the community ever look to parson or preacher for political guidance; on the contrary, any forthright political pronouncement by a religious leader is as likely as not to provoke criticism on the grounds of unwarranted interference in matters outside his concern. In all three respects the long-dominant concepts of the connexion between religion and education have been largely emptied of meaning. Nothing reveals more clearly that Wales has become not much more than nominally a Christian country.

V.   The Tradition of St. David in Wales*

Saint David 'then enters the synod; the company of bishops is glad, the multitude is joyful, the whole assembly exults. He is asked to preach, and does not decline the synod's decision. They bid him ascend the mount piled up with garments; and in the sight of all, a snow white dove from heaven settled on his shoulder, and remained there as long as he preached. Whilst he preached, with a loud voice, heard equally by those who were nearest and those who were furthest, the ground beneath him grew higher, rising to a hill; and, stationed on its summit, visible to all as though standing on a lofty mountain, he raised his voice until it rang like a trumpet . . .

Afterwards, blessed and extolled by all, he is constituted archbishop of the entire British race, by the unanimous consent of the bishops, kings, princes, nobles, and those of every rank; his city is also declared the metropolis of the whole country, so that whosoever ruled it should be regarded as archbishop.'

This celebrated episode of the synod supposed to have been held at Llanddewibrefi will be familiar to most Welsh people. Generations of Welsh children have solemnly re-enacted the scene in St. David's Day festivities – though without miraculous results! The quotation given above, comes from the first biography of the saint, where it represents, in more senses than one, the high point of his career. We cannot, unfortunately, believe most of the details as the saint's biographer recorded them. They come from a biography which was not written until five hundred years after the saint was dead. Admittedly, they were then set down by a writer who had exceptional opportunities for acquiring information about his subject; but his work is, like most medieval saints' lives, an amalgam in which legend heavily overlies facts. Yet, symbolically, the story embodies an important truth. David's voice has, figuratively, been lifted like a trumpet for many centuries in Wales, and his pre-eminence among the Welsh saints has for long been beyond dispute.

The undoubted facts concerning David's life, however, are perilously slender and can quickly be summarized. We have no certain knowledge of the dates of his birth or death; but there is no doubt that he flourished in the sixth century and he may have died in the year

*First published in Owain Jones and David Walker (eds.), *Links with the Past: Swansea and Brecon Historical Essays* (Llandybie, 1974), pp. 1–20.

589. He was one of those illustrious monk-missionaries of the Celtic Age of Saints. Though, like others of his kind, he may have taught and peregrinated in other Celtic lands outside Wales, there is every reason to suppose that the main theatre of his activities was his own native region of West Wales, of Ceredigion and Dyfed, particularly within a triangle bounded by Mynyw (St. David's), Hen Fynyw (near Aberaeron), and Llanddewibrefi. In this area he founded and became abbot-bishop of his chief church at St. David's. He belonged to a group of western saints, the other two most celebrated of whom were Teilo and Padarn. They appear to have been members of a second generation of Celtic monks in Wales who were, in general, more ascetic and less romanized in outlook than the previous generation to which saints like Illtud or Dyfrig belonged. This is attested by the name 'Dewi Ddyfrwr' or 'David the Waterman' which later generations attributed to David. It is possible that there is a substratum of truth in the traditions of his royal or noble birth and of his education by Paulinus. There may also be an important and genuine memory preserved in the story of his connection with the synod at Llanddewibrefi. Though there is no firm historical evidence that such a meeting took place, it is by no means impossible that there was a synod there in which David took a leading role, even if it was not as supernaturally marvellous an intervention as his biographer recounted.

Two points seem to stand out about David's career. The first is that at this stage, in his own lifetime, David was very much a regional figure whose influence and associations were largely confined to those parts of West Wales where he was born and where he chiefly laboured. Even the Welsh form of his name, 'Dewi', betrays his western affiliations, for it is peculiarly characteristic of the western or Dimetian dialects to drop the final 'dd' sound which would have been expected in a Welsh name derived from the Latin form *Davidis*. (In contrast with 'Dewi', the other Welsh form of the name is 'Dafy*dd*'). The second point to be noted is that in his own lifetime David was neither a 'national' figure nor a patron saint recognized and revered throughout the whole of Wales – indeed, the concept of Wales as a separate country or the Welsh as a nation cannot properly be said to have existed in the sixth century. David was only one of a large number of Celtic 'saints', i.e. that remarkable band of monk-missionaries who swept through all the Celtic lands in an extraordinary wave of evangelizing activity. There is no firm evidence whatsoever that he enjoyed any special position of pre-eminence among his fellows during his lifetime.

During the five centuries or so that lay between David's own age and the first biography of him written by Rhigyfarch *c*. 1095, references to the saint are very scanty. Such as they are, they suggest that he was well-known in Ireland and Brittany, possibly even better known there than in some parts of Wales. The earliest reference to him may well be an inscription belonging to the first half of the seventh century on an early Christian stone monument at Llanddewibrefi, which is thought to record the grave of one Idnerth who was killed trying to defend David's church against pillage. David is also mentioned in two early Irish sources: the Martyrology of Oengus the Culdee, dating from *c*. 800, where the date of his feast is given as 1 March; and the Catalogue of Irish Saints, now thought to date from the ninth or the tenth century. A further reference to him comes in the life of St. Paul of Léon, written in 884 by a Breton monk called Gourmonoc, the main interest of which is that it gives us the first mention of the *cognomen* 'Aquaticus' or 'Waterman', an acknowledgement of David's asceticism, which was to be strongly underlined in later lives of the saint himself. Then comes the first reference to him in a British source, Asser's Life of King Alfred, which is thought to have been completed about 893, where the author mentions 'monasterium et parochia Sancti Degui' ('the monastery and church of Saint Dewi'), and the form given of the saint's name strongly suggests that the author was a Welshman writing for a Welsh audience. There are further references to David in tenth- and eleventh-century calendars from Glastonbury and Sherborne, indicating perhaps that his cult had been introduced into Wessex by Asser and had survived there afterwards. Perhaps the most significant of these early references to him is that to be found in an early Welsh prophetic poem, *Armes Prydein* ('The Prophecy of Britain'), reliably dated to about the beginning of the tenth century. It reveals David in a new and striking light, as a symbol not primarily of Christian virtue but of patriotic pride and warlike prowess. The poem prophesies that a confederation of the Welsh, Irish and Danes of Dublin, along with men from Dumbarton and Brittany, will unite to fight under the banner of David to defeat and drive out the hated Saxons. It expresses the view of that party in South Wales that was opposed to Hywel Dda's policy of recognizing the overlordship of Saxon rulers. David is the only saint mentioned in the poem, and this seems to suggest that for the men of South Wales, at least, he had now achieved a primacy among Welsh saints. All in all, however, the David of the Dark Ages remains a shadowy and elusive wraith.

He emerges into much clearer historical light towards the end of the eleventh century about the time of the Norman conquest of Wales. Round about the years 1090 to 1095, probably nearer the latter than the former, the first life of the saint was written in Latin by Rhigyfarch, descendant of a Llanbadarn family famous for its learning, and son of Sulien, a much-venerated bishop of St. David's. Rhigyfarch's work depicts David's career as one of superlative lustre and distinction. He first performed miracles from his mother's womb and continued to do so throughout his lifetime; he lived a life of impressively austere and unworldly sanctity; he visited Jerusalem and was made archbishop by the patriarch there; such were the force of his example and the power of his preaching, especially at Llanddewi-brefi, that, by the acclamation of all, he became archbishop in succession to the aged and failing Dyfrig; and he then transferred to his own church at St. David's the seat of that archbishopric which had previously been located at Caerleon. David's life and work as chronicled by Rhigyfarch were unfailingly holy, miraculous and successful. Yet we need not believe that the biographer very largely made the whole story up out of his own imagination. On the contrary, steeped as Rhigyfarch was in the learning and traditions of David's region and his church, he must have had access to a body of existing materials for his biography. Some fragments of these may already have been reduced to writing. There also probably survived a memory of the outstanding incidents of the saint's life in the form of a *passio* or sermon delivered in church on the day of the saint's commemoration. We may be sure that there was an already ancient and revered body of hagiographical lore. This had been steadfastly preserved and, no doubt, greatly added to by oral transmission over the five centuries since David's death. The memory of a core of real happenings in the life of the saint was retained; but, in keeping with the general tenor of Dark Ages tradition, these events were all too readily infused with a dramatic, highly-coloured, and supernatural quality which raised them far above the level of ordinary existence. Moreover, major and popular figures like David attracted to themselves scattered fragments of legend and tradition as magnets do iron filings. Rhigyfarch was also familiar with a mass of Irish saints' lives and was much influenced by their conventions. So that, one way and another, the bare facts of the saint's life soon became thickly coated with fable. It was this inextricable mass of truth and legend, hitherto chiefly preserved by word of mouth, that appears first to have been given shape and permanence in Rhigyfarch's life of the saint. Thereafter, his work became the basis of all other medieval lives of the saint by authors like Gerald of Wales, or John of Tynemouth, whose life of David was included in Capgrave's widely-known collection of saints' lives, or the Welsh version first preserved in the famous Book of the Anchorite of Llanddewibrefi in or about 1346. Rhigyfarch's labour in transforming David's life-story from an oral to a literary tradition proved to be of crucial significance. Not only had he given it a much more artistic, certain, and lasting shape, but he had also introduced it to a wider and more influential audience of the literate public; a public made up very largely of clerics, to some of whom David's achievement would be of special interest.

The tone and timing of Rhigyfarch's work were not coincidental. In part they were dictated by the need to assert the rights of St. David's diocese in opposition to those of Llandaff in the boundaries dispute between the two dioceses, and Rhigyfarch's life of David may well have been intended as a counterblast to the claims put forward for St. Cadog and, by implication, the diocese of Llandaff in Lifris's life of St. Cadog. Rhigyfarch was even more concerned, however, to stave off the Norman threat to the territorial and ecclesiastical independence of Wales. When he wrote, Normans were not only swarming into south and south-west Wales and laying greedy hands on Welsh territory, they were also imperilling the independence of the Welsh Church. The key to the independence of the Church lay in the status of St. David's. That in turn depended on the pre-eminence which had been accorded to the saint in his own lifetime. Hence the overwhelming emphasis placed by Rhigyfarch on David's supremacy:

> To all men the holy bishop Dewi is the supreme overseer, the supreme protector, the supreme preacher, from whom all men

received their standard and pattern of living virtuously.

To all men he was their regulator, he was their dedication, he was their benediction, he was their absolution, their reformation. To the studious he was instruction; to the needy, life; to the orphans, upbringing; to widows, support; to fathers, a leader; to monks, he was their rule; to non-monastic clergy, the way of life; to all men he was all things.

In fact, Rhigyfarch gave two different versions of how David had become archbishop. In one, David was advanced to the dignity by the patriarch of Jerusalem; in the other he was chosen archbishop by the acclamation of the whole people after his triumph at Llanddewibrefi: 'he is constituted archbishop of the entire British race, by the unanimous consent of the bishops, kings, nobles, and those of every rank.' The most important point, however, was that his city was also 'declared the metropolis of the whole country, so that whosoever ruled it should be regarded as archbishop.'

Rhigyfarch's argument was that just as David had been recognized archbishop in his own lifetime so his authority as primate rightfully belonged to his successors. If this had been accepted it would have rendered the Bishops of St. David's and their suffragans among the other Welsh bishops independent of any authority wielded by the Archbishop of Canterbury. There is, in fact, no evidence at all to prove that there had ever been archbishops at St. David's in the sense in which men of the eleventh and twelfth centuries understood the nature and functions of archbishops. Nevertheless, St. David's may well have enjoyed a place of more indefinable authority and influence among the Welsh. This may already have been recognized by no less a figure than William the Conqueror himself, who went on pilgrimage to St. David's in 1081. The Conqueror, though he had a rough, conventional piety, was not the sort of man to go on pilgrimage to a remote Welsh shrine just for his soul's health. He may well have intended his visit to be a demonstration of power over this nerve-centre of Welsh ecclesiastical and patriotic loyalty.

Whatever King William I's intentions may have been, there need be no uncertainty about the motives of those churchmen of the twelfth century who battled for recognition of St. David's as an archbishop's see. They stood for the independence of St. David's and, through it, the independence of the Welsh Church from Canterbury.

This battle was only partly and secondarily one about the independence of Wales as such; it was primarily an ecclesiastical contest for
the independence of the see and had been deeply influenced by the
successful assertion of the independence from Canterbury of the
archbishopric of York and by many other similar controversies of the
period. It was a tussle in which a man like Bernard, the first Norman
Bishop of St. David's, could take part on behalf of the diocese: as
could Gerald of Wales – himself three parts a Norman despite being
styled 'Cambrensis'. The champions of the diocese, it need hardly be
added, failed to establish their contention. There was, however, one
highly significant outcome as far as David himself was concerned.
His supporters seem to have succeeded in obtaining recognition of his
cult from Pope Calixtus II some time between 1119 and 1124. David
was the only Welsh saint ever to achieve such a distinction in the
Middle Ages, and in a Church increasingly dominated by the papacy
it vastly enhanced his status and prestige. Furthermore, support in
the struggle for the primacy of St. David's had not been confined to
South Wales; it had also gained the goodwill of the powerful princes
of Gwynedd in the north. Increasingly during the Middle Ages
David was winning an undisputed place for himself as the patron
saint of the whole of Wales.

During the medieval centuries there is eloquent testimony to the
esteem and affection in which David was held. First of all, there were
the large number of churches and wells dedicated to him – 53
churches and 32 wells – far outnumbering the dedications to any
other Welsh saint. The oldest of these go back well beyond the Middle
Ages, back to the time of the saint himself or soon after; but many of
the dedications were undoubtedly medieval in origin. Interestingly
enough, though, not a single church was dedicated to him in North
Wales in medieval times. Then again, David occupied an interesting
and relatively important place in the liturgy of the medieval Church.
In his own diocese and in churches dedicated to him his feast was
celebrated weekly, probably on Tuesdays. In the liturgy for this
commemoration he was described as 'pugil britannorum, dux et
doctor walicorum' ('champion of the Britons, the leader and teacher
of the Welsh'). Nor was his fame confined to his own diocese and
country. In 1415, Henry Chichele, Archbishop of Canterbury and
formerly Bishop of St. David's, ordained that David's feast should be

observed throughout the province of Canterbury as a major festival. One of the features of the celebration of such a feast would be a reading of the saint's life, or some parts of it, as the lessons appointed for the service. It was for such a purpose, among others, that Rhigyfarch and Gerald had composed their lives of St. David.

Medieval pilgrims, inevitably, found David's shrine an immense attraction. It became celebrated throughout Wales as a holy place, two visits to which were worth one to Rome, while three visits there were equal to a journey to the Holy Land itself. This reputation found frequent expression in medieval literature and, no doubt, in the oral traditions associated with it. A particularly popular prose text of the medieval period was the Welsh version of Rhigyfarch's *Vita* of St. David. The oldest surviving text of it dates from 1346 and is contained in the celebrated *Llyfr Ancr Llanddewibrefi.* ('The Book of the Anchorite of Llanddewibrefi'), one of the two richest manuscript collections of Welsh prose texts. Llanddewibrefi was one of the oldest and most venerated churches linked with the saint's name, and the Welsh version of his life may be best understood as being as much a part of a patriotic protest against the rapidly-growing exploitation of the Welsh Church by the English State in the fourteenth century as Rhigyfarch's Latin text was against the Norman incursions in the eleventh century.

In contemporary Welsh poetry the sanctity of David's life and the beauty of his church, the power of his own miracles and the wonder-working virtues of his shrine, are interwoven in the characteristic bardic paeans of praise. One of the best examples of medieval poetry addressed to the saint is the *cywydd* by the Cardiganshire gentleman-poet, Ieuan ap Rhydderch (*flor. c.* 1430–70). This poem, like others of the same kind, is based on the life of the saint by Rhigyfarch, which the poet might have known in either the Latin or the Welsh version of it. It refers to David's royal birth and to all the more important events and miracles recorded in the life, with particular attention being paid, as might be expected of a Cardiganshire poet, to the synod at Llanddewibrefi, where David was said to have preached so sonorously that he could be heard as far away as St. Dogmael's ('Clywad ef . . . mal cloch yn Llandudoch deg')! Ieuan ap Rhydderch was also ecstatic in his praise of the beauties of the church at St. David's which he likened to a second Jerusalem or

Santiago de Compostella, and, of course, he stressed the merits of the pilgrimage there:

Cystal o'm hardal i mi	Myned deirgwaith, eurwaith yw,
Fyned dwywaith at Dewi	Â'm henaid hyd ym Mynyw,
A phed elwn, cystlwn cain,	Y mae'n gystal â myned
O rif unwaith i Rufain.	I fedd Crist unwaith . . .

('To go from my district twice to David is as good as if I went in blessed company to Rome. To take my soul three times to Menevia, blessed work, is equal to going to Christ's grave once.')

In medieval poetry, too, there survives another strand of special interest. This is the continuing association of David with the prophetic tradition in medieval Wales which foretold the coming victory of the Welsh over the English in battle. In an age when patron saints were expected to give prompt and effective aid on the field of battle this was not surprising. It was thus to be expected that in the most dangerous and long-lived of the rebellions of medieval Wales, that of Owain Glyn Dŵr, St. David and his church should have figured prominently. The rebel leader was himself powerfully moved by ancient Welsh prophecies and claims. One of the major policy aims evolved in the course of his rebellion was to free the Welsh Church from the jurisdiction of Canterbury. This was to be achieved by elevating the Bishop of St. David's into an archbishop ruling over an independent province. It was a logical enough outcome of the long association of St. David and his diocese with prophetic themes and patriotic struggles for independence.

Clearly, then, in the course of the Middle Ages David came to be regarded as the patron saint of all Wales, whose feast day on the first of March, already associated with the wearing of the leek, should be fittingly kept up by Welshmen. It was only proper that that most successful of all medieval Welshmen, Henry Tudor, should, after he had become King Henry VII, make a monetary allowance to his fellow-countrymen to celebrate St. David's Day in style at court. We may also recall how that fiery patriot, Fluellen, in Shakespeare's *Henry V* says to the king 'And I do believe your Majesty takes no scorn to wear the leek upon St. Tavy's Day.' Though Henry V was born in Monmouth this reference of Shakespeare's may well preserve a recollection of Henry VII rather than Henry V.

With Henry VII we reach the threshold of the Reformation, which brought with it a severe crisis for medieval saints and their shrines. To ardent Protestant reformers the very eminence which David and his church enjoyed as an attraction for pilgrims made them an object of suspicion. Reformers looked with horror on shrines, relics, pilgrimages, saints' cults, and the like; and they showed an undisguised contempt for the 'monkish legends' and 'superstitions' which had given birth to them. St. David's church was not immune from their censure. The first Protestant bishop of the diocese, William Barlow (1536–47), violently assailed the earlier traditions of his cathedral. He was only too eager to bring to an end the medieval régime at St. David's, which he denounced in unmeasured terms as 'ungodly image service, abominable idolatry, . . . popish pilgrimages, deceitful pardons, and feigned indulgences'. Indeed, he thought his cathedral was so far gone in papistical practices that the only hope for the diocese was to remove the see from St. David's to Carmarthen. Barlow's plan did not succeed. It was hotly and successfully resisted by his own chapter, nor was it ever mooted by any subsequent bishop.

Although the Reformation did not destroy David's cathedral it did, nevertheless, severely mutilate the position he had held in medieval life. Inevitably, he now lost his former place in the liturgy; equally inevitably, the pilgrimages to his shrine were brought to an abrupt end, though there may have lingered for a long while a secret attachment to them in the hearts of many people. Nearly all the earlier Welsh poetry, which had usually been closely geared to the need to publicize the shrine of St. David and pilgrimages to it, disappeared when the pilgrimages went. Furthermore, the old prophetic poetry in which St. David had figured as the champion of the coming victory of the Welsh became almost completely muted when the Tudors had come to the throne. Indeed, when Robert Ferrar, a Yorkshireman who was Bishop of St. David's from 1547 to 1555, tried to please the Welsh people of his diocese by referring sympathetically to the old prophecies of Merlin concerning the triumph of the Welsh, he was severely censured by some of his own canons, themselves Welshmen, for doing so.

Yet, dented though the saint's reputation may have been by the Reformation, destroyed it certainly was not. He continued to thrive in the sixteenth century and for long after. There were probably two main reasons for this. First, there continued to be a strong secular patriotic urge to celebrate his day, and we know that in London and elsewhere good Welshmen insisted upon wearing their leeks and feasting in honour of their national saint on the first of March. Their festivities did not always commend themselves to Englishmen. In 1640 a Welshman provoked by English antipathy allowed his patriotic indignation to get the better of him to such an extent that he was indicted for manslaughter. On St. David's Day, 1667, Pepys recorded in his diary that he saw 'the picture of a man dressed like a Welshman, hanging by the neck' on a pole a-top a merchant's house. London bakers in the seventeenth and eighteenth centuries were fond of making gingerbread 'Taffies' on St. David's Day in the form of a skewered man. Even that opprobrious nickname 'Taffy' may itself be derived as a result of the partiality of the Welsh for swearing by their saint's name, since 'Taffy' is thought to be a caricature of the Welshman's way of pronouncing 'Davy' as 'Tavy' or 'Taffy' (*OED*).

Secondly, and perhaps nearly as important, was the rehabilitation of the Celtic Church by Welsh Protestant reformers themselves. This is in itself a long and interesting story, but without going into the details of the argument the attitude of Welsh reformers can be put briefly thus. In the great days of the Celtic Church, among whose heroes none had been mightier than David, the British Church had been a kind of early Protestant Church free from the corruptions of Rome. So, they argued, the Reformation in Wales, far from being the imposition of new-fangled and alien errors, as its Roman critics claimed, was in fact a return to the bright dawn of the Celtic Church. By a remarkable stroke of poetic justice the chief protagonist of this point of view was none other than the outstanding Tudor bishop of St. David's, Richard Davies. This distinction drawn between the purity of the Celtic Church and the corruptions of the Roman Church, however doubtful its actual historical foundations may have been, could well have been crucial to the survival of the reputation of St. David and his contemporaries. Without it they might easily have been swept into the limbo of unworthy survivals from a 'superstitious' and 'monk-ridden' past. As it was, however, this notion of the glorious independence and evangelical purity of the early British Church survived strongly through a succession of influential Welsh

authors like Charles Edwards in the seventeenth century down to
Theophilus Evans in the eighteenth.

When we come to the eighteenth century we have to focus our
attention on the Welsh patriotic societies, which flourish, not in
Wales, but in London. Odd as this may seem at first sight, the explanation for it was really very simple. There were in Wales no towns of
any consequence, nor any independent institutions like a court, an
academy, a university, or an aristocracy, around which a sense of
Welsh patriotism could crystallize. Only in London were there ardent
Welshmen in numbers, wealth, and inclination sufficient to sustain
patriotic societies. One of the most enjoyable as well as one of the
most important activities of these groups was their annual celebration of St. David's Day, which they kept up in style with a church
service and a sermon, followed by a good – sometimes too good –
dinner. Across the Atlantic Ocean, astonishingly enough, the
practice took root among Welsh exiles as early as 1729. The historic
Welsh Society of Philadelphia, the earliest of its kind in America and
the oldest surviving such society in Pennsylvania, first met on
1 March 1729 to honour St. David with the traditional banquet and
Welsh singing. Among the Welsh of this American colony, as among
a number of London-Welsh societies like the Ancient Britons, the
Cymmrodorion, Gwyneddigion, and others, the fitting commemoration of St. David was unmistakably a prime focus for their patriotic
sentiments. So devoted were they to the practice that one of their
leading members, David Samwell, when he was thousands of miles
away on a voyage of discovery in the South Seas, contrived to
remember his patron saint and namesake on 1 March 1777.

It may, however, be asked, 'What had all this to do with Wales
itself?' The answer is that the members of London-Welsh societies
maintained a close and continuing contact with fellow-countrymen
back home in Wales. Moreover, the ideals and practices of the
London-Welsh societies were to exercise a profound influence within
Wales itself after about 1815. By this time Wales was becoming distinctly wealthier and more prosperous than at any previous time in its
history. The effects were to be seen in the growth of new, richer, and
more literate groups of professional men, shopkeepers, and skilled
artisans in the rapidly-growing little towns of Wales. Outside Wales,
in some of the larger English cities like Liverpool and Birmingham,

there were also groups of Welshmen who tended to cling together. Men of this kind, in Wales and amid the exiles, were hungry for knowledge, for entertainment, and above all for identity and reassurance. The editor of one of the earliest Welsh-language periodicals put it very well in 1828: 'In comparison with earlier times,' he wrote, 'the present age can be described as the *age of books – the age of readers* – the age when everyone is eagerly extending his hands to the tree of knowledge . . . It would have been unbelievable even at the beginning of this century that the printing-presses of Wales should have given birth to so many monthly publications as well as to a multitude of books on all aspects of knowledge.' Literacy and prosperity in Wales, as elsewhere in Europe, encouraged a greater sense of national awareness, and its outcome was the founding of a whole crop of patriotic societies. The 1820s were quite a remarkable decade for the founding of such societies, which usually went by the Welsh name of Cymreigyddion, or less often by the English title of Cambrians. There was hardly a single market or industrial town in Wales which did not have its society or societies, and Welsh exiles in England were equally active. Eagerly following the lead given by London-Welsh societies, they encouraged *eisteddfodau*, literary and historical studies, and, as the highlight of their year, they celebrated St. David's Day. Their normal practice was to hold a church service, attended by all patriots resplendent with leeks, and this was followed by as lavish a dinner as they could rise to. At the dinner the usual order of the toasts was: 'The King and the Church', 'the Principality of Wales', and the 'Immortal memory of Saint David', followed by a bewildering, not to say intoxicating, miscellany of other toasts.

These dinners celebrating St. David's Day became widely popular and were, on occasion, attended by some distinguished but unexpected guests. When the Society of Ancient Britons dined in London on 1 March 1828 their chief guest, loyally wearing his leek, was none other than the heir to the throne, the Duke of Clarence, later King William IV. The dinners also spread to some improbable places. In *The Life and Letters of Rowland Williams* (1874), p. 41, Williams gives an entertaining description of how Welsh patriotism invaded Cambridge University on St. David's Day, 1839:

'There has been for the first time here a Welsh dinner on St. David's Day, and though I am not much given to such things, yet I assented to attend, whereupon Herbert [Lord Powys's heir] was made president, and myself vice-president, and we presided accordingly, making speeches and praising Wales to infinity. I believe there really was no kind of panegyric which some orator or other did not lavish on ourselves or our country. We declared that the language was music, the people the best of all peoples, and the country the best of countries. We had the Hughes', or the infant harpists, there by way of music.' The scene and the proceedings were typical enough of such dinners. This kind of sentiment was not perhaps very profound, but it was characteristic of the extended awareness of Welsh patriotic feeling in the first half of the last century. Nor were celebrations of this sort confined to the United Kingdom. The exodus of thousands of the Welsh overseas gave rise to the familiar nostalgia of exiles and the desire to found societies which might help to preserve common links and memories. In the United States alone, more than a hundred such Welsh societies, nearly all of them called St. David's Societies, have been traced. The focal activity which brought and held the members together was the punctilious observance of the patron saint's day. This usually followed the familiar pattern long established in the homeland: religious services on the preceding Sunday, a dinner on the saint's day, followed by toasts and speeches extolling the glories of the Welsh past and the particular contribution of Welsh immigrants to the land of their adoption. In other countries like Canada or Australia, where the Welsh emigrated in any numbers, similar associations came into being.

Some of the most conspicuous leaders of early nineteenth-century patriotism in Wales were a group of Anglican clerics, most of whom were associated with the diocese of St. David's. They were given a notable lead by that outstanding Bishop of St. David's, Thomas Burgess (1803–1825), himself a leading advocate of the idea that the early British Church had originally been free of the influence and corruption of Rome. These Welsh clergymen, as can be imagined, had a special interest not only in the early history of Wales generally but in its ecclesiastical history in particular. For all of them St. David himself was an object of the deepest pride and affection. One of the most attractive figures among them was Thomas Price (*Carnhuanawc*), vicar of Llanfihangel Cwm Du, in Breconshire. Author of an unusually influential history of Wales written in Welsh, he stoutly upheld St. David's virtues and the unbroken memory of them in subsequent ages, though he firmly repudiated what he regarded as no more than legend. Referring to the celebration of the saint's day in his own times, he argued that it 'offered an opportunity for the Welshmen to meet together to nurture patriotism and to support those practices and institutions that tend to the honour of our nation and our native country'. Similarly, another of the same group, Rice Rees, whose book, *An Essay on the Welsh Saints* (1836), was for long regarded as a classic on the subject, after discoursing at length on the subject of St. David, concluded, 'he has long maintained the highest station among the saints of his country; and . . . he professes the fairest claim to such distinction'.

In an age of rapidly-burgeoning patriotic sentiment and deep religious allegiance, St. David's place in the affections of Welshmen was secure. Not only in the ranks of members of the Established Church but also among the rapidly-growing numbers of Nonconformists was he venerated. Many aspects of his reputation made him particularly congenial to the latter. His ascetic self-restraint, his reputation as a drinker of water, and his emphasis on hard and regular work seemed to fit in admirably with the Nonconformist ethic of sobriety, moral fervour and self-improvement. As early as 1816 a leading Nonconformist minister and historian, David Peter of Carmarthen, had written very warmly of David's life and labours in his *Hanes Crefydd yng Nghymru* ('History of Religion in Wales'), a book very widely read and admired by his fellow-Nonconformists. Although earlier generations of Nonconformists had tended to view the patriotic societies with some suspicion and disfavour, by mid-century many in their midst were taking an active part in their work, including the celebration of the patron saint's day.

With the spread of schools and compulsory education in Wales a new and very influential trend was apparent by the end of the century in the shape of the regular celebration of St. David's Day in schools. This was true even of those areas where the Welsh language had died out, and quite recently one elderly man from an anglicized area told me that he and his contemporaries always enjoyed St. David's Day, if only because it gave them a break from routine and a half-day's holiday!

It only remains to discuss briefly why the tradition of Saint David has persisted so powerfully in Wales for so long. First of all, it may be suggested that the very remoteness of the saint in time has been an important reason. This has worked in two ways, the one positive and the other negative. The positive aspect is that David goes back right to the beginnings of Welsh history, back to the heroic age of the Saints and Arthur. The concept of the saint-hero, the prince-bishop, upright of life and fearless of conduct, one of the original shapers of the Welsh mind and spirit, appeals to very deep-seated instincts. Negatively, the very fact that he is so remote that little can be certainly known of him has meant that he has not been too closely tied to any one phase or aspect of our history; he has not become 'dated'. Even the legends about him, when they had to be rejected as historical truth, remained artistic and profoundly appealing. It is noticeable how warmly children respond to them. It is as if they filled a deeply-felt need for heroic virtue, divinely-maintained and celestially-rewarded.

A second reason may be that the Welsh, over a large part of their history, have had very few national institutions around which their sense of identity could be focused – no independent monarchy, no court, no representative institution, no separate body of law, educational system, or church. Nor have they had many heroes who were men of action. So that those national emblems and heroes they do have are wont to loom correspondingly larger in their estimation and affection. It might readily be agreed, for instance, that David plays a larger part in Welsh patriotism than does St. George in England or even St. Andrew in Scotland. Only Patrick in Ireland can vie with him in this respect within the British Isles.

Thirdly, the saint's connection with Christianity was extremely important. Over a large part of their history the Welsh have tended to be deeply conscious of their Christian heritage. The remarkable thing about St. David, however, is that his inextricable association with the Christian religion is one that can be and has been appropriated by Christians of many different persuasions. Roman Catholics have claimed him as one of the earliest and most brilliant pioneers of the universal Roman Church as it has evinced itself in these islands. Anglicans, on the other hand, have seen him as the illustrious representative of that native British Church which had not come under the yoke of Rome and which was the true spiritual mother of the Church of England, the Church in Wales, and other Christian Churches in this island. Yet Nonconformists, for their part, have often felt able to depict David as a simple, God-fearing Welshman, scornful of the pomp of the Establishment, and true to what they liked to think of as the natural Welshness, fervour, and austerity expressed in Welsh Nonconformity.

Finally, St. David has, from very early times, been associated with patriotic as well as religious aspirations. He has been portrayed as the champion of the Welsh hardly less than of Christ. One of the most typical characteristics of patriots in any age is their addiction to the past; but they will borrow from the past and interpret it in ways that particularly suit their purpose. (They are not alone, of course, in that endearing human foible). In this context is has been the astonishing versatility of David's roles that has so largely contributed to his fame. So, for instance, the Welsh of 930 AD in *Armes Prydein* wanted him as a champion in their fight against Wessex and its rulers. Rhigyfarch and others insisted upon his claims in opposition to the Normans. Medieval pilgrims saw him as a wonder-working purveyor of health for body and soul with a special affection for his fellow-countrymen as his votaries, while to their soldier-contemporaries he was a lieutenant of the God of battles, striking his enemies and sparing his friends. Sixteenth-century reformers, on the other hand, succeeded in rejecting most of what had made him desirable to their medieval predecessors and looked to him as an early embodiment of their own most cherished ideals of ecclesiastical polity and patriotic endeavour. London-Welshmen of the Augustan and Romantic Ages found in him a most ancient and venerable representative of their nation's distinctive identity and culture. Undoubtedly, it is as a symbol of religion and culture, not of politics and statecraft, that he has been most potent. That is why he came so very much into his own in the nineteenth century, when he appeared to epitomize so completely the values of civilization over barbarism, the triumph of light over darkness. A patron saint probably had a more natural and assured place then than he has now. In our own day his role may be somewhat reduced. In an increasingly secularized society, in which nationalism tends to take a sharper and more militant edge, there are not lacking those who advocate abandoning David for a more combative national symbol – a Llywelyn ap Gruffydd or an Owain Glyn Dŵr.

An ancient Celtic saint may seem less appropriate for the role of the nation's father-figure.

Yet there continues to be a deep and strong current of regard for St. David. In a recent one-volume history of Wales, Dr. Gwynfor Evans reaffirms with striking emphasis the continuing patriotic appeal of the patron saint. The Age of the Saints he regards as the Golden Age of Welsh history, and of St. David he writes, 'It is impossible to think of a patron saint for Wales more worthy than he, for David is one of ourselves, a Welsh-speaking Welshman who worked in our midst and suffered for us.' Another quotation provides a deeply-moving reavowal of the undying religious inspiration of the saint. It comes from a recent sermon preached on St. David's Day in the saint's church by the former Dean of St. David's, the Very Reverend T. E. Jenkins: 'We need have no fear that St. David will be forgotten . . . His name will always live, his spirit ever inspiring the people of God in this land, and beyond it, to greater fidelity in bearing witness to God who wishes to make Himself known in those to whom He thus entrusts His honour.'

The Welsh version of Rhigyfarch's life of St. David relates how the saint, as he felt his life ebbing away from him, preached his last sermon and proclaimed the blessing. He is then said to have uttered these words:

> Frodyr a chwiorydd, byddwch lawen a chedwch eich ffydd a'ch cred, a gwnewch y pethau bychain a glywsoch ac a welsoch gennyf fi.
>
> ('Brothers and sisters, be joyful and hold fast to your faith and belief, and do the little things you heard and saw from me.')

We cannot, admittedly, know for certain that these words were actually spoken by him; yet their direct and touching simplicity makes us want very much to believe that they were. For they seem to carry the secret of why so many Welsh men and women over fourteen hundred years have responded to his ageless and abiding appeal.

VI.   Language, Literacy and Nationality in Wales*

It can be an extremely dangerous anachronism to talk too facilely of a sense of nationality among the men of the Middle Ages. Yet they were, inevitably, aware of differences which existed between various racial or linguistic groups. By the fifteenth century they had become more conscious of them, so that English representatives at the Council of Constance (1414–18) could claim for their nation equality with the French, 'whether', as they said, 'a nation be understood as a race, relationship, and habit of unity, separate from others, or as a difference of language, which by divine and human law is the greatest and most authentic mark of a nation and the essence of it.' Now any Welsh poet of the fifteenth century would have assented readily enough to the general proposition embodied in that declaration. If he had been asked whether he was aware of anything distinctive about his language and the literature which was the highest and most enduring form of expression to be found in it, he would have answered emphatically in the affirmative. He would proudly have directed the enquirer's attention to an unbroken continuity in the Welsh poetic art which went back for close on 1,000 years to the sixth-century Taliesin, the first acknowledged master of it. He would, moreover, have extolled the way in which Welsh had been protected, cherished and enriched by generation after generation of a powerful order of poets and littérateurs. Although this pride was evinced at its most intense in the bards, it was by no means confined to them; it was just as characteristic of their patrons. For centuries the princes of Wales had been the poets' mentors. Following the extinction of princely independence at the end of the thirteenth century, leading families of gentry and the higher clergy stepped forward to assume the role of patrons and protectors. Not only families of native Welsh origin either; many families of non-Welsh extraction were anxious to share in the prestige deriving from the patronage of literature – an unusual example of cultural diffusion.

The literature of medieval Wales, whether poetry or prose, was essentially an oral one; it was an art intended for the ear not the eye.

---

*Originally delivered as a lecture to the Annual Meeting of the Historical Association in Bangor in April 1970. I have kept as closely as possible to the spoken idiom. Subsequently published in *History*, 56 (1971), 1–16.

The long and arduous period of apprenticeship and instruction in the strictly-regulated bardic and literary schools was by word of mouth. The master poets or professional declaimers (*datgeiniaid*) declaimed their verse aloud in patrons' halls. This did not necessarily mean that they were illiterate. Many of their verses, and much of the prose, including the laws, were transcribed and preserved in manuscripts which were lovingly treasured by poets and patrons alike. The practice became much more widespread from the middle of the fifteenth century onwards when it was, no doubt, briskly stimulated by the readier availability of paper in place of the more expensive parchment previously used for manuscript copying. There may well have been more medieval lay people able and anxious to read than has often been supposed. But there were obvious and severe restrictions on literacy in the Middle Ages. There was almost no incentive for many laymen, even of the upper class, to learn to read. As far as the poets were concerned, they had very strong reasons for favouring restricted literacy of a kind which anthropologists have often observed in societies and literatures at a comparable stage of development in more recent times. The bardic mystery was an arcane lore to be confined to initiates who wished to preserve its secrets. Oral transmission had immense archaic value in so self-consciously conservative a poetic art. Finally it was important to channel access to such books as existed through an authorized teacher. Even so, despite the limitations of an oral tradition, knowledge of the literature and appreciation of it were widely diffused in medieval Wales.

Poets were not only the guardians and exponents of language and literature. They were, by age-old convention, under an obligation jealously to conserve a three-fold 'memory of the Island of Britain'. The first of the three strands was the 'history of notable Acts of the kings and princes of this land of Brittaen and Cambria'; the second was the language of the Britons; and the third was to keep 'the genealogies or descents of the nobility, their division of lands and their arms'. The poets, then, were the sentinels of a potent sense of nationality closely linked with language. The essentials of the bardic sense of history were that the Welsh were the descendants of the ancient Britons, one of the oldest and most 'honourable stocks in the world – sprung from Brutus and the Trojans'. (There was a very strong myth of Trojan descent of the same kind in medieval France.)

Their origins made them the rightful rulers of Britain, treacherously deprived of much of their territory by the usurping Saxons. But they were destined to recover their rights, as the messianic prophecies of the poets over centuries assured them. Under the charismatic leadership of a son of destiny, one of their own princes and a descendant of the rightful royal house of Britain, i.e. a Welsh ruling house, they would ultimately defeat the Saxons. The persistence of these concepts of nationality, through centuries of hardship, disappointment and setback, is one of the most extraordinary things in the history of medieval Wales. The apparent vindication of the prophecy in the person of Henry VII could appear to many of his Welsh contemporaries almost as supernaturally wonderful as a medieval romance.

The importance of these achievements of the poets for the future history of Wales can hardly be overestimated. They had shaped, fostered and perpetuated a distinctive Welsh consciousness of nationhood. It was founded principally on descent; for a pedigree was as important to a people as to an individual. The prime characteristic was pride in lineage – the claim to be sprung from the oldest, most authentic and most illustrious of the inhabitants of the island of Britain. Language and literature were inextricably linked with this pride and were very important. But they were secondary tokens of nationality; they were the badge of the superiority of the truly *British* inhabitants sprung from one of the greatest peoples of classical antiquity over the lesser breeds of Saxons, the offspring of pagan barbarians.

For many poets and others the triumph of Henry VII was the fulfilment of these medieval dreams and aspirations. Little did they or anyone else then suppose that within half a century of the battle of Bosworth Henry's son's realm would be plunged into revolutionary changes.

As we move to these changes of the age of the Renaissance and the Reformation, say from the 1530s to 1660, we find ourselves in the midst of great cultural and social shifts, all of which tend to promote a rapid and widespread increase in literacy. It is not too much to say that in many European countries we witness an intellectual and educational revolution. The extension of the authority of the State combined with the ambitions of up-and-coming classes to make a much wider degree of formal education and training indispensable for many of the laity. The resurgence of trade and the emergence of new industries called for a greater number of literate merchants and craftsmen. The Renaissance stimulated curiosity not only in classical languages, texts and literatures but also in the vernaculars. This was to be an age of grammars, dictionaries and literary criticism, through which the vernaculars were to be helped to become no less worthy of status and distinction than the classical tongues. In more than one European country a standard literary language or dialect triumphed over its competitors: the *langue d'oil* over the *langue d'oc* in France; in Spain, Castilian over Galician and Catalan; Tuscan over all other versions of Italian; and in Germany the German of Luther's Bible. The Reformation, for its part, was a religion of conversion and, like others of its kind, it was a 'religion of the book'. It laid particular emphasis on the need for a return to the Word and its true interpretation. Wherever it took root, it tended not only to appeal to those who could already read but greatly added to their number. In addition, as its adherents knew all too well, a trigger which released the most dynamic reforming forces was the appeal in the vernacular. But more important than all of these and, indeed, a major source of strength to all of them was the invention and diffusion of the art of printing. 'The subtle science of printing books,' said a contemporary, Werner Rolewinck, was the 'art of arts, the science of sciences, by whose swift operation a desirable treasure of wisdom and knowledge, yearned after by all men through their natural instinct, hath leapt forth as from the depths of hidden darkness to enrich and enlighten this world that is seated in darkness.' He was right to set such store by printing; it had, without doubt, revolutionized the media of education, knowledge and literature, formal and informal.

All these influences were radiating among the more sensitive and intelligent Welshmen of the period. Had it been simply a question of assimilating these trends into the established literary and cultural modes of Wales, this would in itself have been a formidable enough operation. But alongside these developments came others which had no less crucial significance for the Welsh and their language. By Acts of Parliament passed between 1536 and 1543 Wales had been politically united to England. In the process, English became the official language of government, administration, law and justice; and without knowledge of it no one might hold office in Wales. In 1549 when the first English Book of Common Prayer was promulgated it looked as if English might become the language of religion in Wales as well. (It ought to be made clear, of course, that there were many in Wales, especially among the upper classes, who already had a knowledge of English; but this was the first time it had been formally placed in a position of official superiority and dominance over the Welsh language.)

The dilemmas of the age presented themselves most starkly to two or three generations of lively and active humanists in Tudor and Stuart Wales. They were men who were thoroughly imbued with an appreciation of the age and authenticity of the Welsh literary achievement and they were steeped in that spirit of patriotism that derived from the ancient British descent. They had also drunk deeply and avidly of the springs of the Renaissance ideals at the universities and elsewhere, and they had no illusions that if Welsh literary culture was to continue to thrive it must be refreshed and fructified by this new source of revivification. Many of them were ardent Reformers who were convinced that if Protestant tenets were to have any genuine meaning for their countrymen they must be presented in the vernacular. When these men dwelt upon all these things they were haunted by a double vision of peril and opportunity.

The *peril* they saw was that the Welsh language would lose its place of honour in Wales; that English would become the language of learning and civility; spoken, read and revered by all the intelligentsia; Welsh would meanwhile degenerate into a mere peasant *patois*. The man who saw this first and most clearly was one of the greatest Renaissance scholars produced in Wales, William Salesbury. (His family offers an outstanding illustration of that cultural diffusion among non-Welsh immigrants referred to earlier.[1]) He was aware of the crisis as early as Henry VIII's reign. The prospect that appalled him was that the same fate might befall the British language

---

[1]The origins of the Salesbury family are obscure. Earlier claims of their descent from Adam of Salzburg, a member of the eleventh-century ducal house of Bavaria, have been shown to be spurious. The family may well have originated in Herefordshire, and members of it are first traced in the Vale of Clwyd, Denbighshire, as yeomen in the first half of the fourteenth century (before 1334). By the sixteenth century they were the most powerful gentry in the country.

in Wales as had overtaken it in Cornwall and Brittany, that it would become 'full of corrupt speech and well-nigh completely lost'. Not that he and men like him were anti-English. On the contrary Salesbury applauded Henry VIII's 'excellent wisdom' in ensuring that 'there shall hereafter be no difference in laws and language' between the Welsh and English, remembering 'what a bond and knot of love and friendship the communion of one tongue is, and that also by the judgement of all wise men it is most convenient and meet that they that be under dominion of one most gracious Head and King shall also use one language'. What Salesbury wanted to safeguard against was that the spread of English should not reduce Welsh to be the language only of the farmyard and the market-place. This was a degradation unthinkable for a literary language so ancient, so renowned, so uncorrupted, so capable of better things.

These better things were the *opportunity* of which the humanists thought the language capable; that Welsh should adapt itself and its literature to the cultural demands of the Renaissance and Reformation, as other European languages were doing. In particular, they saw how the printing press had revolutionized the situation. Fortunately for Wales the Act of Union, though it had proscribed the use of Welsh for official purposes, had not forbidden the printing of books in Welsh – possibly because such an eventuality had never been envisaged! Welsh humanists were profoundly convinced of the crucial importance of printing for the future of the Welsh language. They appreciated the value of manuscripts, of course, and indeed the sixteenth and seventeenth centuries were to be a glittering era of Welsh manuscript copying. But they knew manuscripts to be frail and insecure instruments whose significance might all too often be unappreciated, with the result that they could end up, as Siôn Dafydd Rhys said, 'in the hands of children to make dolls of them, or of shopwives to pack up parcels, or even of tailors to make patterns'. If the treasures of the past were to be preserved and knowledge of them extended to scholars and littérateurs elsewhere in Europe, if the labours of humanists in the present were to be fully rewarded, then the printing press must be used. As the author of the first Welsh printed book (1546–7), Sir John Price, wrote: 'And now that God has given printing in our midst to multiply knowledge of his

I. Chepstow Castle *(Crown Copyright, R.C.H.M. Wales)*

II. Dolbadarn Castle *(Crown Copyright, R.C.H.M. Wales)*

III.   Caernarfon Castle *(Crown Copyright, R.C.H.M. Wales)*

IV.   Raglan Castle *(Crown Copyright, R.C.H.M. Wales)*

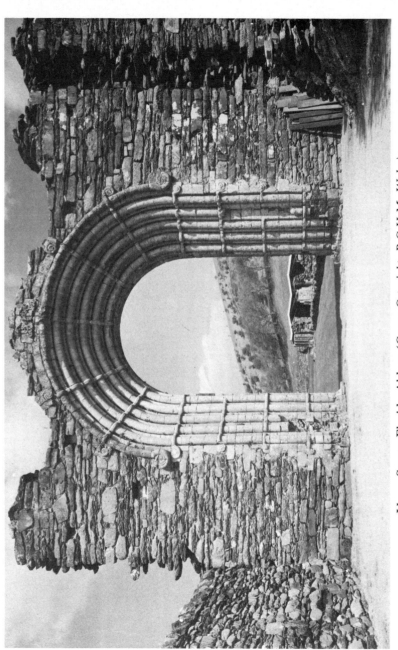

V.   Strata Florida Abbey (*Crown Copyright, R.C.H.M. Wales*)

VI. Tintern Abbey (Crown Copyright, R.C.H.M. Wales)

VII. Saint David's Shrine, Saint David's Cathedral
(Crown Copyright, R.C.H.M. Wales)

VIII. Memorial Stone to Llywelyn ap Gruffydd ('The Last'), Cilmeri, near Builth (*Crown Copyright, R.C.H.M. Wales*)

IX. Singleton Abbey, University College of Swansea (*Roger Davies, Esq.*)

EMIGRATION ! !
UNITED STATES & CANADA

CARDIFF
DIRECT TO
NEW YORK!
(Without calling at any intermediate port) by the

SOUTH WALES ATLANTIC STEAMSHIP COMPANY
LIMITED.

STEERAGE PASSAGE, £6 : 6 : 0
TO

New York, Baltimore, Boston, Portland & Philadelphia

FROM

All Parts of WALES and the South of England.

Including abundance of well-cooked Provisions served by the Company's Servants.

☞ STEWARDESSES CARRIED BY THESE STEAMERS.
AND MATTRESSES PROVIDED FREE.

A duly QUALIFIED SURGEON is attached to each Steamer.

Passengers BOOKED THROUGH to any Town in the United States, or Canada, at the Lowest Rates.

Parties securing Tickets in Europe or the United States for themselves or friends, are particularly requested to guard themselves against disappointment by seeing that the Ticket is for the CARDIFF LINE OF STEAMERS.

For further Particulars apply to any of the Company's Agents; or, at the

Company's Offices, 1, Dock Chambers, Cardiff.

An advertisement of 1875
Published by Glamorgan Archive Service
Poster Number 1

X.   Poster Advertising Emigration to the U.S.A.
(Glamorgan Archives Service)

blessed words, it is proper for us, as it has been for all other parts of Christendom, to participate in that blessing with them, so that so excellent a gift should not be without its fruits for us as for others.' The supreme achievement, as all these early humanists were agreed, would be the translation of the Bible and the Order of Service into Welsh; this for religious motives even more than cultural. The translation was brought about in two main stages: the Prayer Book and New Testament in 1567, and the whole Bible in 1588. It was accompanied in the period down to 1660 by the publication of a number of other miscellaneous printed books: religious and didactic works mainly, but also grammars, dictionaries, literary criticism, etc. Admittedly, the output of a few dozen Welsh books printed in the first century or so of Welsh printing looks meagre in comparison with the vast output of the press elsewhere. It was also disappointing even in terms of what Welsh humanists themselves had undoubtedly hoped for. This was probably inevitable. All sorts of explanations for it have been advanced: the anglicizing policy of the English State and the materialism of the Welsh gentry; the conservatism of the poets and the apathy of many Welsh people. Without denying that each of these causes contributed to the failure, it may be suggested that the most important reason is one of a different kind, namely that the literary ideals of Welsh humanists had developed faster than Welsh society. The Renaissance inspiration was one which would flourish fully only in a courtly and urban milieu. Welsh society was still that of a poor pastoral community. It did not have the economic and social resources adequately to sustain a printed literature of the new kind. At the same time, too many of its sons who were most sensitive to its literary and cultural needs had heard the siren calls of the new awakenings and could no longer rest content with the customary *genres* of the Middle Ages. Without ignoring the effect of other causes it is this which seems best to explain the gap between the ambitious aspirations and the limited output.

Nevertheless, what was achieved constitutes a much greater break-through than the mere counting of books would suggest. First, there had been ensured the continuity of the literary tradition in Wales, and the persistence of a deep and lasting affection and regard for it. It was an unquenchable conviction that the historical, linguistic and literary traditions of Wales were as old and honourable as those of Hebrews, Greeks and Romans which lay at the heart of the passionate affirmation of the necessity for keeping alive and vigorous this distinctive inheritance. Second, Welsh had become the language of religion. This had profound consequences for the future. It may well have done more than anything else to safeguard the continued existence of the language at all. Quite definitely it ensured its survival as a literary language; for the Bible became the standard and safeguard for all future Welsh literary expression. The biblical translators, especially William Morgan and John Davies, deliberately ensured that the vocabulary, idioms and standards of the bards should be preserved in all their purity in the Welsh version of the Bible; and that at the very time when the bardic order, hitherto the guardians of the language against decline or corruption, were markedly in decay. Thus was ensured, moreover, that at least one major element among the educated classes, the clergy, would have an incentive to preserve, cherish and extend their knowledge of Welsh and the publication of books in Welsh. Third, there is little doubt that it stimulated a wider measure of literacy. It is impossible – at present, anyway – to measure this with any accuracy. But the most frequently reiterated theme in justification of publishing these books was that they were being aimed at a large body of Welsh who *could* read Welsh but no other language; and most of whom could not be reached by manuscripts. Like all Protestant reformers they had an irresistible compulsion to make scriptural and devotional literature as widely available as possible. Fourth, they had succeeded in associating the Reformation with the emotive patriotic and literary inheritance of Wales. Leading Reformers eloquently and plausibly depicted the Reformation as a return to the pristine purity of the Church of the ancient British – as, indeed, the fulfilment at its most sublimated level of the prophecy of the restoration of the ancient glories of Wales. Finally, what happened in Wales is in startling contrast with what happened in other Celtic countries and regions of the British Isles. In none of the others does the native language become the language of religion in the same way. Nor is there anything like the same conscious and energetic response to the challenge of the new age and the printed book. Herein, perhaps, lies the essential key to the difference in the subsequent fate of Welsh and that of Celtic languages elsewhere. It possibly explains why Welsh survived so strongly. It certainly explains why there persisted a profound respect for the language, as well as affection and habitude, into a swiftly changing society of a later period.

Turning now to the period from the Restoration to the Industrial Revolution, say *c.* 1800, when we look at the state of Wales for about three-quarters of a century after the Restoration, it seems at first glance as though many of the springs of the preceding era were running into the sand. The process by which the gentry had become anglicized had proceeded very far, and many of the middling and smaller families among them seemed to become submerged and lost to view. Anglicization also appeared to be spreading to the episcopate and the higher clergy, especially under the Hanoverians. The intense and dedicated activity of manuscript copying had largely withered; and manuscripts themselves lay mouldering and neglected in the libraries of now apathetic gentlemen. The bardic order had become extinct by the end of the seventeenth century. Geoffrey of Monmouth and much of the myth of the glorious British past had now become steadily more discredited. All this seemed likely to paralyse that hopeful and self-confident patriotism of earlier Welsh humanists and squires. Small wonder that the age from 1660–1730 has been characterized in Wales as one of torpor. Focusing our attention more sharply, however, may enable us to see that it is an age of gestation rather than torpor.

The decisive factor continues to be that association of Welsh with religion. It is a concern for the religious well-being of the Welsh, reinforced of course by motives of preserving the established order and forestalling social tumult, that accounts for the publication of by far the great majority of Welsh books. It is the same motives that explain the efforts made to circulate books more widely and cheaply and to multiply the number of those able to read them. We may note, first of all, the dramatic rise in the actual number of Welsh books. Three times as many different titles were published between 1660 and 1700 as between 1540 and 1660. Between 1700 and 1740 there were about three times as many again as between 1660 and 1700. Moreover, printing-presses began to be established in Wales itself in increasing numbers from the beginning of the eighteenth century onwards. Most of these Welsh books were of a religious kind;

many of them Bibles, Prayer Books and Catechisms. Large numbers of them were sponsored and circulated free or at reduced prices by the charitable societies like the Welsh Trust in the 1670s and '80s and by the S.P.C.K. from 1699 onwards.

Equally impressive is the parallel attempt being made to augment the number of those who could read. From 1650 onwards, beginning with the schools established under the Commonwealth, through a succession of charity schools founded by the Welsh Trust, and the S.P.C.K. down to Griffith Jones's Circulating Schools of the years 1737–61, enormous inroads were made into illiteracy in Wales. Jones's schools particularly deserve comment. They represent the most striking experiment in mass religious education undertaken anywhere in Great Britain or its colonial possessions in the eighteenth century. Altogether he claimed to have taught about 150,000 Welsh children to read Welsh and about twice that number of adults (see pp. 200–16). Neither should we forget the considerable amount of informal instruction that went on. That amazing man, Iolo Morganwg (1747–1826), of whom more later, tells us that he could not remember the time when he had not been literate in 'both my native languages', having been taught at home by his mother. Nor was this at all exceptional, he claimed, 'It is a usual thing in Wales for a few young, and sometimes older persons of both sexes to attend for an hour twice or thrice a week at a place where a good-natured neighbour . . . will give them some instructions in reading Welsh and often in writing.' Iolo was prone to romanticizing admittedly, but his evidence tallies closely with that of the very different Erasmus Saunders: 'Even the common people . . . take pains privately by reading or discoursing to instruct one another in their houses.' There were, therefore, many earlier informal precedents for the extraordinarily successful Sunday Schools established all over Wales towards the end of the century. And the progress of the Methodist Revival was undoubtedly a consequence of this growing literacy.

It must readily be admitted that we cannot as yet quantify the extent of literacy with any precision. But there seems to be no doubt that there was a very substantial increase in the number of literates. Literacy, after all, can never be only a matter of being able to read; it must also be a question of the reading matter available and the incentive to read and to continue reading. In all these respects the story was one of growth and progress. The literacy achieved was a restricted one in many, perhaps most, instances – no more than an ability to read in Welsh. But its effects could be seen in the slow rise of an eighteenth-century Welsh reading public of a new kind. Authors were no longer dependent solely on wealthy patrons or charitable societies to bear the cost of publishing their books; increasingly they were seeking the support of advance subscribers. And the striking fact about these subscribers, from mid-century onwards, was that they were drawn not only from gentry, clergy and professional men, but also from among shopkeepers, craftsmen, drovers, farmers and even shepherds.

The motive force behind much of this activity was socio-religious – a desire to save souls and make good citizens. Griffith Jones said that he was not concerned with the fate of the Welsh language 'abstractly considered'; his solicitude was centred on the 'myriads of poor ignorant souls' who 'must launch forth into the dreadful abyss of eternity and perish for want of knowledge'. But, in fact, at a number of points even Griffith Jones shows himself to be the heir to an earlier patriotic regard for the language. He appeals to 'the prophecies of old Taliesin written above a 1,000 years since' and claims for Welsh: 'she has not lost her charms nor chasteness . . . she still retains the beauties of her youth, grown old in years, but not decayed'. He refers also to the opinions of contemporary antiquarians, quoting with evident approval and deference the opinions of the Abbé Pezron that the Welsh and the Bretons have 'the honour to preserve the language of the posterity of Gomer, Japhet's eldest son and the nephew of Shem; the language of those princes who passed for great deities among the ancients' (see also pp. 22–4). This quotation serves as a graphic reminder that the charity school movement was not without some links with that other major cultural force of the period, the antiquarian revival.

There were in the eighteenth century successive surges of anti-quarian and scholarly activity, all of them inextricably associated with the history and language and literature of Wales. They began with a man of impeccable scholarly standards, Edward Lhuyd (1660–1709). This most formidable of Welsh polymaths was a serious and critical student of antiquities. He was fully and properly convinced that he had to have a thorough knowledge of Welsh and other Celtic languages in order to understand some of the oldest and most important sources relating to British antiquities. Unfortunately this promising start was not maintained; and the more dubious voices of a number of false prophets began to gain wide credence. The Abbé Pezron's contentions in his *Antiquity of Nations* that 'the common origin of all European tongues was none other than Celtic' and Bullet's even more far-reaching claim in *Mémoires sur la langue celtique* that it was a 'dialect of the original language communicated by the Creator to the first parents of mankind' carried a very seductive appeal. It gained added attraction by becoming mixed up with the eighteenth-century passion for Druids, of whom the Welsh bards were thought to be the lineal descendants. Welsh writers had, ever since the sixteenth and seventeenth centuries, been captivated by the notion that Welsh poets were the descendants of ancient Druids, but it was not until the eighteenth century that it achieved its full flowering. An unusually influential source was Henry Rowlands's *Mona Antiqua Restaurata* (1723) which tried to prove that Anglesey had been the chief seat of Druidic worship. It was all very exciting, and very flattering to patriotic sentiment, but far from conducive to the more scientific approach laid down by Edward Lhuyd.

Much of the enthusiasm for this kind of antiquarianism was focused on the Welsh societies founded in London – the Cymmro-dorion in 1751, the Gwyneddigion in 1771 and the Cymreigyddion in 1794. Founded primarily by clubbable men for clubbable men, these societies existed chiefly for social contact and conviviality; and the sights of most of their members were never raised far above this level. But within them was a small core of more dedicated and better-informed enthusiasts; mostly middle-class and professional men, like the Morris brothers of Anglesey or the two rather tragic clergymen-poets, Goronwy Owen and Evan Evans. They saw them-selves as ardent descendants of the ancient Britons, and passionate upholders of the worth and dignity of the Welsh language and literature, though in some respects woefully ignorant of their true nature. They were alarmed by the signs of decay and disintegration which they saw as a result of the death of the bardic order and the apathy of the gentry. So they set themselves the task of the 'cultiva-tion of the British language' and 'a search into its antiquities'. It has to be confessed that disappointingly little ensued by way of tangible results in the publication of ancient literature.

Later in the century this antiquarian interest was injected with a potent infusion of romanticism, notably from Iolo Morganwg and William Owen-Pughe. Both were men of immense if often misapplied erudition; each of them was indefatigably energetic. They shared the preoccupations and predilections of romantics everywhere: the discovery of ancient poetry (and even the fabrication of it); a passion for medieval literature and an urge to publish it; an unbounded admiration for the 'noble savage' and a craze for all that was simple, spontaneous and pristine in folk-life and ways. This was not, in fairness to them, merely a theoretical devotion; they were responsible for some very remarkable publications, including an edition of poems by Dafydd ap Gwilym, a grammar and dictionary, and, above all, for the monumental *Myvyrian Archaiology*, which was much the bulkiest collection, however uncritical and even spurious in parts, of ancient and medieval Welsh verse and prose hitherto published. They surrounded the patriotic societies in London and in Wales, now and in the nineteenth century, with the distinctive aura of romanticized patriotism. They also left their mark very clearly on the Eisteddfod, to which Iolo attached his most successful and long-lived invention – the *Gorsedd* of the Bards of Britain. This, he claimed, had survived in unbroken succession from the Druids to the Glamorgan of his youth, an institution of which he was the sole surviving member after 1798.

It may appear odd that this antiquarian and romantic patriotism owes so much to London-based societies. It becomes more explicable when we recall that Wales had no capital nor even one town of any consequence, no university, no representative institution, no Welsh-speaking aristocracy. Only in London did wealth and inclination combine to provide an appropriate setting. Nor should we forget Acton's dictum that 'exile is the nursery of nationality'; Welshmen are proverbial for their *hiraeth*, that nostalgia for home and kin that defies exact translation. In London these Welsh exiles sought to preserve the old institutions that they had left behind them. They were reacting sharply against two kinds of change which they thought were in danger of ruining the rural Wales they had known: the onset of industry and the rise of Methodism. Ironically enough, in the nineteenth century, their own patriotic urges were ultimately to infect and capture industrial and Nonconformist Wales.

When we look at nineteenth-century Wales it becomes immediately apparent that it was industrialism and Nonconformity which supplied the dynamics of Welsh life. Each was, as it turned out, to be infiltrated and, to a greater or lesser degree, won over by the earlier linguistic and patriotic consciousness. Both contrived to make the Welsh more literate and more aware of their nationality. At the outset this would have seemed distinctly improbable. Many of the early industrial entrepreneurs were English immigrants, and English was unmistakably the language of commerce and industry at their higher levels. Lower down the social scale, attracted by new employment opportunities, many non-Welsh immigrants streamed in from Ireland and England, and not all of them, especially in sea-port towns and the eastern fringes of Wales, were fully absorbed into the Welsh-speaking population. Nonconformity, on the other hand, was admittedly more indigenous than industry. But it had been much more concerned with salvation than language and with piety than culture. It frowned upon the worldly vanities associated with the more carefree and, in its eyes, more sinful society of old Wales. It suspected the activities of the eisteddfod and the literary and patriotic societies as providing occasions for carousing, roistering, and other fleshly pursuits unbecoming the elect of God. On the face of it, industry and dissent appeared to represent so complete a break with the Welsh past as not to be susceptible to the transmission of that earlier patrimony of conscious pride in language, literature and nationality. And, indeed, for part of the nineteenth century this was largely true. The mantle of the eighteenth-century patriots fell on the shoulders of Anglican clerics and gentry – men associated with the rural areas and the Established Church. For the first three or four decades of the nineteenth century these were the chief mentors of the eisteddfodic and literary movements.

Industrialization was, however, transforming the potentialities of Welsh social and cultural life. It gave rise to a phenomenal internal migration. The Welsh were colonizing their own country, and most of the inhabitants of the industrial areas were Welsh by origin, speech and culture. In this context there was a marked difference between them and Irish and Gaelic speakers; a difference which reinforces the point made earlier about the language of religion. The Welsh in their search for industrial employment were not obliged to abandon their language along with their old rural homes. They could take Welsh with them to new industrial towns and villages – they even contrived to do so very successfully in London or Liverpool or Manchester or even the United States, as well as in Wales. Furthermore, industry and trade were bringing wealth into Wales on a scale previously quite unprecedented. Not just to towns like Merthyr or Llanelli or Blaenau Ffestiniog which were essentially creations of the Industrial Revolution, but to many old market-towns and seaports as well. For the first time there existed a sufficiently large Welsh-speaking *urban* population and a wide enough margin of prosperity to support flourishing societies and institutions; most important of all to sustain a really vigorous publishing industry for Welsh books and periodicals.

All this was being heavily reinforced by the phenomenal spread of Nonconformity, nowhere more rapid than in the new industrial areas. The chapels were intensely Welsh in character. Their commitment to achieving literacy among all their members was typical of that of all the more strongly Protestant forms of worship and belief; and it was their Sunday schools which taught adults, as well as children, to read, discuss and treasure the classic Welsh prose of the Bible. Their emphasis on the Calvinist virtues of restraint, sobriety, industry and self-improvement was an invaluable adjunct to the ethics of an industrial society. Chapels offered an outlet, elsewhere provided by politics or conspiracy or riot, to the craving for self-expression and the search for justice. They also supplied a framework for men to associate in broad-meshed fellowships or closely-knit small groups. Before mid-century their suspicions of political activity, of the eisteddfod and the patriotic society were fast being eroded. Initiative was rapidly passing from Anglican to Nonconformist leadership.

These nineteenth-century developments just described find expression in a positive explosion of Welsh-language publication. Much of the output continued to be religious in character; there were, for instance, some 370 editions of the Welsh Bible published between 1800 and 1900, as compared with 31 editions before 1800. Alongside the Bible there appeared every year scores of volumes of theological expositions, sermons, religious histories and biographies, and the like. There was also a great mass of books of more secular interest: histories of Wales, Welsh poetry, lives of eminent Welshmen – one such biographical collection was published in 1867–70 as a volume of 1,300 pages, without help or subsidy of any kind. There was a wide range of works on miscellaneous general knowledge, which finds its peak in an extraordinary Welsh encyclopaedia in ten volumes published between 1856 and 1879 by Thomas Gee of Denbigh. It required of him an initial outlay of £20,000, but was sufficiently successful for him to embark on a second edition ten years later. In all it has been estimated that close on 8,500 Welsh books were published in the nineteenth century, as compared with 1,100–1,200 in the eighteenth century. Perhaps the most convincing testimony to the liveliness and profitability of the Welsh book-market at this time is that English and Scots publishers found it worth their while to commission Welsh authors, publish Welsh books and maintain their own sales representatives in Wales. For the only time in history, probably, a Welsh author could expect to make something like a decent profit out of his writings.

Still more striking and more widely-ranging in its influence is the growth of a Welsh-language periodical and newspaper press. Whereas there had been a number of abortive attempts to found such publications in the latter half of the eighteenth century, by 1870 there were about 30 such flourishing periodicals (most of them of a religious nature) and a number of newspapers. Particular importance should be attached to these periodicals because of the regularity and continuity with which they could influence readers over a long period of years. Perhaps it is not possible to appreciate this fully until one has immersed oneself in one or more of these periodicals or newspapers through a number of volumes. Only then does one get the sense of a going concern and the full flavour of indoctrination. There is a wide spectrum of periodicals and each has its own particular style and approach; but the most important among them also have much in common. One is struck by their extensive scope; they include not only theology and moral uplift, but also a broad coverage of parliamentary and foreign news, together with a good deal of denominational news. There's also a lot of history, poetry and many items of interest on the kinds of science and general knowledge of special appeal to nineteenth-century readers. Of the actual reader-ship we know as yet far too little. If, however, we assume that it consisted of no more than an élite of ministers and church elders – and that, surely, is a fairly safe assumption – then we can reasonably calculate that such a group was strategically placed to mould an informed public opinion among the Welsh-speaking population over practically the whole of Wales for the first time. It must also have created an awareness of political, social and cultural issues among significant new social groups for the first time. Its effect was to make for a much stronger sense of ideological cohesion and solidarity, especially among Welsh Nonconformists who now constituted the large majority of the population. What was lacking for a long time was effective political organization. Professor Ieuan Gwynedd Jones has strikingly shown how effectively and speedily the Liberation Society was able to supply that organization in the 1860s. He would agree that for a generation beforehand the periodical literature had created a propitious climate of opinion.

This situation of an articulate, self-conscious public opinion finding expression through its own vernacular; sustaining and in turn being sustained by a thriving press; often sharply critical of a landowning class and an established church speaking a different language and upholding different cultural modes, must provoke reflections on the parallels it offers with the nationalisms of Eastern and Central Europe at this time. And it is significant that nearly all the Welsh words for 'nationalism', 'nationalist', and 'nationality' listed by the standard University of Wales Dictionary appear for the first time either at the very end of the eighteenth century (1798 in two cases) or in the nineteenth century, most of them during the 1850s and 1860s. The question that readily prompts itself is, 'why was there by the middle of the nineteenth century no significant demand for the setting-up of an autonomous Welsh nation-state?'

It wasn't because the Welsh were ignorant of the kind of national-ist aspirations that existed in Europe and Ireland. They knew of and admired men like Mazzini, Kossuth and O'Connell. But they applauded their radicalism not their nationalism. The radicalism they regarded as being relevant to their own aspirations, the nationalism they did not. Partly this is to be explained by the specific nature of Welsh patriotism from Tudor times onwards. Even those most devoted to it had never regarded it as being anything but fully compatible with loyalty to, indeed enthusiasm for, the British Constitution. What Lewis Morris in the eighteenth century called 'congruency of opinions in religion and politics' mattered far more than differences in language and culture. This kind of loyalty had been strengthened by the long wars of 1793–1815, first against what was depicted as French 'atheism' and later against Napoleonic tyranny. Welsh opinions are also to be explained by the fact that for many of the more influential leaders their literacy was not confined to the Welsh language. Iolo Morganwg was one of a number who thought in terms of two native languages, and much of whose thinking was conditioned by extensive reading in English as well as in Welsh. In the industrial areas, by the middle of the nineteenth century, many of the Nonconformists' Sunday schools were conducted bilingually. The most decisive consideration, however, was that Welsh attitudes tended to be moulded by the dominance of middle-class values during most of the nineteenth century. Men engaged in industry, business or the professions might be suffused with patriotic sentiment but they also saw the economic value of being part of the United Kingdom. They eagerly accepted all the advantages that the connection had to offer, since they could share in them on equal terms. Added to which many of the Continental nationalists were committed to revolution; a procedure unthinkable, and indeed unnecessary, in the eyes of Welsh radicals.

The period from mid-nineteenth century to about the end of the 1880s was the high-noon of the kind of Wales just described. This was when it was at its most thriving, confident and optimistic; the halycon days of Nonconformist, middle-class, Liberal ideas. It preserved much of its élan right down to the First World War. Some of the finest literature written in Welsh for centuries was written in the first quarter of the twentieth century. It was all the more remarkable because it necessitated the abandonment of many of the most cherished criteria of Victorian Wales, because it was the work of men and women who could never make writing their livelihood on account of the smallness of the Welsh book-market, and because it had had to be achieved without much in the way of help from a cultivated and leisured aristocracy or upper middle class. The wonder was not that there were so many false starts and wrong turnings but that so broad and commendable a highway was struck in the end. Yet in retrospect we can see that the achievement it embodied was being subjected to acute and painful strains long before 1914.

In the 30 or 40 years before 1914 we can see the operation in Wales of forces present in other European countries bringing about what E. H. Carr described as the rise of new social strata to full membership of the nation. This resulted from the decisive triumph of industrialism, especially in the heavy industries of South Wales; from very rapid emigration out of the rural areas and the even steeper rise in the number of industrial workers; from the growth among the latter of more militant political and trade union postures; from the introduction of compulsory education and the extension of the franchise. This constituted a process by which concepts of a nation could become increasingly democratized; and it could lead to an intensified and more aggressive nationalism in the twentieth century. It did so in a number of European countries; but not in Wales, where what had hitherto been the firmest bases of national consciousness became increasingly undermined in the twentieth century.

Looking at the Welsh language first, we observe it being subjected to much severer pressures of competition. It is not always realized how much the pattern of industrial migration changed after *c.* 1860, with the creation of a railway network and the full opening-up of the coalfields. Into north-east and south-east Wales there poured a mass-migration of English speakers in numbers too large to be assimilated by Welsh-speaking communities. This is probably the most important single explanation for the decline in the number of those speaking the Welsh language. When enough English speakers came in not to *have* to learn Welsh to maintain normal social existence, a community became bilingual and from there it was but a short step to becoming predominantly English in speech. The effects of migration were reinforced by other factors. Compulsory education usually led to the extension of English because what many Welsh people then wanted was that their children should leave school with a good knowledge of how to read and write in English. Even more far-reaching was the impact of the Welsh county schools set up under the Intermediate Education Act of 1889. They provided much greater educational opportunity and vastly increased social mobility; but they creamed off, especially from the rural areas, many of the abler children and sent them out in shoals as teachers, ministers, doctors, etc. Even those of their pupils who remained had been educated largely in English. The same years saw the rapid spread of daily newspapers – all of them in English. Later generations have seen comparable pressures from the effects of two world wars, tourism, the internal combustion engine, the cinema and, above all, broadcasting. And there are two crucial points to keep in mind about the relationship between Welsh and English: (1) Welsh is not in competition with another small language like Irish or Gaelic but with a world language, and (2) most people in Wales do not have to learn English the hard way but can pick it up very easily. The results of this in relation to the number speaking Welsh have been very serious. In the census of 1891 the percentage of Welsh speakers was 54.4; by 1921 it had fallen to 43.5; by 1931 it was 36.8; by 1961 it was down to 26; and by 1971 it had slumped to 20.8 per cent.

The effects on literacy can be readily guessed. Illiteracy has been eliminated in Wales. It is worth noting that official figures for illiteracy in Wales in 1851 were distinctly higher than for any other part of Great Britain – at 55 per cent, compared with 49 per cent for north-western English counties and 31 per cent in south-eastern counties. But this referred to a particular sort of illiteracy, an inability to read and write in English. This actually insulated the Welsh language and did not necessarily mean that the people concerned could not read Welsh. Since 1870, however, formal education has placed a high premium on literacy in English. Literacy in Welsh depended much more heavily on domestic and voluntary sources of education, many of which, notably the chapels, have become much weakened in their hold. It took some time for the full impact of this to be appreciated. For a long time there was no problem about learning Welsh, the difficulty appeared to be to acquire a knowledge of English. Nor did people realize how quickly the process of anglicization could take place, and how difficult it was to reverse, once started. Now in mid-twentieth century the contrast between Welsh publishing today and that of 100 years ago is depressing. Many Welsh periodicals have disappeared and others are on their last legs. Although a surprisingly large number of Welsh books are published, it would be virtually impossible to produce them without a considerable government subsidy.

One of the clearest consequences of all this has been to produce a more divided sense of nationality between the English-speaking Welsh and the Welsh-speaking Welsh. English-speaking Welshmen are, as a rule, not apologetic about their Welshness or without pride in it. They are conscious of an amalgam of many traits which shade them off from the English or the Irish or the Scots: a separate history, a prevalent radicalism in religion and politics, a dislike of class distinctions and snobbery, a warmth and ebullience of temperament, a deep attachment to their own kin and locality, a love of singing and rugby football, and the like. They often view with keen regret the decline of the Welsh language and confess, a little ruefully, that they wish they could speak it. But, in general, they have not been willing to think of their Welshness as the determining test of their political or cultural allegiance. A large majority of them, indeed, have hitherto judged it to be largely irrelevant to the most serious social and political issues of the twentieth century. They moved from the dominant Liberalism of the era from 1868 to 1914 to the almost equally monolithic Labour allegiance after 1918 – a transference of loyalty brilliantly documented in Dr. Kenneth O. Morgan's book, *Wales in British Politics, 1868–1922*. The extreme, but logical, socialist point of view was put by the late Aneurin Bevan in the first Welsh Day debate in the Commons in 1944 when he argued that there was no special solution for Welsh economic difficulties that was not a solution for the same problems elsewhere in Great Britain; 'there is no Welsh problem', he insisted flatly. On the other hand there were other members in his own party who would have agreed with what Robert Richards, the Labour member for Wrexham, said in the same debate, 'Wales is a nation which in its tradition, history, language and literature is quite distinct from England. There are many people in Wales who are more concerned about the culture of Wales than about the economic life of Wales.'

VII.   The Gentry of Wales*

Four reasons, at least, make me shudder at the prospect of trying to survey within the space of a single essay the characteristics of a social group so much discussed, often vilified, and not infrequently misrepresented in Wales as the gentry. First, there is the long time-span involved. The age of the gentry in Wales may be said to have lasted from about the time of the Glyn Dŵr Rebellion (1400–1415) – though some families were conspicuous well before that time – to the outbreak of the First World War. Those five centuries witnessed many and distinct phases in the history of the gentry which have to be all-too-roughly telescoped together in what follows. Second, though Wales is a small country it nevertheless covers thirteen counties, between which there are many differences as well as similarities. The disparities between those of the north and the south are reasonably well-known; yet contrasts just as great exist between east and west, which are often overlooked: Merioneth and Cardigan, for instance, have far more in common with one another than the former has with Flint or the latter with Monmouthshire. Within individual counties there can be remarkably sharp divisions, of which the gulf between Welsh-speaking northern Pembrokeshire and English-speaking southern Pembrokeshire is the most clear-cut example. Third, within each county there has been great diversity among the families who could be classed as gentry. Some survived for pretty well the whole of the five hundred years under review: Bulkeleys at Beaumaris, Vaughans at Nannau, Prices at Gogerddan, Morgans at Tredegar, Philippses at Picton. Others lasted no more than a few generations. But in each county, from the sixteenth century onwards, there would at any one time have been anything from about a dozen to thirty or forty families who formed the ruling élite, the county gentry, though its composition might change markedly over the centuries. It is with their representatives that this essay will be chiefly concerned. It should be recalled, however, that beneath them, and especially from the fifteenth to the early-eighteenth centuries, in each shire there were literally dozens of minor gentry families. Finally, in any discussion

*The substance of this essay was first delivered as a lecture at an Easter conference at Dyffryn House, Glamorgan, in 1974, organised by Mr. Trefor Owen, Curator of the National Folk Museum of Wales, and his colleagues.

of this kind it is difficult to escape from that image of alienation stamped on the gentry by a good deal of recent Welsh historiography. In this they figure as traitors to their Welsh inheritance, economic and social oppressors of their tenantry, estranged from the mass of the nation by barriers of class, language, culture, religion and politics. In general they have had a singularly 'bad press' in the Wales of the last 150 years or so. It is not the purpose of this short essay to 'defend' or to 'rehabilitate' the gentry but only to examine, as concisely and impartially as possible, the part they have played in the history and the historiography of Wales. Given that the period involved is long and the gentry's circumstances multifarious, their portrait has to be delineated in a series of broad, not to say coarse, brush-strokes, inevitably lacking in detail, subtlety and chiaroscuro.

* * *

The origins of gentry families varied widely; but, broadly speaking, they were of two kinds: the native gentry and the incomers (*advenae* as they were often known in the pedigrees of south-east Wales). The native gentry liked to claim descent from the princely families of early Wales, and a number of them could with justice do so. From early medieval times the gently-born in Wales were notoriously pedigree-conscious and inordinately proud of a long and exalted lineage; a pride which they transmitted to later generations. That very characteristic product of Elizabethan and early-Stuart Wales, Sir John Wynn of Gwydir (1553–1627), voiced their sentiments in an oft-quoted passage: 'A great temporal blessing it is, and a great heart's ease to a man to find he is well-descended, and a greater grief it is for upstarts and gent. of the first head to look back unto their descents being base in such sort.' In the literature of Elizabethan and Stuart England it became a stock joke to tease the Welsh on account of their obsession with ancestry and their insistence upon their descent from the Trojans. One contemporary satire of the kind ran thus:

Py Got, they be all shentlemen
Was descended from Shoves own line,
Part human and part divine . . .
And from Ffenus, that fayre Goddesse,

> And twenty other shentle poddies,
> Hector stout and comely Paris,
> Arthur, Brutus, King of Fairies.

That satirist, of course, had been unable to resist indulging in flights of vastly-exaggerated poetic fancy. But many Welsh gentlemen did, in all seriousness, trace their descent back to the princes and kings of old Wales. One Brecknock family even went so far as solemnly to claim as its founder one of the knights of King Arthur's Round Table, who was in turn reputed to be descended from 'Belin the Great, Emperor of Great Britain'. To be able to cast illustrious pedigrees and to praise the antiquity and distinction of their patrons' genealogy with few concessions to modesty or reticence was one of the most essential items of the stock-in-trade of Welsh bards. Closely linked with that tradition was the powerful desire to claim descent from those ancient British, so persuasively depicted by Geoffrey of Monmouth's *Historia Regum* as the high-born descendants of the Trojan race (hence the sarcastic references to Venus, Hector, Paris and Brutus in the satire quoted above). How genuine the claims to princely lineage were, it is not always easy to tell. The bards, in their more unbuttoned moods, were wont to accuse one another of 'cooking the books', of claiming long and exalted descent for an upstart in return for his patronage. Yet there is no doubt that genealogy was one of the most carefully-cultivated bardic arts and that whatever far-fetched claims might be made concerning the earliest ancestors, a number of the gentry families were genuinely able to trace their origins to the leading Welsh families of the twelfth and thirteenth centuries. Indeed, the embarrassment was that so many relatively poor and obscure freemen in Wales could lay claim to lordly descent, which led to John Earle's comment that in Wales 'they are born with heraldry in their mouths and each name is a pedigree.'

As for the *advenae*, they sprang from very diverse sources. Some might derive from fairly old families of Continental origin; the Stradlings of Glamorgan, for example, were originally a Swiss family who had settled in England and Wales during the reign of Edward I. Others were old English garrison families like the Hanmers of Flintshire. Some sprang from distinctly obscure beginnings, like the Bulkeleys, who came from Cheshire to Anglesey in the first half of the fifteenth century, or the Salisburys, who settled in Denbighshire in the fourteenth century. But all those families who emerged into prominence in the fifteenth and sixteenth centuries, whatever their origins, looked for illustrious predecessors and ancient lineage. The heralds and bards were nearly always ready to oblige them in a search for the necessary evidence for a lengthy and honourable pedigree – witness Sir Thomas Smith writing in Elizabeth I's reign: 'If need be a King of Heralds shall give him for money arms newly-made and invented with crest and all; the title whereof shall pretend to have been found by the said herald in perusing and viewing old registers.' Thus the Salisburys, leading family in Denbighshire though they may have been in the sixteenth century, were no better than yeomen two centuries earlier; but ingenious pedigree-hunters found for them an appropriate forbear in the person of one Adam of Salzburg (whence derived the name 'Salisbury'), a grandson of the Duke of Bavaria, in the time of William the Conqueror. Similarly, the Herberts, grandest of all the Welsh families of the Tudor age, equally fictitiously linked themselves with Herbert, chamberlain to Henry I, as their great ancestor. Many of the immigrant *advenae* families had 'gone native', intermarried with Welsh families, and patronized Welsh bards, who added their own certificates of gentility to the family's status.

Certainly, this pride in ancient descent and its associated insignia of coats-of-arms, genealogies, mottoes, and the other trappings of gentle birth continued unabated down to recent times. Glamorgan furnishes an interesting example of it. Many of the leading gentry families of the county claimed as their progenitor Iestyn ap Gwrgant, a celebrated prince of Glamorgan at the time of the Norman incursion at the end of the eleventh century. It is virtually certain that Iestyn himself knew neither coat-of-arms nor motto, but later heralds and bards confidently attributed both to him. The splendid Welsh watchword assigned to him, 'A ddioddefws a orfu' ('He who suffered, conquered') was later appropriated to themselves by his descendants, the Williams family of Blaen Baglan and Aberpergwm. When the first Glamorgan County Council came into being in 1888 it took over the motto and retained it until the demise of the old county council in 1974; it is still retained by one of the three successor authorities, the Mid Glamorgan County Council.

Nevertheless, however stoutly gentlemen affirmed their high-born antecedents, real or imagined, birth of itself was hardly enough to warrant the status of a gentleman. Undoubtedly, such standing could not be maintained for long unless lineage was reinforced by economic sufficiency. The point is neatly illustrated by an encounter recorded by the antiquary, John Leland, in the course of his journeys through Wales *c.* 1536–39. Leland told of his meeting with one of the family of Leyshon of the parish of Baglan near Neath, who proudly boasted his descent from Iestyn ap Gwrgant and averred that his family had been in Glamorgan 'in fame before the conquest of the Normans'. It was a claim which had obviously made a deep impression on the antiquary; but he could not forbear from adding the comment that though this man was of ancient stock he was 'now of mean lands about £40 by the year'. In other words, Leland had grave doubts whether a long line of descent, unsupported by comfortable circumstances and broad acres, was enough to qualify a man to be regarded as a gentleman. In the changing economic circumstances of the two hundred years from about 1440 to 1640 there is no doubt that Leland's attitude was becoming increasingly prevalent.

Although the process of acquiring gentry estates can be discerned in embryo as early as the fourteenth century, or even the thirteenth in a few exceptional instances, it was the circumstances of the two centuries from about 1440 to 1640, and the opportunities which they offered to those who had the wit, enterprise or luck to seize them, which enabled the gentry to lay the economic basis for their domin-ance over a long period. This was the classical era for the formation of gentry estates in Wales. An essential part of the contemporary conception of a gentleman was that he did not need to live by the work of his own hands, and that usually meant that he had to own enough land to live off the rents and the labour rendered to him by others. Conditions in Wales were conspiring to make this much more readily achieved than had ever hitherto been conceivable. From the fifteenth century onwards there occurred the final disintegration and disappearance of the earlier communal social and economic institu-tions which had been characteristic of medieval Wales. In the Normanized areas of the south and the east the old manorial organization was fast breaking down and the Marcher aristocracy were either becoming absentees or disappearing. From the débris emerged a new structure of gentry-landowners, rent-paying tenantry, and wage-earning labourers. In *pura Wallia*, Welsh Wales, the older institutions based on groups of kinsmen and lands held in common were likewise collapsing under pressure from thrustful individualism. Earlier obstacles, legal and tenurial, to the creation of individual holdings were fast disappearing; and forceful and ambitious men were not slow to acquire and extend the nuclei of landed estates.

Moreover, for a variety of reasons, the land market became much more fluid during the century or so from Henry VIII's reign to that of Charles I, and it made considerably more land available for purchase and lease. The severe inflation of the period – the worst known to British history before that of the last twenty years – squeezed the smallest freeholders and tenants particularly hard and made it more difficult for them to hold on to their land in face of the pressures from more powerful neighbours. Again, the dismantling of much of the structure of the medieval Church by Reformation changes brought a large acreage of ecclesiastical land, especially former monastic possessions, on to the market. The Crown, too, was willing – on occasions was obliged, on account of a desperate need for income – to grant, sell, or lease wide stretches of its own possessions in Wales to those who had earned its favour or who could afford the going rate for rent or purchase. Lastly, the royal policy of introducing English legal practice relating to the succession to land and the tenure of it made it easier for landowning families to consolidate estates and to transmit them less divided to successor generations.

This, too, was an age which offered enterprising men outlets for making money from a miscellany of sources in trade, industry or the professions. If, however, they wished to translate financial success in such ventures into lasting social recognition and esteem they knew they must invest their profits in land, for their own benefit and that of their heirs. To take but two examples from many: Thomas Middleton and John Herbert. Middleton left North Wales for London to become in time one of the city's leading merchants, but he invested his profits in estates around Chirk Castle, where his descendants have lived until the twentieth century. Sir John Herbert, second son of Matthew Herbert of Swansea, an Oxford-trained lawyer and a brilliant linguist, was engaged on a succession of major diplomatic negotiations for Elizabeth I, eventually rising to become her second secretary of state and one of her leading privy councillors. The money he made was applied to the purchase of Neath Abbey with some of its estates, and much of his handiwork in transforming the former abbot's house into an imposing gentleman's mansion can still be seen among the abbey ruins (see also, pp. 69–70).

Estate-builders rarely 'had it so good' as they did during the early modern centuries, when the nuclei of most of the big estates of Wales were first laid down. A majority of these acquisitions remained in the hands of the original families for three or four centuries. A number have been broken up only within living memory; a handful still remain – against almost all the odds – in the possession of some families. Two of the notions associated with the acquisition of landed estates showed quite astonishing vitality and persistence. One was the enduring concept of the true gentleman as a country landowner, preferably living on his estates, with a direct concern for his tenants. Writing as late as 1926 H. M. Vaughan, who had a very remarkable knowledge and understanding of Welsh squires, declared that an 'estate with tenants is an absolute necessity to the true squire, who must therefore own an immediate personal interest in all land legislation, as well as in the ordinary matters of local administration'. When in the 1960s I once drew Vaughan's observation to the attention of the former Lord Lieutenant of Carmarthenshire, Sir Grismond Philipps of Cwmgwili (d. 1967), himself the embodiment of many of the virtues of the old squirearchy, he declared himself in full agreement with it. The other point worthy of note was the power which the concept already mentioned exercised over successful 'nabobs' and industrialists of the eighteenth and nineteenth centuries. Few of them in Wales could resist the compulsion to acquire social cachet by purchasing land and buying, or building, houses similar to those of long-established county gentry. By a strange coincidence I have spent many years of my life in association with two of such houses, Cyfarthfa Castle and Singleton Abbey. I went to school at Cyfarthfa Castle, Merthyr Tydfil, a handsome, castellated, mock-medieval building, erected in 1824–5 in a magnificently landscaped park by William Crawshay II, one of the most successful of the early ironmasters of Wales. For more than thirty years I have been associated with Singleton Abbey, Swansea, an imitation-Tudor structure now part of University College, Swansea, also set up in a superb park in the year 1823 by John Henry Vivian, the copper king of South Wales.

The gentry's economic power was matched by their social pre-eminence. From the fifteenth century onwards there had been emerging an ever more unmistakably hierarchical landed society, a society of deference, in which the leading gentry exercised, and expected to exercise as of right, an unchallenged domination over lesser men: smaller freeholders, tenants, servants, and labourers. It was conspicuously revealed in the outward symbols of influence and superiority. The characteristic country-houses, the manor-houses of the gentry, increased markedly in number, most notably from about 1580 to 1640. (The whole process has recently been splendidly recorded in Peter Smith's outstanding book, *Houses of the Welsh Countryside* (1975)). These houses, often surrounded by their parks, were essentially peaceful and unfortified in character; they betrayed not a hint of the turbulence and insecurity so frequently displayed in the domestic architecture of contemporary Ireland or Scotland, but rather underlined the confident and unthreatened position of the gentry of Wales. True, some of the medieval castles survived as homes for the upper class, but even when they did they were changed into something altogether more civilized and palatial, as at Raglan or Carew (see pp. 49, 61).

All these houses had more space, comfort, light and privacy. They were also noticeably better furnished and fitted out, in a way that emphasized the plainly recognizable wide and growing gap between their contents and those of the houses of lesser men. There now ensued an era in which the gentry's pride and consciousness of rank found free and prominent display in their homes and their churches, in wood and stone, and glass and paint. Family portraits and effigies, for instance, became more numerous and splendid; more than any other feature, possibly, they express that sense of a continuing claim to superiority, prosperity, confidence, and a belief in the ongoing hereditary privilege of the family. During the next two or three centuries many of these houses would be enlarged, extended, or even rebuilt on a grander scale. Their furnishings and fitments would simultaneously become even more lavish and elegant. Not a few of the older and smaller gentry homes would, by the end of the eighteenth century, have been relegated to the rank merely of substantial farmhouses, like Plas Iolyn near Pentrefoelas, once the home of the vigorous and powerful Prys family and, early in the sixteenth century, a house that commanded the rapturous encomia of poetic admirers.

Economic power and social dominance had been accompanied from the sixteenth century onwards by the enjoyment of assured political, judicial and administrative authority. Between 1534 and 1543 came those Acts of Parliament which merged Wales fully with England. They introduced into the whole of Wales English law, parliamentary representation at Westminster, and the English methods of local government and justice; and the implementation of the whole system was firmly lodged in the hands of the leading families of county gentry. The working of all these institutions was based on the shires, into which the whole of Wales had been divided for the first time in 1536. The shire became, and remained until the end of the nineteenth century, the essential unit of politics, defence, justice, and administration. It was the constituency for the return of members of parliament, the recruiting-ground for the levy of troops for home defence or foreign service, and the sphere of jurisdiction for the indispensable local court of justice and administrative body – the Quarter Sessions, composed of the justices of the peace within the county. All the key offices within this network of authority – member of parliament, deputy-lieutenant, sheriff and justice of the peace – were reserved for members of the county gentry. Their ancestors had often held local power in earlier times, as agents of the Crown or the great medieval Marcher lords, but never with such a sense of constitutional right and permanence as the Tudor statutes had conferred upon them. It was hardly surprising that contemporary observers commented with evident approval on the advance in political and legal status which they believed these changes had conferred. Rhys Merrick of Glamorgan declared that, as a result of them, 'life and death, lands and goods, resteth in the monarchy and not in the pleasure of a subject', while George Owen of Pembrokeshire maintained that the Crown had redressed 'enormities' and established 'good and wholesome laws' among the Welsh, and given them 'magistrates of their own nation'. Whether those over whom they had been given authority, had their reactions survived, would have been so enthusiastic in their approval is another matter.

Within the Tudor and early-Stuart era there was worked out in practice an unwritten, but well understood, political and social contract between the royal government at Westminster and the gentry in the localities. The former was expected to maintain the independence and safety of the kingdom against any foreign enemies or extraneous forces, including the papacy and the Roman Church; to ensure internal peace and the stability of the existing social and religious order; to dispense reasonably prompt and impartial justice and legal redress; and to preserve the rights of persons and property. It also had the duty to respect the voice of the political nation as expressed in Parliament and to entrust jurisdiction and power within each county to the leading families there. In return it could expect from the squirearchy loyalty, co-operation, and a willingness to shoulder public office and responsibility. Within their own localities the gentry would act as a voluntary bureaucracy, which would raise and officer troops for the Crown, keep the peace and dispense local justice, collect the fines and levy the taxes, maintain the Church 'by law established', implement legislation, run the administration, and carry out instructions from the Privy Council. It was a system which, for most practical purposes, lasted until the end of the nineteenth century, though the coming of the Industrial Revolution and the rapid growth of new-style communities had by then imposed upon it crippling limitations.

An arrangement not without its weaknesses, it was from time to time subjected to severe strain. In the seventeenth century, during the reigns of Charles I and James II, it appeared as if the monarch was defaulting badly on his part of the bargain – though it has always to be remembered that the Welsh gentry were almost unbrokenly Royalist in the Civil Wars and that many of them evinced strong Jacobite sympathies in the eighteenth century. There were shortcomings, also, in the attitude of the gentry towards the régime. It took them a long time to overcome their inclinations to violence and wilfulness and to accept that their own instinctive reactions must be curbed in the interests of their public responsibility. It is probably true to say that they never entirely eliminated their sense of private and class prerogative attaching to their office as parliamentary representatives and magistrates. Right down to the last century politics were regarded as the preserve of gentlemen, and tenants and lesser mortals were expected unquestioningly to follow their lead. Out of such attitudes sprang much of the bitterness of political clashes and controversies over the 'screwing' of tenantry at elections and the eviction of them for voting disobediently. There was the same deeply-felt resentment at the way in which landowner-magistrates administered the Game Laws in their own narrow interest and at their snobbery in trying to exclude from the bench men who had made their money in trade or who were Nonconformists in religion.

To do them justice, however, we should not overlook some of the more estimable features of the system. The deep attachment of the gentry to Parliament, the common law, trial by jury, constitutional and legal safeguards for individual freedom, and the whole paraphernalia of judicial rights and constitutional liberties as embodied in the working of British political and jurisdictional arrangements was not without its practical fruits. Life, liberty and property were more secure in England and Wales than most European countries; there was more freedom and less oppression; and censorship of written and spoken opinions was far less in evidence. Nor were the ruling class devoid of a real sense of public duty and responsibility which they regarded as being inseparable from the privileges of gentle birth.

Inextricably linked with politics and administration was another fundamental and, as it turned out, permanent change of the sixteenth century which the gentry were able readily and successfully to absorb and turn to their own interest: the abandonment of the medieval, papally-ruled Church in favour of a Protestant and largely Erastian form of worship and organization. In consequence the State, and its representatives in the counties, i.e. the gentry, acquired much more authority over the Church. A substantial part of its former property in the form of land, tithes, and advowsons passed into their keeping – very often to the detriment of the clergy and their parishes. Endowments which ought to have supported a more sufficient clergy, better parish schools, more effectual charitable relief, and a more active religious life were siphoned off by landowners as a virtual supplement to their rent-income, while their rights of presentation

to livings were more usually exercised in their own or their depend-
ants' interests rather than those of religion. By the opening of the
seventeenth century the attachment of the gentry to a Protestant
establishment was largely secured. However much a mass of vestigial
remains of papist belief and practice survived among the common
people, the ruling class for the most part had little doubt where their
allegiance lay. Only a minority of recusants or crypto-Catholics
survived in their midst. The bulk of them had been won over to the
Protestant camp and there they firmly stayed; partly because of
their intense dislike of the foreign influence of Rome and Spain and
their fear of a Catholic Ireland; partly because the Church was an
essential and integral component of the Tudor régime which had
done much in their interest during the course of a century; partly
because their control over church and religion was enhanced;
partly because of the use of the vernacular in worship and the
patriotic appeal of reformed religion; and last, but not necessarily
least, from religious conviction, because it seemed to a number of
them that they had emerged from a 'time of blindness' to the 'second
flowering of the gospel', as one of their bishops put it. Their willingness to be wooed away from the old faith may have saved Wales
from dreadful disasters. Had the gentry remained attached to the
church of their medieval forefathers, the mass of the people would
surely have followed their lead. Wales would then have been in
much the same sort of situation as Tudor and Stuart Ireland. Being a
smaller country within easier reach of England, it would probably
have been more forcibly subdued, with consequences conceivably
more tragic than those which befell Ireland.

The alliance between squire and parson was much strengthened
after the traumas of the Civil Wars and Puritan rule. Each thereafter
felt a more urgent need of the other; stability in politics, religion
and society seemed inseparable from an unassailable ascendancy for
an Anglican establishment. The landed gentry became firmly,
almost bigotedly, Anglican in allegiance; so much so that when in
the nineteenth century a majority of the Welsh people had become
Nonconformist by conviction the schism created thereby in Welsh
society became one of the bitterest sources of antagonism and
dispute.

Another major shift of emphasis in the early modern era had been a new eagerness for the upper classes to provide their children with an ampler measure of formal education. A whole new spectrum of career opportunities had been opened for those who had had the training to be able to grasp them. If the gentry were going to take a more active and responsible part in local justice and administration they needed education to do so effectually. Aspiring younger sons who hoped for careers in the public service or the professions had little chance of attaining them without having been to grammar school, university or inn of court. The Reformation thrust to the forefront its claims for literacy, private meditation and judgment, household worship by the devout paterfamilias, and the grave responsibilities of the godly magistrate. Renaissance ideals insisted that a gentleman must aspire to be the complete courtier, a man of trained mind and refined susceptibilities, able to play his part in war, government and public affairs, but with a lively appreciation of literature, philosophy, history, music and the visual arts. Few measured up anything like fully to all these elevated criteria, but the influence of the new incentives created the contemporary boom in education, the lavish foundation of schools, colleges and fellowships, and the entry of a palpably larger number of gentlemen and their sons into educational institutions. The Welsh gentry were as keen as any to avail themselves of such facilities, in England as well as in Wales – at least until the Civil Wars, though after the Restoration this urge for education lost a good deal of its impetus. Two of the least happy features of this drive for education were that it was confined almost entirely to the gentry and some of the more substantial yeomen and that it found no means of establishing a broad-based system of parish schools, embracing the sons of tenants as well as of landlords in the way that Scottish schools did. Moreover, unlike the Scottish lairds, the gentry of Wales were separated from the mass of the people by the nature of the education they received. For much of their education was, when not an instruction in the classical tongues, an English-language education which contributed towards setting up a further cultural barrier in addition to the obstacles of class and wealth between them and the rest of the populace.

Virtually inseparable from the issue of education is the complex and thorny subject of language and literature. It has to be recognized at the outset that in the sixteenth and seventeenth centuries the

Welsh gentry became more accustomed to the English language and to making more use of it than they had previously done. Their contacts with England and the English were closer and more frequent on a number of planes – political, economic, social and educational. Acts of Parliament had made English the language of law, justice and government; and while they did not proscribe the use of the Welsh language they had certainly put it in an inferior position and entrusted authority only to those who had an adequate knowledge of English. In addition, the rapid extension of upper-class literacy and the revolution in communications achieved by the spread of the printing-press made English much more readily accessible to the literates in society than it had ever been before. Even the most ardently patriotic authors of Welsh books, like William Salesbury or Bishop William Morgan, recognized the importance of English to their compatriots as an invaluable medium of instruction and entertainment, with a printing-press producing a torrent of printed English books in sad contrast to the meagre trickle of Welsh ones. The incentives encouraging the gentry to learn and use English were strong and numerous; those inducing them to maintain their Welshness were few and weak.

It was this apparent willingness on the part of the gentry to sell out their national birthright which has brought them in for the severest censure in recent times. The indictment against them, at its most critical, can be summarized thus. Until the 1530s the gentry took a deep pride in the Welsh language and were the enthusiastic patrons of Welsh literature. The terms of the legislation of 1536–43 were deliberately calculated to offer the lure of status and power to them in return for a willingness on their part to sacrifice their language, and their sense of nationality, of which it was the chief ingredient. Having eagerly swallowed the deadly bait they rapidly became anglicized in speech and cultural affiliations. They ceased to patronize bards and writers, and Welsh literature went into steep decline. They had become Wales's 'lost leaders', separated from the people *(y werin)* by a yawning chasm of class, wealth, status, language, and culture, and, later, were to be divided still further by politics and religion.

The hypothesis is neat and, at first sight, persuasive. Closer scrutiny of the historical reality raises doubts; life was, as usual, more complex and loose-ended than theory. For a long while before the legislation of the 1530s there were many of the Welsh gentry who had already acquired a knowledge of English and who believed that there was great value in doing so. Moreover, long after the Acts were passed many Welshmen saw no incompatibility whatever between accepting with open and willing hands any benefits that Tudor policy had to confer upon them and yet at the same time maintaining much of their traditional Welshness; for example, one of the most prominent themes of later-sixteenth-century or early-seventeenth-century Welsh poetry directed to the gentry is the poets' eager eulogy of any office such as that of sheriff or justice of the peace which their patrons may have held. Nor did those patrons desert the Welsh language and literature until well into the seventeenth century, even later in some instances in the remoter shires and among the more conservative families.

That a sad decline in Welsh literature set in during the sixteenth century is undeniable; but to attribute it solely to the 'language clauses' of the Act of Union is an example of the fallacy of arguing *post hoc ergo propter hoc*. It takes too little account of some massive contemporary social and economic forces which are likely to have contributed much more to the nature of the changes than did Tudor legislation. We need, for instance, to assess more carefully and realistically to what extent contemporary inflation eroded the bases of the recruitment and remuneration of the bards. It must have made the customary nine-year-long apprenticeship of the bardic schools extremely difficult to maintain; the normal rewards for the poets' verses may well have become sadly inadequate; and the frequent complaints by poets of the 'miserliness' of patrons may, partly at least, be reflecting the latter's failure to take account of the fall in the value of money in the payments they made. Again, we have to ask ourselves what was the impact of the printing-press and the new Renaissance evaluations of literature? Sir John Price of Brecon was a devotee of Welsh literature and manuscripts; he was also sufficiently concerned about the language to publish the first Welsh printed book. But his own well-stocked library contained, inevitably, far more books in French and Spanish as well as English and classical languages than in Welsh. And what of the social function of literature? For a considerable time into the seventeenth century, gentry patrons still seemed to require that Welsh verse should continue to serve its ancient and immemorial function of praising the patron's status as a gentleman by descent, marriage alliances, public office, personal characteristics and local influence. Traditional poetry was, nonetheless, fighting a losing battle against other rival means of asserting gentility – through the College of Heralds, manuscript genealogies, and conspicuous expenditure on housing, costume, jewellery, or other ostentatious expressions of rank and substance comparable to those made familiar to the Welsh gentry by their counterparts in England. There may well be reason to conclude that we have not been asking all the right questions about this subject, or even to have been asking questions at all, as opposed to making assumptions.

* * *

Thus far, discussion has ranged very largely round the 'golden age' of the gentry in the sixteenth and seventeenth centuries. It has confined itself largely to those abiding characteristics which gave the pre-industrial period of gentry dominance a unity and flavour of its own and which, to a surprising extent, survived the Industrial Revolution and lasted down to 1914. But though the gentry pre-served much of their position and privilege intact until then, this should not disguise from us the underlying challenge they faced from industrial society. From the eighteenth century onwards whole areas were being turned over to industrial pursuits, and before the middle of the next century industrial workers in Wales would outnumber those engaged in farming. In the industrial regions there would be no role of much consequence for an agrarian gentry unless they were themselves willing to devote some, at least, of their energies to becoming industrial entrepreneurs. Even then, the growing industrial population, whether masters or men, would be unlikely to look to landed proprietors for leadership. But it was not only in the major industrialized zones that the new economic forces were exerting their influence. The ripple effects of growing trade, wealth and population were spreading into rural areas as well; into the old market-towns, seaports, rural industries, even into agriculture itself. An impressive consequence was the growth of a larger element of men engaged in the professions and in business. Some among them looked around for leadership and reassurance to new sources of inspiration, to the more radical notions – usually much diluted – concerning trade and politics of disciples of Jeremy Bentham or the Manchester School. Gradually, this kind of opinion became bolder and more vocal, finding expression in societies, lectures, public meetings and, much most forcefully of all, in the press, a vigorous and rapidly-growing organ of opinion in Welsh and English.

This rising tide of nineteenth-century attitudes was not, of course, confined to Wales, nor was it finding its chief sources of ideological inspiration inside Wales. But its expanding strength and confidence came to constitute a particularly serious challenge to the Welsh gentry. Hitherto, they had drawn much of their strength from being associated with the ruling class of England and Wales as a whole. This was now being turned against them in two ways. First because the opinions and influence of a middle class based on trade and industry were much stronger in England than Wales, and sympathizers in Wales drew heavily on these superior resources in ideas, confidence and organization. Also, because of the close ties of the gentry with England, the Church of England, and the English language, they could be and were depicted with increasing conviction as 'aliens' or, at least, 'half-aliens'.

As Welsh, or more accurately Nonconformist, Wales grew more self-conscious and more vocal in its public stances, it evolved a whole complex of social values which were increasingly critical of, even diametrically opposed to, those of landowners. The conflict can here be outlined only under very broad headings. Economically, there were patent clashes of interest between industrialists and landowners; but what was unusually significant was the way in which the Nonconformist radicals tried, and largely succeeded, in allying industrialists and industrial workers with tenant farmers to establish a greater sense of solidarity between them than between tenants and landlords. Socially, as well, inherited landed wealth was depicted as being less acceptable or defensible; on the contrary it was portrayed as the preserve of a privileged class of idle parasites living on prosperity being created by others. When the system was shown at its worst, extending to younger sons, brothers, or hangers-on who were accused of living in slothful luxury by exploiting outmoded institutions of state, public service, armed forces, judiciary or church at the expense of the industrious elements in the community, it became peculiarly repugnant to radicals.

The links between such attitudes and the emergence of a political stance hostile to that of the gentry need hardly be stressed, since the growth of radical and Liberal politics is the best-documented theme of the history of nineteenth-century Wales. Almost equally well known is the parallel clash of religious allegiance between the Anglican landowners and the mass of the populace. What does need pointing up, however, is that this was not only a conflict of sectarian principles, it was also a violent clash of two rival conceptions of social morality and manners. The landed class was associated with the morality of old rural Wales, with its easy-going acceptance of custom-honoured delights among all classes of drinking, dancing, womanizing, sports, cock-fighting, hunting, horse-racing, gambling, revels, patronal feasts, wakes and the like, all of which had become anathema to the earnest, puritanical, thrifty-minded, self-improving Nonconformists. Nowhere was the confrontation between the two worlds more sensitively or artistically portrayed than in Daniel Owen's novels, *Gwen Tomos* and *Enoc Huws*. If the attraction of the old lay in its warm, simple, tolerant humanity, that of the new dwelt in its intense moral and spiritual discipline. The characteristic frailty of the one was its prone-ness to a heedless, earthy sensuality; that of the other was its tendency to a stifling, moralizing, self-righteous hypocrisy. Each set of values had its merits, and the one could have complemented the other; but all too often there was no dialogue between the two but only a slanging-match. Because the values of the new found expression so strongly in the Welsh language in pulpit, press and platform they seemed to throw into ever sharper relief the non-Welshness of Anglican and anglicized land-owners and their agents. There was, in fact, little that was distinc-tively Welsh in the content of Nonconformist radicalism; apart from the language in which it was expressed there was almost nothing in it which could not have been paralleled in similar circles in England, Scotland or the United States of America. Nevertheless, in Wales itself, then and since, it has often been invested with a particular mystique and aura of indigenous Welshness.

By the end of the nineteenth century there had been formulated a strongly condemnatory stereotype of the Welsh gentry which has hardened into something closely akin to an orthodoxy of Welsh historical interpretation. It presents the image of a selfish, privileged élite, which had driven between itself and *y werin* a broadening wedge of economic, social, linguistic, religious, political, educational and ethical differentiation. The sternest critics among historians with nationalist sympathies would push the case for the prosecution back to the sixteenth century, contending that ever since Henry VIII's days the gentry had been the willing quislings of Machiavellian English state imperialism; the men who connived at the making of the anglicized modern Wales and the unmaking of the truly Welsh Wales of earlier ages. Dr. Gwynfor Evans has been unrelentingly severe in his condemnation of them as 'a sterile class, who took much out of Wales without putting anything back. They declined into a clique of useless landlords, parasitic and anglicized.'

Perhaps it hardly needs saying that these criticisms are less a portrait than a caricature; a caricature drawn by honest and well-intentioned interpreters, but men who were opposed to the gentry on most counts. Like all caricatures it contains an element of truth and reality, but it also exaggerates and distorts. It is a view of the gentry as seen from outside by their antagonists – Liberals, Socialists, Nonconformists, men from Welsh-speaking chapel backgrounds and egalitarian industrial milieux. There was, on balance, more to be said on behalf of the gentry than their Welsh critics have always allowed.

We can agree that in their treatment of their tenants they looked for a degree of deference, obedience and loyalty to themselves which would now seem to most people to be hopelessly out of place in personal relationships, but was not necessarily seen as degrading or unnatural in earlier centuries. But whatever may be thought about that aspect of their relationship with their tenants, they were immeasurably less harsh and oppressive than were their opposite numbers in Ireland, nor had they anything remotely like the appalling 'Highland clearances' of Scotland to answer for. It might also be claimed for them that their record compared distinctly favourably with that of, say, the coalowners in their treatment of the miners. Socially, they had the merit of never having been an exclusive caste, and there was never any suggestion of their having

treated their tenantry in the way in which the mass of the Third
Estate was treated in France before the Revolution, or as serfs were
treated in Eastern Europe or Tsarist Russia in the nineteenth
century. Politically, no doubt, they were mostly Tories who believed
that government existed primarily in the interests of the landed
classes for whom all the most valuable perquisites must be reserved;
and they resented bitterly the nineteenth-century extension of
democracy as a reversal of the natural and divinely-ordained order
of authority. Yet to their credit they accepted much that was best
and freest in British constitutional life. They were nothing like as
obscurantist, reactionary or savage as their counterparts in the
majority of European countries. In most circumstances they never
maintained a censorship or secret police, and only rarely suspended
habeas corpus. Their dominance never reached the point where many
of their antagonist had to live in enforced exile convinced that the
régime could only be changed by bloodshed or revolution. Even the
most fervent of Nonconformist radicals never believed that anything
more than constitutional means would be needed to overthrow the
Tories, and such violent outbursts as there were in the form of
upheavals like the Rebecca Riots or the 'Tithe War' were generally
short-lived and untypical aberrations from the norm of political
protest.

In their religious allegiance they were, admittedly, out of touch
with the majority and committed to maintaining an unacceptable
ecclesiastical privilege and establishment. It is frequently held
against them that they found Anglicanism more congenial to them
for social reasons rather than for those of religious conviction. That is
difficult to deny; but the converse is just as true of the Nonconformists. The commonly-held assumption in Wales that Nonconformity
triumphed because it was a truer and more valid expression of
Christian belief *per se* will hardly hold water. Closer examination
has revealed that social incentives for tenants and workers to become
chapelgoers were as powerful as the pressures on landlords to remain
churchgoers. Furthermore, whatever the shortcomings of the Church
of England and its adherents, as an established church it was
decidedly more tolerant and less repressive than most state churches.
It was never so completely the creature of an authoritarian state or
political reaction as to provoke the savage and relentless anti-

clericalism witnessed in a number of European countries.

Finally we come to the vexed issue of language, culture and nationality. It would be idle to pretend that no gap existed between the gentry and the people or that the former's record was anything but unimpressive. Yet it can reasonably be submitted that the sins were those of omission rather than commission. It was not so much that the gentry worked directly against the Welsh language or Welsh culture than that they did nothing for them. When the reinvigoration of the Welsh language and Welsh publications got under way in the nineteenth century it got little support from the landed classes, though decidedly more from some of the Anglican clergy. In the main, however, it was perforce the astonishing phenomenon of a small nation of farmers, shopkeepers, workers and ministers pulling themselves up by their own cultural bootstraps, largely unaided by the privileged orders. Even so, it may be doubted whether the remote and tepid attitude of the gentry was ever as fundamentally damaging to the Welsh language as the narrowly utilitarian criteria of some of the most successful Welshmen engaged in trade and manufacture. The former saw it as a harmless, picturesque, even reassuring survival from the wholly deferential and rural society of the past; whereas to the latter it appeared as an outmoded obsolescence seriously retarding the wheels of progress in the brave new world of business and industry. Some of the more enlightened and thoughtful among the gentry were prepared to defend the Welsh language in print with warmth and spirit, notably A. J. Johnes and Thomas Phillips. Both were profoundly disturbed by the alarming effects on the religious allegiance of the Welsh brought about by the neglect, even contempt, shown by most of the bishops appointed to Welsh dioceses for the Welsh language. Johnes gave it as his firm conviction that the 'crying abuse of the Church in Wales, and the fundamental cause of all the defects peculiar to the Church in that country, is the system of conferring her bishoprics on Englishmen. For the last century not one individual has ruled a Welsh diocese who possessed the faintest knowledge of the language of the people!' Similarly, Thomas Phillips argued that 'In recommending that those children, whose native language is Welsh, should be so instructed in their own tongue as to read it with understanding, expression is given to convictions, not formed hastily, but after much deliberation; and it may be earnestly urged upon the members of our National Church, how vitally important it is that true views of this question should be formed and inculcated. If children, whose ordinary language is Welsh, are taught to read English only, their minds can rarely be influenced, nor can much knowledge be given them in the limited period over which their school instruction extends.' Such attitudes might be thought to compare not unfavourably with the views of men like David Davies, the railway-builder and coal-exporter, who contended: 'If you wish to continue to eat black bread and to lie on straw beds, carry on shouting, "May the Welsh language live for ever!" But if you wish to eat white bread and roast beef, you must learn English.' Or again, there was the Unitarian-minister turned banker, Lewis Lloyd, who deplored the absence from Welsh libraries of 'books such as those of Dr. [Samuel] Smiles and others, which show to the young what is possible through determination, education, culture, honesty, sobriety, prudence and perseverance. Many a Welshman, after coming into contact with the literature of the English, has agonizingly wished, "O that I might not return to begin my life again: I would be sure to make something of it!" (I owe the quotations from Davies and Lloyd to the kindness of my friend, Professor Ieuan Gwynedd Jones).

Though by the nineteenth century few members of the gentry were at ease in the Welsh language and most of them had little or no command of it, they were by no means indifferent to a sense of nationality as they understood it. Undeniably they conceived of themselves as part of a landed order which constituted the hereditary ruling class of the whole of the British Isles, but that did not preclude those families who were of native Welsh origin – and they still constituted the majority – from avowing Welshness. They were continuingly proud of their Welsh antecedents; but ancient patrician descent, centuries of unbroken connection with locality, estate and tenantry, and generations of the exercise of authority and acceptance of obligations were of greater consequence in their eyes than linguistic affiliations. These notions of cohesion and continuity, which belonged more appropriately to an earlier era and a simpler rural community, had been overtaken by events. They found diminishing favour in a society becoming more insistent upon the claims of language and democracy.

When social groups and institutions, together with the rationale evolved to uphold them, have outlived their function and value, they are apt, in the later stages of their existence, to be censured to the point of distortion and even travesty by the proponents of new groups and ideas which seek to oust them. The Welsh gentry have long been the subject of such animadversions, and the unflattering image of them adumbrated by their critics still largely holds the field. It is no part of the business of this or any other historian to take upon himself the mantle of counsel for their prosecution or defence. His is the more complex and, maybe, more thankless task of suggesting approaches that might help to set the record rather straighter.

VIII.   The Welsh in Tudor England*

On 1 August, 1485 a force of 2,000 men, described with scant courtesy by a French chronicler as the worst rabble one could find, set sail from Harfleur for Milford Haven. Three weeks later, on 22 August, their number augmented by contingents recruited *en route* in Wales and the Midlands, they fought and defeated the army of Richard III of England on Bosworth Field. His contemporaries believed that the dead king had lost the ordeal by battle; divine favour had given his adversary Henry Tudor victory and a crown. Henry Tudor – Henry VII as he now became – had taken as his banner the Red Dragon of Wales; a standard he later presented in triumphal gratitude at St. Paul's. It was a heraldic symbol of ancient right and power that, for the rest of his reign, Henry never seemed tired of displaying.

Henry and his Red Dragon had a particular significance for Welshmen. To some of them it might even have looked as if he were, indeed, the son of destiny *(mab darogan)* come to vanquish the usurping Saxons and to restore the progeny of the ancient Britons to their rightful place of rule over the whole island, as the Welsh bards had for centuries foretold. No doubt the more rhapsodic extravagances of the poets were taken with a large pinch of salt by seasoned and hard-headed Welsh leaders; yet even the latter might nonetheless be looking for something like a new deal. They might be thinking of that promise made by Henry in a letter to at least one of his Welsh followers that he had come to deliver his countrymen from 'such miserable servitude as they have piteously long stood in'. They were hoping, in short, for more careers open to Welsh talents. And, a century later, historians looking back at what had happened after Henry's victory, certainly saw it as having achieved just this. George Owen, writing late in Elizabeth's reign, recalled how 'since the time of Henry VII and Henry VIII that we were emancipated, as it were, and made free to trade and traffic through England, the gentlemen and people in Wales have greatly increased in learning and civility; for now great numbers of youths are continually brought

*This essay was first delivered as the O'Donnell Lecture at the University of Edinburgh in February 1968. It was later given as the O'Donnell Lecture in the Constituent Colleges of the University of Wales during March 1970. I have to thank Professor Kenneth H. Jackson, F.B.A., for originally suggesting that I should deliver a talk on this subject.

up and maintained at the Universities of Oxford and Cambridge and in other good schools in England, where some prove to be learned men and good members in the Commonwealth of England and Wales; some worthy labourers in the Lord's Vineyard; many of them have proved excellent in the Civil Laws, some in Physic, and other laudable studies, wherein they are found nothing behind other nations'. Lest you should think this is just George Owen's parochial pride, let me direct you to the same kind of testimony in that most impeccable of English Elizabethan antiquaries, William Camden, who speaks of the Welsh having plentifully yielded 'martial captains, judicious civilians, skilful common lawyers, learned divines, complete courtiers and adventurous soldiers'.

Still, we should not overemphasize the importance of Bosworth in encouraging the Welsh to go to England. The phenomenon of Welsh migration there was a good deal older than 1485. The Welsh of the Middle Ages lived in a mountainous country of limited resources and restricted opportunities. They were a fecund and energetic people not unwilling to look for wider scope outside their own country, especially after the Edwardian Conquest of 1282–3. Many of them sought a martial outlet; at Crecy, Poitiers and Agincourt there were hundreds, perhaps thousands, of Welshmen. In mid-fifteenth century a Welsh soldier of fortune, Mathew Goch – the 'Matago' of terrified French remembrance – was the horror of French chronicler and civilian alike, though he died defending London Bridge against Jack Cade. Others found more peaceful avenues into the royal service. Henry VII's own grandfather, Owen Tudor, went to court and charmed Henry V's royal widow. Their son, Jasper, was one of the shrewdest and most indestructible of Lancastrian leaders, while on the Yorkist side another Welshman, William Herbert, was one of Edward IV's most trusted advisers. An almost equally important route for advancement lay through the great aristocratic entourage. Owain Glyn Dŵr himself spent some time in the retinue of Henry of Lancaster and in that of the Arundels. Owain's father-in-law, Sir David Hanmer, was one of Edward III's leading judges and reminds us that some Welshmen found distinguished careers in the law. Others rose in the Church, like Philip Morgan, Bishop of Worcester and of Ely, and a major figure in the diplomatic and political life of Henry VI's reign. A few became prosperous merchants. One of these, Lewis John, became a successful landowner, the son-in-law of two earls – successively not simultaneously! – a financier, a diplomat, a member of parliament and one of Henry V's Council. Nearby English towns and cities like Bristol, Shrewsbury, Oswestry or Chester, had a number of well-to-do Welsh merchants within their walls. Other migrants were humbler drovers and clothdealers. Each year, large droves of lean cattle from Wales, 'the Welsh runts', were driven overland along well-trodden routes to the English Midlands, Smithfield, and even to Kent and Essex. Similarly, considerable quantities of Welsh flannel and friezes were taken by packhorse across the border for sale in English markets. There were also great throngs of wandering seasonal labourers who descended on English counties only for a few weeks at harvest time, though doubtless some of them never returned home at all. The numerous Welsh students at the universities were well-known for their patriotic ardour and tendency to unruly behaviour. In the English border counties the influx of permanent Welsh settlers was on a sufficient scale seriously to alarm the English inhabitants, who launched a flood of angry petitions to Parliament on the subject at the end of the fourteenth century and the beginning of the fifteenth. So Henry VII's victory had not begun anything new. Many an ambitious or needy young Welshman had felt the urge to 'go East, young man!' – east of Offa's Dyke, long before 1485.

For all that, Camden, Owen, and their contemporaries were not wrong in thinking that Henry VII's accession had made a significant difference. In all the spheres so far mentioned, and in many new ones besides, there were, after 1485, fresh, enhanced, and more numerous opportunities for Welshmen. They now went to England in larger numbers than ever before and made a much more palpable impact on the life of that country. So that by James I's reign Ben Jonson could claim that Wales had long been 'fruitful of loyal hearts . . . a very garden and seed plot of honest minds and men'. 'Whence', he asked, 'hath the crown in all times had better servitors, more liberal of their lives and fortunes?'.

The fact of the influx of Welshmen into Tudor England is plain enough; but there remain problems in trying accurately to document it. Our sources, though fuller in the sixteenth century than earlier, often remain patchy and insufficient. Even when they are reasonably informative it is not always easy to identify a Welshman as such. It may not be too difficult if the ubiquitous 'ap' is present in his name, or if a vestige of it survives as in Penry or Powell. A name like Llewellyn or Hopkin also offers a reasonable presumption of Welshness. But names like Exmewe, Trew, Goodman, or Flood are not immediately recognizable as Welsh, yet we know that men bearing those names and coming from Wales had distinguished careers in England. Finally, it hardly seems possible to quantify the extent of Welsh migration. Only rarely can we come anywhere near to doing so – in those instances where the institutions have kept fairly full registers or records, e.g., the universities or the inns of court, or more unexpectedly, the Shearers' Guild at Shrewsbury, one-third of whose members, at least, are thought to be Welsh. In other realms we have to be much more imprecise. For instance, we have reason to suspect that there were a considerable number of Welsh among the London paupers; but we are not yet in any position to estimate just how many. Let me give just one example of the difficulty. In 1582 when Queen Elizabeth was 'in her coach near Islington taking of the air, her highness was environed with a number of rogues'. Some 200 of them, 'none of whom had been about London above three or four months', were rounded up and dealt with 'according to their deserts'. Many of them were specifically said to have come from Wales, but we cannot be sure just how many, nor can we tell how representative this group of paupers and vagabonds was.

Nevertheless, however imprecise and impressionistic the picture has to be, it is incontrovertible that many Welshmen found their way into Tudor England and some of them carved a notable niche for themselves in Tudor life. It is with these notables, the 'learned men and good members in the commonwealth' as George Owen describes them, that this essay will be chiefly concerned. What we hope to do is to reveal the wide and diversified range of professions and occupations in which Welshmen distinguished themselves and to illustrate each by reference to some particularly noteworthy representatives.

We might begin by looking at the ways in which many of them

went to England to prepare themselves for the future, whether that was to be spent in England or at home in Wales. The traditional methods of the Middle Ages were still much in evidence. Attachment to the royal service, as we shall see, was still the major highway to success. Service in the great noble households continued to hold its attractions – and its disasters! Many of the ill-starred second Earl of Essex's boisterous and ambitious henchmen who shared in his spectacular eclipse in 1601 were Welsh; foremost among them his steward and *éminence grise*, Sir Gelly Meyrick. For others, whose hopes lay in the world of commerce, apprenticeship – preferably to a successful London merchant – was still the best opening. Young Richard Clough of Denbigh was first the apprentice in London, and later the trusted deputy in Europe, of Sir Thomas Gresham, whose fabulous success among English merchants on the Continent he shared. Clough left still-visible traces of his experience in the Low Countries in the stepped gables of his house at Plas Clough and the even more remarkable Antwerp-style house that he built at Bachegraig. Yet at least one of the greatest London-Welsh merchants, William Jones, began his career in the city as a mere porter. He was, perhaps, the kind of Welshman who, 'when they came to London were very simple and unwary, but afterward by conversing a while and by the experience of other men's behaviour, they became wonderful wise and judicious' (Thomas Wright, 1601). Not all were as lucky in rising to the top like Jones. Some fell prey to the sharks which shoaled prodigiously in the murky waters of the London underworld. Among those on whom such predators battened was the Welsh poet-adventurer, Tomos Prys. He wrote one poem 'to show that London is hell' *(Cywydd i ddangos mai uffern yw Llundain)* and another to 'show how a young man was cheated of his money through drabbing and dicing when he first went to London' *(Cywydd i ddangos fel y siomed gŵr am ei arian pan aeth ef i dref Llundain gyntaf rhwng caru merched a chwarae disiau)*.

However, one of the most noticeable innovations of Tudor society was the fashion for formal education. Some of the greatest enthusiasts for it, according to Humphrey Llwyd, were the Welsh:

> There is no man so poor among them but for a while will set his sons to school to learn to write and read, and those whom they find to be apt they send to the universities.

The grammar schools, springing up like so many mushrooms in all parts of England, attracted pupils from Wales. Shrewsbury, on the border, might have been expected to exert a strong pull; but other famous schools more distant – Westminster and Winchester, for example – also had close connexions with Wales. Historians of Westminster school, commenting on the abnormally large number of Welsh-born pupils to be found there, have attributed it to the fact that for sixty years the deans of Westminster were Welshmen.

From Westminster and other schools many young Welsh lads went on to the universities, just as young Owen Lewis went from distant Anglesey, first to Winchester, then to New College, Oxford, where he remained as a fellow until 1562, when Elizabeth's religious policy drove him into a long exile and the tenure of the Italian see of Cassano. Only from Caius College, Cambridge, were Welshmen explicitly excluded, along with the 'deformed, dumb, blind, deaf, lame, mutilated, and those suffering from contagious diseases'! At the universities they might be in danger of acquiring other things besides learning, if we are to judge by what one Welsh squire wrote to his son:

> Keep company with honest students who abhor evil courses such as drinking and taking tobacco, to their own loss and the discredit of their friends and parents, who sent them to the university for better purposes.

It was even suggested that it would be better to make friends with English students:

> I had rather that you should keep company with studious honest Englishmen than with many of your own countrymen, who are prone to be more idle riotous than the English.

A large number survived all the insidious temptations to idleness, tumult and debauchery, and went on to become scholars of some eminence at both universities. At Cambridge in Henry VIII's reign, William Glyn (Marian Bishop of Bangor) became Lady Margaret Professor of Divinity, was later President of Queen's College, and weighty enough a controversialist to be chosen by Queen Mary to debate with Latimer and Ridley in 1554. At Oxford, William Aubrey and John Griffith were successively Regius Professors of Law in Elizabeth's reign and were recognized as outstanding teachers of the subject. All Souls' College, with its strong legal tradition, had so many distinguished Welsh fellows in the sixteenth century as to make us suspect some national 'log-rolling' in the choice of them. Most of the Tudor Principals of New Inn Hall, Oxford, were of Welsh origin, and Jesus College, it need hardly be said, was in 1571 founded by a Welshman, Hugh Price, for Welshmen.

Nor were Welsh aspirants lacking for the 'third university' of the realm, the inns of court. It becomes possible to trace them fairly exactly after about 1560, when the admission registers indicate the county of origin of those admitted. It is clear that during Elizabeth's reign a growing number of Welshmen were seeking admission. At the most popular among Welshmen, Lincoln's Inn, there were 12 Welshmen admitted between 1570 and 1580, 13 between 1580 and 1590, 24 between 1590 and 1600 and 40 between 1600 and 1610.

In thus presenting themselves as acolytes in all these temples of learning these Tudor Welshmen, despite the growing influence of Renaissance ideals in their midst, were not impelled by a single-hearted devotion to culture. They were, first and foremost, equipping themselves for a career.

In terms of careers the greatest attraction of all was the royal service. Though there were plenty of medieval precedents for this, the harsh penal legislation of Henry IV's Parliaments against the Welsh had, in the fifteenth century, acted as a deterrent. It took the more benign climate of Henry VII's reign for the thaw really to set in in the cold war of relations between the Welsh and the English Crown. Henry's own undisguised pride in his British descent and his fondness for Welshmen, not to mention his dependence on them, marked a real turning-point. He, after all, was the supreme example of the local boy from Wales who made good. Many of those Welsh who had fought for him at Bosworth remained in his service. At the topmost reach of all, next only to Henry himself and the King's most influential adviser, was the man he described as 'carissimus avunculus', ('dearest uncle') Jasper Tudor, now made Duke of Bedford, and loaded with office, lands and honour, befitting the immense services he had rendered. Many others surrounded Henry in more modest roles. David Owen was his chief carver, Lewis Caerleon his doctor; Piers Lloyd, one of his many Welsh yeomen, was made customer at Calais 'for true and faithful service', and another yeoman, Edward Apryse, received from the King a beer-house in Fleet Street appropriately named 'The Welshman'. Though Henry's successors on the throne made no boast of their Welsh blood, the attraction of Welshmen to the service of the King begun by Henry continued under its own momentum.

Relatively few of them could aspire to the innermost corridors of authority and influence. This privilege was restricted to the tiny *élite* in whom rank, talent and dependability combined to make them the sovereign's natural advisers. Not more than two or three families with Welsh connexions could confidently tread within this charmed circle. Chief among them were the Herbert Earls of Pembroke. Though the first earl moved the family's headquarters to Wilton, he had been born in Wales and showed his love of the country by his patronage of Welsh books and writers. He had skil-fully avoided too direct a personal commitment in all the tangled politics of the age and had, in the graphic metaphor of a contempo-rary, 'leaned on both sides the stair to get up'. 'Get up', he certainly did. He was a major figure at court and in council down to his death in 1570. So too was his son, the second earl, who was also sufficiently Welsh in sympathy to be known as 'llygad holl Gymru' ('the eye of all Wales'). The only two other families with Welsh connexions of broadly comparable rank were the Somerset Earls of Worcester and the Devereux Earls of Essex.

Apart from these great families there were one or two individuals who penetrated to the heart of politics. (I leave out William Cecil, tempting though it would be to include him on the grounds of some Welsh connexions). Perhaps the greatest might-have-been of Elizabethan England was Sir Thomas Parry, controller of the Queen's Household and one of the first members of her Privy Council. For a year or two, until his death in 1560, Parry formed with the Queen and Cecil what Sir John Neale has called an inner cabinet of three. Had Parry survived, this corpulent knight from Wales, imperishably preserved in one of Holbein's memorable portraits at Windsor, might have been one of the crucial figures of the Elizabethan political scene. Another splendid character of

Shakespearean proportions was Sir John Perrott. Reputedly the bastard son of Henry VIII, he was a tempestuous and choleric personality, entrusted with high office in Ireland and in 1589 made a member of the Privy Council. But like that other stormy petrel from Pembrokeshire, Robert, Earl of Essex, Perrott too fell foul of powerful enemies at Court. He was put in the Tower for treason and died there before he could suffer execution.

In the next category of royal servants came those who, lacking aristocratic birth or connexions, nevertheless by their own talent and training achieved high office as leading civil servants and career diplomats. Many of these would in the Middle Ages have been ecclesiastics. There are some survivors of the type in the reigns of Henry VII and Henry VIII. The clerk to Henry VII's first parliament was John Morgan, an Oxford man and doctor of laws, who later became the first Welshman to be Bishop of St. David's for over a century. Another such was Richard Gwent, also an Oxford doctor of laws, close confidant of Cromwell and Cranmer, and the man singled out for the responsible and ticklish task of presiding over Convocation during the 1530s and 1540s. But clerics were, in this more secularized age, rapidly being ousted by laymen. Thus Sir Edward Carne of Ewenni graduated as a doctor of civil and canon law. But he never entered holy orders, though he remained a devout son of the Church and became lay chancellor of Salisbury diocese in 1541. Carne was widely employed on diplomatic missions by Henry VIII, including his suit at Rome for the annulment of his marriage to Catherine of Aragon. Yet he ended his career, paradoxically enough, as Catherine's daughter's ambassador at Rome – the only independent English representative maintained abroad during Mary's reign. Another leading civil servant, William Thomas, clerk to Edward VI's Privy Council and an influential adviser to the young king, moved much farther away than Edward Carne from the medieval Church and from medieval political theory. Thomas spent five years in Italy, where he immersed himself in a profound study of the language, arts and history of the nation which, he was convinced, flourished 'in civility (i.e. culture) most of all other at this day'. On his return he published a perceptive history of Italy and an Italian grammar. He had also learnt to know, appreciate, and imbibe much of Machiavelli's political philosophy, being one of the

first, if not the very first, in this country to do so. Still more interesting was his pioneer role as an advocate of the cardinal value of
teaching the vernacular language and assigning to it an honourable
place in the curriculum. 'To triumph in civil knowledge, as other
nations do', he contended, 'the means must be that each man first
covet to flourish in his own natural tongue' – though it was English
he was here referring to, not Welsh.

Closely associated with royal servants of this kind were the leading
Welsh lawyers of the day. The legal profession was more than
ordinarily attractive to men whose talent and ambition exceeded
their birth and possessions. In a highly litigious age none were more
fervent in prosecuting their lawsuits than the Welsh: 'they will
wrangle and contend with another so long as they are worth a
groat', said Ortelius. William Harrison, the Elizabethan antiquary,
was perhaps exaggeratedly severe on the excessive keen-ness of the
Welsh to litigate in London:

> 'Our Welshmen do exceed of all that ever I heard, for you shall
> here and there have some one odd poor David of them given so
> much to contention and strife that without all respect of
> charges he will up to London, though he go barelegged by the
> way and carry his hosen on his neck (to save their feet from
> wearing) because he hath no change. When he cometh there
> also he will make such importunate begging of his countrymen,
> and hard shift otherwise, that he will sometimes carry down
> six or seven writs with him in his purse wherewith to molest
> his neighbour, though the greatest quarrel be scarcely worth
> the fee that he hath paid for any one of them.'

So there was seldom any shortage of Welsh suitors in London for good
Welsh advocates to lack clients. The lawyers who succeeded there
were sometimes able to invest their profits in land to set themselves up
as the heads of new or resuscitated landed families. One of them,
David Williams, who began life as the son of a substantial yeoman-
freeholder of the upland parish of Ystradfellte in Breconshire, had
risen to become Justice of the King's Bench. On the basis of his
success at the bar and on the bench he became the founder of the
well-known gentry family of Williams of Gwernyfed, Breconshire.
One of his most celebrated judgments was in the famous case of the
post-nati, which determined the legal status of King James I's

Scottish subjects after the union of the Scottish and English crowns.

In the second half of the sixteenth century a positive galaxy of Welsh stars shone in the legal firmament. They often collaborated on legal occasions of major consequence. When the Queen visited Oxford in 1566 three out of the four Doctors of Civil Law called upon to debate in her presence were the Welshmen, William Aubrey, Hugh Lloyd and Robert Loughor. In 1571 Aubrey was again sitting with two other Welsh judges, Henry Jones and David Lewis, to determine the exceptionally thorny and vital issue of whether or not Mary Queen of Scots's ambassador, the Bishop of Ross, was amenable to the jurisdiction of English courts in respect of his activities on behalf of his mistress. Aubrey, the great-grandfather of the antiquary, John Aubrey, was involved in a whole series of major judgments in ecclesiastical, international, constitutional and maritime law, in many of which he was associated with other leading Welsh judges. Himself the cadet member of a well-known Breconshire family, he bought wide estates in Wales and founded the two leading gentry houses of Aubrey of Cantref, Breconshire and Aubrey of Llantriddyd, Glamorgan.

There had been a time when the King's servants among clerics and lawyers had been almost indistinguishable from one another, so frequently had medieval administrators been drawn from the ranks of ecclesiastical lawyers; in the more stormily theological climate of the Reformation the distinction between the two professions was becoming more clearly drawn. Moreover, laymen were taking over a growingly large sector of what had been largely a clerical monopoly. Even so, the clerical hierarchy, particularly at its top levels, remained to all intents and purposes a branch of the royal civil service; even more clearly so in some respects as a result of the breach with Rome. The Welshman who climbed highest on the clerical ladder in the sixteenth century was Thomas Young, a Pembrokeshire man who was Archbishop of York from 1561 to 1568. He was translated there from St. David's at Archbishop Parker's express request because of the rare combination found in him of political acumen with reforming zeal. At York he was active in his double role of archbishop and President of the Council in the North, but he found it an uphill task to forward the Elizabethan settlement in face of dogged opposition. The Welsh cleric with the greatest number of 'near misses' was Gabriel Goodman, Dean of Westminster from 1561 to 1601. He was in the running for elevation to the episcopal bench at least seven times, but he never made it; 'always a brides-maid and never a bride'! As late as 1596 it seemed from Robert Cecil's correspondence that Goodman was virtually certain to be made Bishop of Chester, only to be 'pipped at the post' by his fellow-countryman, Richard Vaughan. It seems strange that a man of Goodman's ability and eminence, who was in close contact with William Cecil for forty years, should have remained unpromoted for all that time. The reasons usually given for it were his opposition to the Earl of Leicester and his reputation as a 'grave, solid man, yet peradventure too severe'; but Leicester had died in 1588 and Goodman's personal characteristics were hardly a disqualification for a bishop, one would have thought. A number of men later elevated to the bench of bishops in Wales began their careers as parish priests or household chaplains in England. Richard Davies, Bishop of St. David's from 1561 to 1581, may early have confirmed the Welsh reputation for eloquence, when he was a parish priest in Buckinghamshire, for it has been suggested that it is he who is referred to by the author of *Petite Palace* where he writes, 'The girls of our parish think that Welsh Sir Richard himself cannot make a better preach than I can'. Griffith Lewis, on the other hand, was a chaplain to the Queen for seventeen years, but complained that in all those years 'he never received any promotion but only the poor deanery of Gloucester'. In 1601 he pleaded for 'the poor and small seat of Llandaff that now in mine old age I may do good in that my native country'. Like Goodman, he was doomed to remain a dean!

But for every son of Wales who went to preach – theoretically anyway – the gospel of peace in England, there were a hundred or more who went to display the ancient martial prowess of the Welsh in the service of the Crown. To a dynasty that had no standing army the loyalty of the Welsh and their readiness to fight for the Crown in an emergency were invaluable. Not only was there not a single serious uprising in Wales during the whole Tudor period – a phenomenon without precedent in earlier centuries – but Welsh troops always seemed to be available to subdue rebels elsewhere. In 1497 at Blackheath, when Henry VII faced a dangerous uprising, that old Welsh warhorse from Dynevor, Rhys ap Thomas, was there with his men to take prisoner the rebel leader, Lord Audley. Or again, in 1549, when the Cornishmen rose up in rebellion in the West Country against an English Prayer Book which they likened to a 'Christmas game', the Earl of Pembroke's contingent of Welshmen was invaluable in putting it down. Yet a few years later, in 1554, the same leader, with much the same troops, could with equal confidence be called upon to suppress Sir Thomas Wyatt and his fellow-rebels, who took up arms against Queen Mary's Roman religion and her Spanish match.

In the many campaigns of Elizabeth's reign in the Low Countries, France and Ireland, her armies were always generously laced with Welshmen. Out of some 100,000 men raised for service abroad, 1585–1602, about 9,000 of them were recruited in Wales, mostly for service in Ireland. The single county of Caernarvonshire was reputed to have provided 150 men who fought at Cadiz in 1596, and between the years 1596 and 1603 some 500 men were required from the county to fight in Ireland. Small wonder, perhaps, that the Privy Council found itself forced to complain that the choice of men was so bad 'as to appear that the men were picked out to disburden the county of so many vagrant, idle and lewd persons rather than for their ability and aptness to do service'. A very seasoned Elizabethan captain, widely employed by the government to help train troops in Wales, Richard Gwynne of Caernarvonshire, had no doubts that Welsh troops would fight most effectually when commanded by Welsh-speaking captains. Writing to Essex in 1598 he urged him to appoint 'none to lead the Welsh but such as hath the language'. From amid the thousands of Welsh rank-and-filers, some of them of dubious quality, a handful of commanders of rare distinction stand out. The *non-pareil* among them was Roger Williams. Veteran of a hundred campaigns in the Low Countries and France, he was well-known to figures of European stature like William of Orange, Henry of Navarre and Alexander of Parma, and warmly admired by each of them. His books on the art of war and on the campaigns in the Low Countries stamped him as a military analyst and commentator of rare percipience as well as a practical soldier of unblemished courage and resource. His commander, the Earl of Leicester, had no reservations about his merits: 'Roger Williams is worth his weight in gold for he is no more valiant than he is wise and of judgment to govern his doings'. He had a pretty turn of rough humour, too. He once came to Court to press a suit. Elizabeth, always fastidious but also anxious on this occasion to be shot of Williams, said, 'Faugh! Williams, I prithee begone. Thy boots stink'. To which he replied, 'Tut, Madam! 'Tis not my boots, 'tis my suit that stinks'.

Many Welshmen were attracted to adventure and profit at sea as well as on land. Not that one can draw a fine distinction between them in an age when most fighting men took naturally to amphibious operations. Most of those who went to sea are, again, obscure and anonymous. Others are hardly more than names: when Sir Hugh Willoughby sailed in search of the north-east passage in 1553 among those frozen to death with him in the inhospitable wastes of Lapland were three Welshmen – Richard Gwyn, carpenter; Robert Gwyn, purser; and Richard Morgan, ship's cook. A few emerged as captains of the front rank. The two most distinguished were Sir Thomas Button, one of the earliest Arctic explorers, and Sir Robert Mansel, the last great admiral in the Hawkins-Drake tradition. Both served their apprenticeship in Elizabeth's reign, but the real glories of their careers lay in the Jacobean era.

However, the Welsh adventurer we seem to know best is not the most illustrious, so much as the most articulate, among them, the buccaneer-poet Tomos Prys. In passing, it is worth noting how these exploits on land and sea seemed often to spark off literary talent among Elizabethan Welshmen. Prys's boon companion, William Middleton, translated the Psalms into Welsh while cruising off the West Indies in a mood of that astonishing blend of piety and privateering not uncommon among Elizabethan sailors. Middleton and Prys also claimed to be the first two men ever to smoke tobacco publicly in the streets of London. But Prys has a stronger claim to remembrance, in Wales at least, as a poet of marked originality if not of great genius. Although he himself decried seafaring as being fit only for wastrels, he obviously revelled in his own misspent youth as a blue-water sailor. He brought into his verses much of the flavour of recklessness, bravado and camaraderie of the seagoing fraternity. It may be interesting to recall one or two short quotations from the bilingual doggerel characteristic of some of his poems. Observe how ruthlessly he thrusts a somewhat reluctant English into the procrustean exigencies of the Welsh *cynghanedd* in the *cywydd* metre:

> By Miri! I see a sail
> Gif sias *er a gefais i.*
> Owt topsail, yw lowt tipsy,
> Gif way, *er y gauaf wynt.*
> *Crio iawnllef, cur anlwc,*
> O Lord! This is too hard lwc.

And he ends on a note of complete mock-disillusionment:

> Before I will, pill or part,
> Buy a ship I'll be a sheaphart.

It is ingenuity rather than inspiration which is the keynote of this lively and amusing verse. It's hard to believe that it was ever meant to be much more than the expression of a rollicking and jocular gusto.

Other Welshmen also had an especial interest in the sea, but of a more pacific and commercial kind. The magnet for these migrants was the profit to be made in the vastly-swelling volume of Tudor trade. In his search for Welshmen in early-Tudor England, the late Bob Owen of Croesor claimed to have traced seventeen tailors and merchant-tailors, twelve clothiers, and ten vintners, all of whom were domiciled in London before 1540. Some leading Welsh merchants are familiar figures: Morgan Wolfe of Chepstow, who became Henry VIII's goldsmith; Thomas Howell, who died in Seville, and whose name is still commemorated in the name of two well-known girls' schools in Wales; or the celebrated Middleton brothers, Thomas and Hugh. But one of the richest and most enterprising of them was William Jones, a man so little known in Wales that he even escaped the eye of that Argus of Welsh biography, Professor R. T. Jenkins. Jones left Monmouthshire, his biographer tells us, because he couldn't pay a debt of ten groats. He came to London to work as a porter; but, because 'his brains were better than his back', he soon gave this up in order to become a factor. In Hamburg 'he made such a vent for Welsh cottons that what he found drugs at home he left dainties beyond the sea'. He became enormously rich, and he ranks as one of the two or three most liberal and far-sighted philanthropists traced by W. K. Jordan among the great merchants of London. He was not the only Welshman of his kind. Among his great merchant-givers Jordan lists at least nine Welshmen, and among the lesser merchant-givers a further 23.

Nor were men of this kind to be found only in London. Every one of the border towns and cities – Chester, Oswestry, Shrewsbury, Hereford and Gloucester, had its quota of them, and Worcester and Stratford some distance farther east are each known to have had a colony of them. Further research would, no doubt, bring a similar situation to light in other places. That metropolis of the west, Bristol, strongly attracted them. In the decade between 1532 and 1542 alone, close on 200 boys and girls from many Welsh counties, though mostly from Glamorgan and Monmouthshire, migrated to Bristol as apprentices. Indeed, one suspects that there would be ample material for a monograph on the Welsh in Bristol during this period. From Bristol some merchants turned eager eyes westward. One of them was Thomas James, originally of Breconshire and father of Thomas James, the Arctic explorer whose voyage is thought to have provided Coleridge with the prototype for his ancient mariner. Thomas James senior was much attracted to the idea of using sea-lions as a source of oil which, as he wrote to Burghley, 'if it will make soap, the King of Spain may burn his olive trees'. Clearly old Thomas James was something of an early Leverhulme *manqué!*

It was not physical horizons so much as intellectual and cultural frontiers that other Welshmen wished to extend. They were found in large numbers in a wide range of scholarly or artistic professions. There must have been nearly as large a proportion of Welsh schoolmasters in Tudor England as there are nowadays in the Home Counties. It comes as no surprise that Shakespeare's best-known schoolmaster, Sir Hugh Evans, should be a Welshman when, in the poet's own native Stratford, there had been just such a Welsh dominie, Thomas Jenkins, whom he may well have counted among his acquaintances. The most talented of these schoolmasters was Leonard Cox, master of the school at Reading Abbey, and author of the first English rhetoric designed as a schoolbook to help 'all such as will either be advocates or proctors in the law or . . . teachers of God's word, in such manner as may be most sensible and acceptable to their audience.' When Reading Abbey was dissolved Cox returned to his home near Caerleon to keep a school.

A number of these pedagogues were music teachers and others were composers. Early Tudor Wales produced a whole nestful of songbirds who migrated into England, many of them becoming court musicians. One of them is thought by those fitted to judge as having been of more than ordinary talent. Robert Jones had the distinction of being included in Morley's list of famous composers in 1597. Musicologists also acknowledge that his Mass and Magnificat marked a distinct advance in musical technique and showed the first glimmerings of the great polyphonic music later created by Tallis and Byrd.

Newly-emerging science stimulated the curiosity of others. An outstanding figure among them was Robert Recorde, born at Tenby *c.* 1510 and educated at Oxford and Cambridge. A scholar with wide-ranging intellectual delight in the study of medicine, Greek, Anglo-Saxon, history and antiquities, he was also a man of accomplished practical bent – a successful physician, teacher, an early Master of the Mint, and General Surveyor of Mines from 1551 to 1558. He is best known as a pioneer mathematical writer, being the first author in this country to write modern treatises on arithmetic, algebra and geometry. The twenty-six editions published between 1540 and 1662 of his first book, *The Grounde of Artes*, give some measure of his success.

Recorde's book was taken up and improved by his younger contemporary, John Dee. Although Dee was born in London in 1527 he was always inordinately proud of his Welshness, tracing his ancestry back to the early Welsh king, Rhodri the Great. He kept up close links with Wales and maintained a profound interest in the history, legends and language of Wales, the *Cambricalingua* as he called it and which he insisted was the equal of Hebrew and Latin. He was perhaps the most versatile intellectual in Elizabethan England, well summed up in William Lilly's judgment on him as 'Elizabeth's Intelligencer . . . a ready-witted man, quick of apprehension, . . . a perfect astronomer, a curious astrologer; to speak truth he was excellent in all kinds of learning'. Generally recognized to have been a formidable geographer and student of navigation, and a first-class mathematician, he has more recently been acclaimed as Elizabethan England's great magus, in whom 'magic, science and religion combined . . . to form one universal vision animated by Hermetic man' (Peter French). But there remains a strong case for thinking that if Dee had not been seduced quite so much by the siren voices of astrology, alchemy, and the occult he might have fulfilled more truly the potential of what was undoubtedly one of the most penetrating and original minds of sixteenth-century England. His famous mirror, in which he claimed to see so many esoteric secrets, has in recent years been acquired by the British Museum. It was typical of Dee that this exotic aid to his magic arts should have been an Aztec mirror of polished black obsidian, associated with an Aztec god who was reputed to use the mirror to foresee the future.

Two Denbighshire men and close friends, William Salesbury and Humphrey Llwyd, were typical Renaissance polymaths. The former, best-known as the translator into Welsh of the New Testament and Book of Common Prayer, was a genuine all-rounder: scientist, lawyer, theologian, historian, linguist, littérateur, author and translator. He spent some years in England and published a number of books in English on a wide range of subjects. He rated his friend, Llwyd, as the equal of Bale and Leland as an antiquary; all three of them were, in his view, 'of any of those parts . . . the most universally seen in history, and most singularly skilled in rare subtleties'. Llwyd showed particular concern for the Celtic element in British place-names and complained in *The Breviary of Britaine* 'how imperfect all the accounts of this Island are, which we have from the *Roman* writers, and how dark for want of a little skill in the old *British* language'. Trained in medicine, and physician to the Earl of Arundel, Llwyd was also deeply versed in music and the arts, in grammar, rhetoric, philology and book-collecting. His co-operation with the European scholar, Ortelius, was a triumph of early cartography, though he is probably best remembered as an antiquarian and for his *Description of Cambria*.

Welsh antiquarians and historians of the period would provide a subject for a lecture in themselves, especially the way in which they took up the cudgels with more patriotic zeal than critical discernment in defence of Geoffrey of Monmouth against what they held to be the calumnies of Polydore Vergil. But a Welsh antiquary for whom I have a particular affection was Thomas Powell, who must surely find an honoured niche in any historian's pantheon for having written one of the earliest guides to the public records.

It would be very tempting to catalogue a bevy of Welsh authors of a whole miscellany of scholarly and literary works written in

English. Some of them, like Richard Whitford, beloved friend of Erasmus and Thomas More, or Robert Parry, author of an early prose novel, or John Owen, the epigrammatist, are highly individual in their contribution. But space will not permit any closer scrutiny of their contribution. Before leaving this aspect of the subject, however, it seems worth making two further points, very briefly. First, that Welsh scholars were generous in their help to English authors. Men as different as Matthew Parker or Edmund Spenser, Michael Drayton or William Camden, all acknowledged this. Second, many of the Welsh had a profound concern for books. John Dee's library was probably the finest in Tudor England; Blanche Parry (see below, pp. 196–7) was Elizabeth's Keeper of the Royal Books; and Bodley's first librarian was a Welshman, Thomas James. A surprisingly large number were involved in the printing trade – no fewer than 345 in the years between 1500 and 1700 was Bob Owen's figure. Richard Jones and Thomas Salusbury were certainly well-known London printers and publishers. John Penry was almost definitely not Martin Marprelate but he undoubtedly played a major role in organizing the press on which the Marprelate tracts were printed secretly. James Roberts, who printed the first quarto of *The Merchant of Venice*, was Welsh enough to include the Welsh motto, 'Heb Dduw heb ddim' ('without God without anything') on his title-page. The Earls of Pembroke were lavish and discerning patrons of English and Welsh literature. Sir John Salusbury, himself a poetaster, moved in literary circles in which he became acquainted with Ben Jonson and probably with Shakespeare. A number of English authors, and Shakespeare particularly, had a soft spot for the Welsh. It may be of some significance that many people with Welsh names lived in Stratford and that a number of Shakespeare's contemporaries on the stage, like Richard Gough, had Welsh names. Shakespeare's friend and executor, Henry Cundell, is thought to have been Welsh; and large claims that the poet himself had Welsh blood in his veins have been made, but remain far from being acceptably substantiated. However, in view of the many and diverse Welshmen in Elizabeth's London, some of them with an active taste for books and the stage, it is understandable that they should appear as often as they do in Shakespeare's plays and elsewhere on the literary scene.

These sixteenth-century Welshmen were, in general, renowned for their loyalty to the Tudors. But there were some notable Welsh opponents to the Crown. More often than not it was a mixture of religion and politics that led some of them to forswear the allegiance that seemed to come naturally to most of their compatriots. Some three or four clerics domiciled in England in Henry VIII's reign pressed their opposition to his royal supremacy to the point of martyrdom. Among them was the brilliant but luckless Edward Powell, one-time fellow of Oriel. His book against Luther had, ironically enough, in Henry's anti-Lutheran phase, been recommended to the King by the University of Oxford as a 'chief and brilliant gem' and Powell himself as the 'glory of the University'. But in 1533 Powell had the rash courage to liken Henry publicly to King David 'who', as he said, 'with his adultery also sat in the seat of pestilence'. Powell paid for his temerity with years of imprisonment and finally with the horrible death of hanging and mutilating.

Henry's daughter, Elizabeth, had many Welsh Catholic opponents, and Wales produced no fewer than 100 seminary priests during her reign. At one early stage in the history of the seminary at Douai one-fifth of its students were Welsh, whereas the population of Wales was only one-twelfth that of England. 65 of these seminarists are known certainly to have come back on the mission to reconvert England and Wales to the Catholic faith; by far the great majority of them to England. Very frequently they courted death and thirsted for martyrdom. Seven or eight Welsh priests, and three laymen, found a martyr's crown, and died with courage and dignity. One of them, John Jones, doubtless voiced the dilemma of them all. At his trial he maintained that he had been guilty of no treason against Queen or country. His judge replied, 'Yet as you are a priest of the Roman Church and have come here against the law this, under the law, is a crime of treason'. To this Jones answered, 'If this be a crime I must own myself guilty, for I am a priest and came over into England to gain as many souls as I could to Christ'.

But some of Jones's co-religionists among the laity were guilty of much more directly treasonable activity. Some major conspirators had perforce to remain abroad, deprived of what Burghley called the 'sweet benefits of their native soil'. A man of this kind was Hugh Owen, an unwavering enemy of the Protestant régime, who became the chief intelligence-agent in Europe to the Spanish Crown in relation to the state of affairs in England and Wales. Another was Thomas Morgan, an agent to Mary Queen of Scots in Europe, who declared that he had 'many means in hand to remove the beast (i.e. Queen Elizabeth) that troubled the world'. Before leaving England, Morgan had been secretary to the actively Protestant Archbishop of York, Thomas Young, until the latter's death in 1568. Doubts were expressed about Morgan's fidelity to Mary Stewart's interests in his own lifetime, and it has recently been vigorously contended that far from being a devoted supporter of Mary he was, the whole time, a secret agent of the English government. Other Welshmen were caught up in conspiracies at home, as were the two who were privy to the Babington Plot of 1586 – Thomas Salusbury, heir to the greatest family in Denbighshire, and Edward Jones, son to Mary I's tailor and master of her wardrobe. Most complex and mysterious figure among them was that characteristic product of an era of cold war, the double agent, William Parry. Parry had unquestionably worked as a spy for the English government and, possibly, as an *agent-provocateur* as well. He later became a member of parliament, and when his fellow-members heard of his alleged plot against the Queen they became so enraged at the thought that one of their own members could become a traitor – a 'mercenary hell-hound' they called him – that they wanted him to be executed in a manner befitting 'his so extraordinary and most horrible kind of treason', as if the fate ordinarily meted out to traitors were not barbarous enough. By contrast, Elizabeth's own sanity and moderation were most commendable; she would agree to no dealing other than the 'ordinary course of law'.

Extreme Protestant opposition to the Crown on the part of Welshmen was much more uncommon. William Thomas was implicated in the Wyatt Rebellion of 1554 and was executed for his share in it. A handful of the more obscure martyrs burned in Marian England were men with strongly Welsh-sounding names, but cannot certainly be proved to have been from Wales. There is no doubt, however, about the Breconshire origins of the Puritan martyr, John Penry. He had a short but crowded career of radical Puritan opposition, which included his major contribution to the organization of that triumph of early English satire, the Marprelate Tracts, and his ministry to the extreme separatist congregation in London. On a distinctly shakily-founded charge of treason, he was executed in 1593 at the age of thirty.

Welshmen there were, then, in Tudor England in large numbers and of many different kinds. But they were not the only immigrant nationality to be found there. In addition to quite a large sprinkling of religious refugees from the Continent – mainly Dutch and French – there were also many Irish and Scots. The Irish were playing a substantial role in English life during the later sixteenth century. Close links between Scotland and England were also being forged, and many Scots took the high road south before James VI of Scotland became James I of England. My point is that this migration of Welshmen was not peculiar to them but has to be seen as part of a wider pattern of movement within the British Isles. It cannot be attributed solely or even primarily to some special relationship between the Welsh and the Tudors created by Henry VII and reinforced by his son. Some of the conditions which led to this migration of peoples were common to all parts of the British Isles and, indeed, to much of western Europe. That outstanding authority on the history of this period, Fernand Braudel, in his great book on the Mediterranean in the reign of Philip II rightly refers to the crucial role of the 'indispensable immigrant' and to what he calls 'les descentes massives' of population from the more mountainous regions to the towns and the plains. This was an age of rapid inflation and growing population which tended to press more than ordinarily hard on the resources of the countries of the poorer Highland Zone of Britain. Those who became footloose there, were attracted to the growth-points of the economy in the Lowland Zone. Recent work on the history of the poor and vagrants has confirmed what a strong pull the richer counties and towns of the English Midlands and the South-east exercised upon them. The more prosperous agriculture, industry and trade found there offered the best chances for craftsmen, impoverished farmers, labourers, and even paupers, pushed out by the pressure of too many hands to employ and too many mouths to feed. Their social superiors – sons and daughters of yeomen, clergy and gentry – may have had more choice in the matter. But it was motives of money, honour or duty, in that order, said Roger Williams, that made them soldiers, and, no doubt, impelled them into many other occupations as well. Their likeliest ladder to attaining any one or more of these objectives, especially if they were younger sons, was to be found in England. Furthermore, the whole process was encouraged by the policies of the Tudor State. The more firmly it asserted its right to rule the outlying areas of the north and west, the more likely its subjects from the periphery were to find their way to the centre of political and economic gravity. In this context there may have been an important difference between the Welsh on the one hand and the Scots and the Irish on the other. Because the Welsh were able, in a way denied to the others, to identify their national susceptibilities with the triumph of the Tudor State they were all the more un-inhibited about making their way to England.

Not that when they got there they all became completely sub-merged and oblivious of their nationality. Some, of course, fairly quickly lost all contact with Wales. The poorer and more destitute they were, the more likely this was to happen; though the son of even so successful a Welshman as Sir Thomas Parry seems to have quite cut himself off from Wales and set up as a country gentleman in Hertfordshire. Other Welshmen were apt to affect English modes and manners with a slavish readiness that made them an object of contempt and ridicule to Welsh authors. These were the type of Dic Siôn Dafydd dismissed by Gruffydd Robert with biting satire as men who, as soon as they saw the spires of Shrewsbury and heard an Englishman say 'Good morrow', promptly forgot all their Welsh. But many, probably most, of them remained unmistakably and unashamedly Welsh. They tended to welcome Welsh kinsmen and friends to their cities of adoption in England and would, as Rowland Vaughan said of one of them, 'steal opportunities to serve some friends' turns'. Just as Thomas Middleton lent money to many a Welshman or, Puritan that he was, nevertheless shielded his Catholic brother. A number of these exiles, having prospered in England, turned to Wales to invest their profits in landed estates: Richard Clough in Denbighshire; the Middletons in Chirk; William Aubrey in Breconshire; and William Owen in Pembrokeshire. Many others remembered their native land with lavish bequests in wills and endowments. Geoffrey Glyn of Doctors' Commons founded Friars' School, Bangor, and Gabriel Goodman was a benefactor to

the borough of Ruthin as well as the founder of its school. William
Jones provided his birthplace, Monmouth, with a whole range of
social institutions. They included an almshouse, a lectureship, and a
free grammar school 'for the instruction and education of 100 boys
in the Latin tongue and . . . other erudition'. For these purposes he
vested in his trustees, the Haberdashers, the vast sum of £9,000. No
other bequest rivals this in scope or imagination; but there are a
great many smaller ones. Here were Welshmen who subscribed
readily enough to the Welsh proverb, 'Cas gŵr na charo'r wlad a'i
maco' ('Hateful the man who loves not the land that bred him').

These Welsh incomers seemed to their English hosts to be easily
recognizable. They have aptly been described as appearing to
Englishmen like 'the most remote and strange of provincials and
the nearest and most intimate of foreigners' (J. O. Bartley). Even
when they conversed among themselves in their own language, they
were readily recognized as being Welsh. Indeed, on the basis of the
frequency with which Welsh was used on the contemporary stage, it
has been suggested that the average Elizabethan playgoer could be
expected to have a smattering of Welsh at his command in the
same way as his modern counterpart would have some knowledge
of French. When the Welsh spoke English their pronunciation and
usage of the language gave rise to idiosyncrasies which were widely
known. Although proverbially fluent and voluble, the Welsh
themselves had occasional misgivings about their mastery of English.
A man of upper-class origin and background like Thomas Madryn
thought it necessary to apologize to the Earl of Essex in 1598: 'If I
have any wise offended you, either in speaking false English or
otherwise in my simple manner of speech, I beseech you to consider
that I am a Welshman.' In a border market-town like Abergavenny,
where English would have been more common than in almost any
other part of Wales, the local Welsh inhabitant was said to have
found it almost impossible to speak English 'without any corruption
from his mother-tongue, which doth commonly infect our country,
so that they cannot speak English but that they be discovered by
their vicious pronunciation or idiotisms'. The Welshman's English
seems to have been easily detected. He was regularly twitted and
satirized by English authors for his speech foibles: the difficulty he
had in pronouncing some consonants, and the dreadful muddles

he made over the use of pronouns, especially his use of 'she' and 'her' as all-purpose pronouns.

The stage Welshman was almost as familiar a stereotype as a modern music-hall comedian's mother-in-law. The stock characteristics of the Welsh reappear time and again: they were impulsive and excitable by nature, warm-hearted but quick-tempered; they had a passionate sense of honour and were fervently, almost aggressively, patriotic (much more so than Irish or Scots characters); they were inordinately proud of their history and lineage as a nation and as individuals; they were as addicted to pedigrees and genealogies as to toasted cheese, leeks and *metheglin* (their native beverage); and they had a great fondness for poetry and rhetoric, music and harps, and mountains and goats. It was not a particularly subtle or profound vignette, but it did set in sharp relief some familiar national traits, and it was usually presented in a generally good-humoured and affectionate way, in which the Welsh normally appeared in distinctly more amiable light than either Scots or Irish.

If the migration of the Welsh into Tudor England was at least not resented by their English contemporaries, it has been the subject of pointedly more critical comment in Wales in recent times on the grounds that it served only to impoverish Wales of its talent. It is a subject which it is not practicable to treat in depth here. But if discussion of such an issue is to be valuable it has to be realistic. First, it has to be borne in mind that this kind of movement into England was nothing new, even if it was much increased in the sixteenth century. Second, many of those who went were *driven* out by economic pressures. Forcibly to have caused them to stay – and it is impossible to conceive how any Tudor government would have found the physical means for effective coercion – might well have driven them to great discontent. Third, others went because they chose to seek wider opportunities than they could ever have found in Wales. I doubt whether it is ever possible to restrain men of spirit and ability from seeking to spread their wings as widely as circumstances will allow them to. A William Thomas or a Roger Williams or a Hugh Middleton could not have been kept at home in Wales in the sixteenth century any more than in the twentieth century Lloyd George could have been confined to Cricieth, Augustus John to Tenby, or Geraint Evans to Cilfynydd.

Surveying the impact made by the Welsh on England it is difficult not to be impressed by the phenomenal success which many of them attained there. The century served to open up opportunities to previously under-used Welsh talents on a scale not seen again until the spread of secondary and university education in this century. Small wonder that contemporaries should have employed images like 'emancipation' and 'seedbed' to describe the phenomenon. Many of those who did best were men who would have been at a marked disadvantage at home – younger sons of landed families, or gifted boys of modest birth and means. They were predictably the people who would be most enthusiastic to avail themselves of the new avenues to advancement opened by better education, increased social mobility, the improved political and legal climate, and economic growth. They seized with alacrity those careers where talent and training counted for more than birth or influence. The age-long, innate Welsh esteem for rhetoric and eloquence may explain why many of them were attracted to those callings where facility in the use of language was an asset – the Church, authorship, publishing, and above all, perhaps, the law, where their successes were more dazzling than in any other profession. The swift progression of many of them in trade is less easily accounted for, but it may be that they, like the Scots, coming from a poor mountain country, were accustomed to being frugal and thrifty and were well-used to having to drive a hard bargain. What all the successful migrants appear to have had in common was a keen ambition, reinforced by the bounding energy, will to succeed, and confidence of being a chosen people, which were typical of the age in which they lived. It was a combination of qualities which took some of their representatives to the top, or near it, in virtually every facet of contemporary achievement.

So far, our discussion has been confined almost exclusively to the *men* of Wales; but at a time when *women* are asking for, and rightly receiving, more attention it might be appropriate to do them the courtesy of leaving the last word with them. Pride of place should probably go to Queen Elizabeth's gentlewoman, Blanche Parry. A relative of the Cecils, she first entered Elizabeth's service when the latter was a three-year-old infant and remained the Queen's servant for the rest of her life. From 1565 until 1590, when she died at the ripe old age of 82, Blanche was the Queen's first gentlewoman. A Welsh-speaking woman from Herefordshire, she was reputed to have taught Elizabeth to speak Welsh, though there is no clear evidence that the Queen ever made use of any knowledge of the language she may have had. A lady of more than ordinary influence with her royal mistress, Blanche was always a good friend to a number of prominent Welshmen and, according to the historian, David Powel, 'a singular well-willer and furtherer of the weal public of Wales'. She lies buried at St. Margaret's, Westminster, just inside the west door under her handsome but rather tight-lipped and spinsterish-looking effigy. For, as her epitaph informs us, though she 'trained was in princes' courts with gorgeous wights' she never married. This, perhaps, specially commended her to her royal mistress, as her epitaph suggests:

> So that my time I thus did pass away
> A maid in court and never no man's wife;
> Sworn of Queen Elizabeth's bedchamber alway
> With maiden queen a maid did end my life.

This epitaph, by the way, is not to be seen at Westminster but at her native Bacton in Herefordshire, where another effigy of Blanche depicts her kneeling at an enthroned Elizabeth's right hand. Both are there preserved in marmoreal perpetuity; everlastingly chaste, as in life we must assume they were; eternally mute, as in life we can be sure they were not.

Many Welsh women must have accompanied their menfolk, or followed them, to England and further afield. In that early outpost of empire, Calais, there was a surprisingly large colony of Welsh and among them were a number of women. Amid the little company of hardy and ill-fated colonizers of Virginia in 1587 were two Welsh women, Jane Jones and Winifred Powell, the wives of two of the men colonizers, John Jones and Edward Powell.

Some of these Welsh ladies of Tudor times made formidable wives; none more than that Amazon among spouses, Catherine of Berain. This much-married lady came to be known as *Mam Cymru* ('mother of Wales'). Having been left the widow of John Salusbury of Lleweni in 1566, in the following year she married the prominent Welsh merchant, Sir Richard Clough, and travelled widely with him in pursuit of his far-flung business interests in Europe. It is of

Catherine that the eighteenth-century antiquary, Thomas Pennant, told a well-known, mildly scandalous, and certainly apocryphal, anecdote. On her way *from* church after burying her first husband she was proposed to by Maurice Wynn of Gwydir. She was obliged to refuse his offer because Sir Richard Clough had allowed even less grass to grow under his feet and had proposed to her, and been accepted, on the way *to* church. She promised Wynn, however, 'that in case she performed the same sad duty (which she was then about) to the knight he might depend on being her third'. She lived to fulfil her alleged promise. She not only married Wynn but also survived him and took as her fourth husband, Edward Thelwall of Plas-y-ward. As a result of these marriages she became the ancestress of a number of notable north Welsh families. Not that she should be in any way censured for her multiple matrimonial ventures. No Tudor widow remained unmarried longer than she, or the usual crop of would-be suitors, could help.

Young Welsh heiresses were also sought after in marriage; and not merely by the sons of the local gentry. Barbara Gamage, heiress of a famous Glamorgan family of that name, was an unusually desirable catch. Her hand was as eagerly sought in marriage as that of any heiress of an industrial tycoon in our own day. The field of suitors was eventually narrowed down to two: Robert, son of Sir Henry Sidney and elder brother to the famous Sir Philip; and Herbert, grandson of Sir James Croft. Henry Sidney and James Croft both had considerable influence at Court, where they belonged to rival factions. The contest brought some of the greatest names in the land to intervene – Cecil, Walsingham, Walter Raleigh, Howard of Effingham, even the Queen herself knew about it. Not that young Barbara had much say in the matter. She had been taken into protective custody, so to speak, by her kinsman, Sir Edward Stradling of St. Donat's. He took a calculated risk and hurriedly married the young woman off to Robert Sidney. The circumstances of the match were hardly such as to enable us to claim that this was a marriage made in heaven. Yet it worked out remarkably well. This young Glamorgan girl became the ancestress of a notable English family. She and her Robert, in that lovely house at Penshurst where their descendants still live, became a devoted couple. His letters to her show a rare and delicate affection. Her memory is still preserved

for us in Ben Jonson's poem on the Sidney home at Penshurst:
>These, Penshurst, are thy praise and yet not all,
>Thy lady's noble, fruitful, chaste, withall.
>His children thy great lord may call his own,
>A fortune, in this age, but rarely known.

(Who said our own was the first permissive society?) So, it is pleasant to be able to report that this romance ended as all good love stories should, and serious academic talks but seldom can, 'and they lived long and happily ever afterwards'.

IX. Religion, Language and the Circulating Schools of Griffith Jones, Llanddowror (1683-1761)

(Originally delivered as a public lecture in a series of four arranged by the Faculty of Education at the University College of Swansea in the session 1961–2, this essay was later published in a volume edited by the late Professor Charles Gittins, *Pioneers of Welsh Education* (1964). Almost all the many quotations in it are taken from Griffith Jones's own writings, especially from his annual reports, known as *The Welch Piety*, on the working of his circulating schools).

By the year 1764 a charity-school project in Wales, which had then been going on for just a generation, was sufficiently impressive to attract attention from as remote and improbable a source as Catherine the Great's Russia. The great Czarina, anxious to improve educational facilities in her own empire, had instructed her representative to make enquiries about methods of popular education in Great Britain. In the course of his report he wrote in the warmest tones of the extraordinary successes achieved by the circulating schools of a Welsh country parson, Griffith Jones of Llanddowror in Carmarthenshire. His enthusiasm was justified. What had kindled it was perhaps the most striking enterprise in mass religious education undertaken anywhere in Great Britain or its empire in the eighteenth century.

The author of the experiment was born, probably in 1683, in a farmstead called Pant-yr-Efel in the parish of Pen-boyr in the upland area where the borders of Carmarthenshire and Pembrokeshire meet. He was the son of relatively humble and obscure parents, and his father died within a few months of his son's birth. Having no father during the formative years of childhood may help to explain not a few of his reactions in later life. Little is known of his boyhood, but one of Jones's contemporaries, a man bitterly hostile to him, in 1752 published an account in sarcastic and partisan vein which may nevertheless preserve the memory of what was to Jones himself a valid and decisive experience. This was a vision of startling clarity of the 'joys and happiness' of Heaven and 'all the secrets of the Kingdom of Darkness'. It left him, so his adversary tells us, with an over-powering conviction of being 'a peculiar instrument for rescuing many souls', 'wonderfully called to be a shepherd of men'. Soon afterwards, he entered Carmarthen Grammar School in order to prepare himself for the priesthood, and after one or two unsuccessful applications he was ordained deacon by the saintly Bishop Bull of St. David's in 1708 and was priested in 1709. In 1710 he became a curate at Laugharne in the vale of Taf in south Carmarthenshire, a pleasant region in which he was to spend the remainder of his days. In 1711 he became curate of Llandeilo Abercywyn, and in 1716 vicar of Llanddowror, a parish in which he remained until his death forty-five years later and with which his name is invariably associated.

While still but a young curate Jones must have struck others as a man of more than ordinary parts and piety. He was soon taken up by a wealthy and distinguished patron, Sir John Philipps of Picton Castle. A staunch Anglican of earnest piety whose self-avowed aim was to 'live not a life of sense but of faith', Sir John was a leading member of the S.P.C.K. and the most enthusiastic founder and sustainer of its charity schools in Wales. It was he who gave the living of Llanddowror to Jones, and he followed this up in 1720 by giving him his sister Margaret's hand in marriage – a match which brought the bridegroom more in the way of connections than connubiality! It was Philipps, too, who sponsored Jones's own efforts on behalf of the S.P.C.K. He informed the society in October 1712 that Jones wished to go to Tranquebar on the Madras coast as a missionary. But, having learnt some Portuguese to fit himself for the task, Jones in the end was deterred not only by the 'belief of his unmeetness and insufficiency' but also by the 'extremely miserable blindness of his own country'.

This 'miserable blindness' he at first sought to dispel by preaching, for which he had prodigious gifts. Contemporaries regarded him as 'one of the greatest masters of the Welsh tongue that ever Wales was bless'd with' and marvelled at his 'superior burst of religious vehemence' that 'like a flaming meteor did beat down all before him'. But not quite all! There were neighbouring incumbents who were less impressed by his torrid eloquence than his tendency to preach in other men's parishes without their consent and to address congregations of as many as three to four thousand in the open air. He was summoned to explain his conduct before Bishop Otley in 1714, but defended himself with a spirited temerity which can best be explained by his being secure in the knowledge that Sir John Philipps was backing him up with the assertion that his defence was 'clear and satisfying'.

He continued, we may suppose, with his preaching and his parochial duties. But there is curiously little information of any significance about his activities in the 1720s. Nor indeed was it until about 1731, as far as can be ascertained, when he was in his late forties that he began the work with his schools on which his claim to remembrance rests. By this time he had become convinced of the marginal impact and the ephemeral effects of preaching amid a population that was largely illiterate and ungrounded in the rudiments of the Christian faith. He had learnt painfully 'how deplorably ignorant the poor people are who cannot read, even where constant preaching is not wanting, while catechising is omitted'. Nearly twenty years later he was to write that it had been found 'in several places that where 60 or 80 (young and old people) came into [his] schools, not above 3 or 4 of them could say the Lord's Prayer, and they, too, in a very corrupt and unintelligible manner, not knowing so much as who their father in heaven was'. It was this 'melancholy discovery of the brutish, gross and general ignorance in things pertaining to salvation' which had given him 'great thoughts of heart and painful concern' and led him to 'wish for, rather than any hopeful prospect of success to set up, Welsh charity schools'. Oddly enough, although Jones had earlier had ample opportunity of observing the S.P.C.K.'s schools, he had evinced little or no interest in this aspect of the society's activities in Wales. It was only when its schools in Wales had dwindled to the point of extinction that he appears to have arrived at the conviction that they were supremely necessary.

In thus pinning his faith in charity schools he was, of course, following a well-trodden path. Professor Jordan's great works on philanthropy have recently accustomed us to thinking in terms of the changing modes of lay benevolence in England during Elizabethan and early – Stuart times. The ethic and pattern of charitable giving were clearly delineated during that period, and education occupied a large sector of this charitable economy. But Wales benefited comparatively little from it. The Commonwealth's Propagation Act of 1650 did more for Wales, but in the end proved to be an abortive experiment in state-aided schools. More attuned to the voluntary spirit and methods was Thomas Gouge's Welsh Trust of 1674–81. This was a charitable venture organized along the lines of a joint-stock company which can justly be looked upon as the typical eighteenth-century philanthropic society, Mark I. Its objects were to set up charity schools and to publish and distribute suitable devotional literature in Welsh. When the S.P.C.K. came to be founded in 1698–9 it regarded itself, as far as Wales was in question, as a mere continuation of the Welsh Trust, although it was clearly much influenced by the work of Pietists of Halle as well. It founded 96 schools in Wales between 1699 and 1727, and distributed a large quantity of Welsh Bibles and other books. But even before the end of Anne's reign sectarian differences had taken much of the steam out of the society as far as schools were concerned, and by the 1720s they had nearly all collapsed. The truth was that all these efforts, commendable though they might have been in theory, had in practice only touched the fringes of the problem. No one concerned with them had properly understood the nature of Welsh society and its particular needs. With a wealth of good intentions and a dearth of genuine insight, they had applied to rural Wales solutions which worked, when they worked at all, only in urban England. It took an ill-educated, hypochondriacal Welsh country parson to show what was really needed.

Not that Griffith Jones at first really grasped that he had got a different answer and the right one. He thought of himself as carrying on 'part of the laudable, but more extensive, labours' of the S.P.C.K. Nor did he at first realize what an enormous responsibility he had assumed, though after the death of Sir John Philipps in 1737 he obviously seems to have felt that the latter's mantle had fallen on his shoulders. By this time, too, he had found a new patron in Madam Bridget Bevan, a lady of rank and substance, who may perhaps be flippantly described as a 'poor man's Countess of Huntingdon'. She proved to be a staunch friend and close confidante with whom Jones was to work in harmony throughout his life. From 1737 onwards, however, the initiative was unmistakably Jones's in a way in which it had never been before. From now until his death in 1761 he was very much the managing director of the concern, on whom its destiny very largely depended.

Already by 1737, his schools, which had begun with a single school in Llanddowror, were in a flourishing state, and had evolved their own characteristics. The concepts governing them were

uncomplicated enough. They were designed exclusively for a religious
end: the salvation of the poor. They were not intended to make their
pupils 'gentlemen, but Christians and heirs of eternal life; . . . not
to elate their minds, but to make them by the grace of God good
men in this world and happy in the next'. Griffith Jones eschewed
any intention of providing any vocational education; he concentrated solely upon religious instruction. 'What better means', he
asked, 'can there be made use of towards reforming the poor? As for
the education of most others, it is commonly directed another way,
viz., to recommend and qualify them for the honours and lucrative
employments of this world, without implanting the most necessary
qualifications of true Christianity in their hearts; which is the chief
and most needful qualification for all stations in life and for the
amendment of the world'. The essential key to such instruction was
'to instruct them in the Catechism and principles of religion'.
Jones regarded catechising as the 'particular and absolutely
necessary kind of instruction for laying the foundation of Christian
knowledge . . . without which . . . the whole building will totter and
fall. It is to want of this we may justly impute the unsuccessfulness
of preaching and other means of instructing and reforming the
people'. However, by a 'proper method of catechising' he did 'not
mean learning only by heart the sound form of words in our Church
Catechism, but explaining to their capacities and inculcating upon
their minds the meaning of it; and confirming the instructions
contained in it with pertinent scripture texts'. But, as was 'very
well known to all pious clergymen . . . catechising is hardly practicable without teaching [the poor] to read', and especially teaching
them 'to read the Holy Scriptures with all the speed that is possible'.
For the 'Word of Truth, contained in the sacred volume', was the
'great and appointed instrument to raise the dead in sin into a life
of righteousness'.

Time and economy were of the essence of this operation, so the
teaching had to be done in Welsh because the population neither
were, nor could be, qualified to 'receive necessary instructions to
secure their eternal salvation in any other language than their own
British tongue'. All that English-language schools had commonly
been able to do in Wales had been to get the children, after two or
three years, 'to learn very imperfectly to read some easy parts of

the Bible, without knowing the Welsh for it, nor the meaning of what they said when they repeated their Catechism'. Hence it followed 'that for the same money there could be but one taught to read English for twelve ... now taught Welsh'. Jones argued strongly that it would be as absurd to teach most of the children in Wales 'Christian knowledge in English, a language they do not understand, as it would be to teach it to the poor English people in French', though he was willing enough to establish English-language schools in those parts of Wales, like south Pembrokeshire or the eastern borders, where English was commonly spoken.

Teachers, though miserably paid at the rate of £3–£4 per annum and placed under humiliatingly strict discipline, seem to have been recruited without much difficulty. They were carefully selected and screened so as to ensure that they were 'not only tolerably well qualified to teach to read, but such as appear to have a more religious impression on their mind than is common'. Before being let loose on their charges, they were brought together for training at Llanddowror, probably in a building which still stood until the early part of this century and was known as Yr Hen Goleg ('The Old College'). Here Jones thought it necessary to have 'them together for some weeks ... under catechetical instructions ... to instruct them ... in easy, familiar explanatory questions upon the Church Catechism, and so through all plain and necessary things in a body of divinity and to set them sometimes to catechise one another'. Further duties laid upon them were 'to warn scholars very earnestly against every vice, particularly against lying, profane swearing, and absence from worship of God, or indecent behaviour in it', and 'also to engage them in the most cogent manner they are able, to learn to do their duty faithfully in that state of life into which it shall please God to call them'.

Working on as narrow a margin of financial backing for his schools as he had to do, 'their subsistence being not much unlike that of the poor taught in them who ... live from hand to mouth only', he had to cut his costs to the bone. After more than a decade of experience of running the schools, he calculated that 'upon a pretty nearly exact computation of all the expenses ... added to the salaries of the schoolmasters ... it appears that about six poor people or children are taught for twenty shillings' and claimed, with some justification, that 'no possible care or circumspection is wanting to cultivate this charity to the utmost advantage, so that every grain of it, if it please God to add His blessing, may produce its salutary fruit'. No money could be spent on buildings, and his normal practice was to secure beforehand the consent and goodwill of a parson or some of his most influential parishioners, so that 'in some places the favour is granted to have [the pupils] taught in the parish church or chapel; sometimes well-disposed persons lend a school-room gratis . . .; and where we are obliged to hire a house, it is on moderate terms'. In what was to be almost the last of his reports, he maintained with unconcealed pride that 'less expense than what costs the building of one schoolhouse in some places had served in this method to instruct several thousands of the poor in a church or chapel or poor cottage'. Expenditure on books was kept to the barest minimum, thanks to the munificence of the S.P.C.K., from whom Jones requisitioned Bibles, Catechisms and works of piety by the thousand. An adequate supply of Welsh Bibles and Testaments was a source of acute concern. Throughout the 1740s he constantly urged the need for a new edition, and he greeted the S.P.C.K.'s edition of 1748 with a rapture tempered only by the anxiety of how to provide copies for all who needed them. Though the new edition was modestly priced at 3s. 6d. (3s. 10d. with clasps) he reported 'upwards of 20,000 desirous to read the Bible, who are not able to purchase it. Such of them as are able to work usually receive the value of their labour in bread-corn, being seldom paid in money'. Two years earlier he had described how 'very few of the Welsh people, even of the farmers, and scarce any at all of the labourers, can at present afford to buy books'.

The schools were usually conducted 'at such times or seasons of the year' as the poor 'could best spare from the greatest stress of their several employments; which in almost all places' was 'between September and May'. Ordinarily, a school lasted for three or four months, and then the school-master moved on to another district. Within six or seven weeks, Jones claimed, the apter pupils had learnt to read Welsh. The phonetic spelling of the language no doubt greatly helped people quickly to acquire a reading knowledge of Welsh; but in some English-speaking districts of Pembrokeshire, also, where English-language schools were established, they 'prospered far beyond what could be hoped for at first. They were soon crowded with scholars, both young and adults, who made a great and speedy progress, not only in reading English, but likewise in knowledge of the Christian belief and doctrines'. The main emphasis in all the schools was on teaching the children. Like all successful pedagogues, Jones had a shrewd appreciation of the importance of influencing the receptive and impressionable minds of the young. 'Training up children in the way they should go', he wrote, 'will . . . preserve great numbers of them from error, vice and profaneness in the future part of their lives. We know by experience that those things which are first fixed in the mind and memory do always make the deepest and most lasting impression'. But from the outset adults were also encouraged to attend no less than the children, and Jones claimed that in most schools the adults made up 'about two-thirds of the number taught in them'. Many more grown-up people, who had 'continued long stupid and careless', were 'impressed with some uneasiness' and thereupon began to 'stir up and try to learn of some or other at home' as opportunity offered.

For more than a generation the schools were a resounding success. The story was not, of course, one of uninterrupted growth; the Circulating Schools, like most other voluntary concerns, had their ups and downs. For example, while there were in 1739–40 150 schools with 8,767 pupils, the number had by 1743 fallen to 74 schools and 4,253 scholars. But they showed remarkable resilience and capacity for survival; so that in 1756–7, despite the outbreak of war and 'how hard it was with the poor, how dear and scarce all bodily provisions were', when Jones himself did 'not expect they would be this year above half the usual number', there were in fact 220 schools with 9,037 scholars, 'more numerous than at any time before'. By 1761, the year of Jones's death, it was estimated that since 1737 there had been set up 3,495 schools in which 158,237 pupils, not counting adults, had been taught. Jones's statistics need modification. The true totals would seem to have been 3,325 schools held in just under 1,600 different places, with 153,835 scholars. These figures include all the children who were enrolled and take no account of irregular attenders, and although Jones estimated that there were two adults to every child attending, this seems too generous a proportion. Even so, the most critical of recent estimates places the numbers taught to read within twenty-five years at 200,000, at a time when the population of Wales numbered probably between 400,000 and 500,000. This is, by any standards, an immense achievement. Given the difficulties confronting Griffith Jones, it is even more astounding.

In the first place, his whole venture was run on a shoestring. It began 'with no other fund to defray the expense of it than what could be spared from other occasions out of a small offertory by a poor country congregation'. Thereafter, it depended on what its founder could raise by his talents as a collector. His pathetically optimistic plea in 1736 'whether parochial officers at the expense of the county stock could not help us' met with as blank a response as might have been expected. Fortunately, there were charitable organizations and individuals who responded readily to Jones's dedicated and unresting importunity. The S.P.C.K. provided him as lavishly as its resources would allow with books, not to mention a whole pharmacopeia of those bizarre drugs and medicaments in which the eighteenth century delighted. Landowners, piously-disposed and philanthropic, like Sir John Philipps, Madam Bevan and Sir John Thorold, gave generously; the latter's openhandedness being particularly commendable since he had no connection with Wales other than through the schools. Three scientists, Stephen Hales, James Stonhouse and David Hartley, less moved by religious enthusiasm than by the Royal Society's ambition to apply science to the rational solution of social problems, made regular and sustained donations. There were also a number of clergymen, especially in North Wales where it was difficult for Jones to exercise personal supervision, who formed a Corresponding Society to carry on the work. In the last resort, Jones depended more heavily on his fellow-clergy, although their financial contributions were necessarily very limited, than almost anyone else. Without their goodwill in allowing him to establish schools and use their buildings, in raising offertories, in catechising and supervising, he would have found it impossible to do anything like as much as he did. Towards the end of his life he rightly admitted that the success of his schools depended much 'under God, on the pious zeal of faithful pastors and their appointment of pious and proper schoolmasters'. To keep up interest among these supporters he published an annual report, entitled *The Welch*

Piety (on the model, doubtless, of Francke's *Pietas Hallensis*), which consisted of a preface, a report by Jones, statistics, and testimonials from clergy and laymen to the work of the schools. But throughout, Jones had to work on the most meagre financial basis. He was never free from 'great thoughts of heart' about 'defraying the expense of so extensive an undertaking, with an unequal provision for it . . . for its best friends know that the supporters of it are but few comparatively.'

Apart from having to be content with few active supporters, he had to contend with serious opposition to the whole idea of his schools. Criticism was concentrated mainly on two aspects of his work: his encouragement of the Welsh language, and the alleged connection between his schools and the rise of Methodism. To the former charge Jones replied that he was not concerned with what became of the language 'abstractly considered', but with 'the myriads of poor ignorant souls' who 'must launch forth into the dreadful abyss of eternity and perish for want of knowledge'. Even so, he advanced a number of arguments on behalf of the antiquity, dignity and purity of the language which betrayed a very considerable affection for it on his part. The second charge of sympathy with Methodism was less easily disposed of. It found expression in a number of hostile pamphlets published between 1750 and 1752, the most virulent and damaging of which was the one by John Evans, rector of Eglwys Gymun, a neighbour of Jones. Its title explains its thesis: *Some account of the Welsh Charity-schools, and of the rise and progress of Methodism in Wales, through the means of them, under the sole management and direction of Griffith Jones* . . . (1752). It was undoubtedly true that Jones's views had affinities with those of the Methodists, that he was on terms of close friendship with their most prominent leaders in Wales, and that some of his teachers were Methodist exhorters. But he himself, in season and out, had protested eloquently and sincerely his devotion to the Established Church and his abhorrence at the thought of subverting it. He claimed that he tried to ensure that his teachers were the 'best disposed members and communicants of the Church of England that we can find willing and qualified', and he insisted time and again that his schools were conducted in a method strictly agreeable to the orders of the Church of England and the rules set by the Archbishop of Canterbury and the Bishop of London for the conduct of the English charity schools. Most of his clerical *confrères* accepted his defence and *The Welch Piety* is full of handsome tributes by parish clergy to the beneficial results of his schools in the renewal of religious life in the parishes.

In what, precisely, lay the secret of his success? It has more than once been pointed out that there was no specifically novel feature to the schools themselves. They were far from being the first charity schools in Wales; literacy and catechising had been given first priority in their predecessors; and the Welsh language had been used by S.P.C.K. schools – in North Wales at least. Even the idea of an itinerant schoolmaster had been mooted earlier: Sir Humphrey Mackworth had thrown out the suggestion in 1719, and 'ambulatory' schools had been tried in the Scottish Highlands. All very true; but the essential consideration remains that *all* these features had never before been successfully combined and stripped of all irrelevancies. What had previously been no more than hints or tentative experiments became the central characteristics of the Welsh Circulating Schools. Jones had grasped intuitively that the typical English charity schools, fixed permanently in a single centre, which earlier organizations had aimed at, could be no more than marginally useful in Wales. They would always be wrecked on three submerged reefs of which their navigators were either ignorant or took little account: the desperate poverty of pastoral Wales; its dispersed and thinly-scattered settlement pattern; and its language. Jones's achievement was to devise a simple and economical design for schools which could be successfully steered past all three obstacles simultaneously. In the first place, holding his schools only for a short time in the slack winter months, he enabled many pupils from desperately poor families to attend whose labour would otherwise have been too urgently needed for them to have spent any length of time in school. Secondly, being peripatetic, his schools got round the difficulty of the absence of many towns or even sizeable villages and the deplorable state of communications in Wales; instead of putting the poor to the expense and trouble of going to schools at a few fixed centres – if indeed they would have done so – the schools went to the poor. Finally, in frankly recognizing the wastefulness of trying to use the English language, the schools were all the quicker and more effective in promoting literacy in Welsh. In doing this, Griffith Jones was unconsciously following a lead given by the two previously most successful groups of diffusers of learning and culture among the Welsh – the bards and the friars; and he was anticipating the method of a later and equally successful institution, the National Eisteddfod. Like so many other successful solutions, Jones's seemed elementarily obvious – after the event!

He was blessed not only with insight but with rare talents for organizing. They enabled him to run his charity schools on a scale and for a length of time hitherto unprecedented in Wales. In a thinly-populated country of notoriously wretched communications, he undertook each year for more than a quarter of a century to establish scores of schools with thousands of pupils, make the preliminary arrangements for them with incumbents, train the teachers, and supervise their effectiveness. He was very largely responsible for raising funds and securing books. He himself wrote a number of the handbooks used, including a tremendously successful work on the catechism; and annually he compiled and published his *Welch Piety*. Such labours might have taxed the resources of the most robust constitution, but Jones enjoyed no more than indifferent health. His letters and writings are from an early date liberally besprinkled with references to his frail and ailing frame, and for thirty years or more before his death he was gloomily expectant that each year was the last of his life. From his youth onwards he was introverted and neurotic, and he showed repeated symptoms of psycho-somatic disorders. Yet however much they may have impaired his physical well-being, these same characteristics released in him extraordinary reserves of nervous energy as occasion demanded.

And occasion regularly demanded with Griffith Jones. For here was a man gripped by a compelling vision and an irrefragable sense of mission. Perhaps from that strange experience in his boyhood onwards, but certainly throughout his adult life, he laboured under a profoundly pessimistic awareness of a world lying under the threat of judgment. He yearned that his fellows 'could·be prevailed on to look over the reckoning of the Last Judgment' with its 'awful decision and tremendous sentence'. To him the England and Wales of his day was a profligate land sinking ever deeper into the mire of degeneracy. He had no doubt that he lived in an age when religion was on the ebb: 'It is too evidently true to be denied, and too grievous not to be greatly lamented, by all serious people, that the Christian cause is much upon the decay and has for many years past lost ground among us, both in its moral precepts and religious duties, and in its peculiar fundamental principles'. He was greatly troubled by the growing strength of intellectual forces hostile to revealed religion, 'Deists, Arians, Socinians, and Sceptics who openly renounce or secretly corrupt the fundamental doctrines of the Christian faith'. What alarmed him even more was the reckless betrayal of their responsibilities by the upper classes of society – their unconcern for their religious duties and the corruption of their morals by growing prosperity. 'If the result of all the wealth drawn together from sea and land be only to make provision for luxury, if the riches of the world are embezzled to support such scenes of riot and ribaldry, as are the reproach and scandal of our age and nation', he thundered, 'what must naturally be the produce thereof but the vile fruit of irreligion, debauchery, and the most corrupt principles of libertinism, deism and atheism, which are but the scum or excrements of sensual excesses?' Moreover, 'the meaner sort of people, always ready to ape their betters in all their vices', were 'too easily and strongly infected by the profane example of their superiors', with the resultant 'utmost danger of continuing to grow up in lying, thieving, cursing, and all scandalous vices'. All this criticism was thoroughly in keeping with the strongly Puritan trend which had remained firmly embedded in the Church of England despite the Civil Wars, and was indeed intensified by Restoration laxities and later by the growth of deism and scepticism. Jones deplored, in characteristic Puritan fashion, those 'sinful lusts of the flesh which, like an insatiable gulph swallow up all', and cast a jaundiced and reproving eye on those 'lewd plays, immodest romances and love intrigues, which poison the minds, captivate all the senses, and prejudice so many . . . against their duty to God'.

Such delinquency, he never doubted, must provoke condign punishment not only in the eternal, but also in the temporal, world. Natural calamities affrighted him with the prospect that 'surely the hand of the Lord is lifted up and His wrath is abroad in the world, whether we see it or no'. Political upheaval and foreign wars terrified him even more. The Jacobite rising of 1745 had been a sore trial to him: 'All our most valuable things . . . lay at stake. Were we not compassed about with fear and danger on every side, dreading to hear the noise of the trumpet, clashings of swords, and stampings of the horses' hoofs to approach us; and the more private, though not less cruel, barbarity of treacherous friends and neighbours, where infatuation and not the fear of God prevailed, who wanted only the encouragement of one blow in their favour to plunder, burn and destroy'? The outbreak of the Seven Years War in 1756 and the surrounding 'fears and distresses and troubles' were the final dread portent that the vials of divine retribution might be about to be opened. Even victories gained in that war did not serve to console him: 'if after so many signal mercies and wonderful deliverances we continue still unholy, unthankful and unreformed, I fear the long suffering of God will only harden us to grow ripe the faster for . . . divine wrath to be poured down on us'. Could so fearful a nemesis be averted without 'humiliation and amendment'? He knew of 'no instance in history, sacred or profane, of a people irreclaimably profane and grown fully ripe for judgment, who were spared without humbling themselves before God'. If 'the wilful infidelity of the Jews, the pride and voluptuousness of the Babylonians, the lewdness of the Persians, the luxury of the Greeks, the debauchery of the old Romans, and the refractory perverseness and irreligion of the Old Britons, were the fore-runners and provoking causes of the ruin of all their empires', would God indeed long bear with a land 'where all these immoralities and every kind of impieties too much abounded'? Jones was nowhere very explicit about the precise nature of the punishment to be visited upon his fellow-countrymen, but what he most seems to have feared was defeat abroad and especially subversion of Church and State at home.

However, he showed not only the Puritans' tendency to denounce, he shared also their profoundly practical concern, that strong sense of humanitarian obligation, that determination to make society fit for the elect to live in, which was die-stamped on the Calvinist ethic. Men would be known by their fruits, and of the fruits of faith none was more estimable than charity, 'the sum of present and future bliss . . . the divine nature and the offspring of God'. And of all the forms which charity took, there could not be conceived 'a more divine, benevolent and godlike charity towards our poor fellow-creatures than that which tends to save their souls'. In this lay the most prudent investment for temporal and eternal returns. 'The almoners of this divine and spiritual charity' had 'Scripture of Truth for their bond of security' and the holy sacraments as its seals. They invested in the surest bulwark against social tumult and disaster, 'For it is certain the established government can have no friends in the world more sincere, faithful and zealous than they who are well instructed in the principles of Christ's holy religion, to fear God, and honour the King'. He went on to warn that 'a general neglect of giving truly Christian instruction to the poor and common people, that everywhere make up by much the greatest numbers, is the ready way to bring in confusion and slavery on the whole nation, in Church and State, to the utter ruin of both'.

But Jones was more than a timorous and unhopeful conservative. He was a visionary fired with a candescent utopian ambition: nothing less than the 'utter reformation of a degenerate age'. To him, morals could not be improved by penal laws or societies for the reformation of manners. Such remedies coped only with symptoms; religious conversion alone, he held, could remove the causes. Before his eyes there floated always a vision irresistible in its compulsion: 'as the gospel, in the beginning of it, was first preached to the poor, and from them went forth and spread all over the earth; what if the Lord will think fit again to restore the gospel to its primitive force and lustre by the same method'? What if, in short, the most terrible fear of the propertied classes – the prospect of revolution by the unprivileged, a nightmare never entirely banished since the Civil Wars of the seventeenth century – could be sublimated into becoming the means of society's redemption? And what if he, Griffith Jones, were the chosen vessel for so mighty a purpose? Because, for all his modest deprecation of himself as 'at best but a very mean and unworthy poor instrument', he never questioned that his enterprise had been wonderfully singled out for divine blessing. It was his hope that 'serious perusal' of *The Welch Piety* would equally convince the reader of the 'goodness of divine love manifested in the rise and wonderful increase of the Welsh charity schools; a work so owned by the glorious Saviour of the World ... stands in need of no arguments to recommend itself to the approbation and esteem of all the children of God'.

A man with a mission can be as infuriating as he is inspiring, and Griffith Jones was both. His philanthropy had in it a pervasive tincture of the self-righteousness and holier-than-thou unctuousness of the professional do-gooder. The loss of his father at a tender age may have acted on him as it has so often done on others in like case. It bred an inner insecurity which craved for reassurance and itched for success and esteem. In the absence of an earthly father he longed to be a chosen son of his heavenly father and, for all his self-depreciation, convinced himself he was one. He could be opinionated, self-willed, domineering, and filled with his own importance, but he was liable to give way to irritability, querulousness and self-pity. Extraordinarily thin-skinned and sensitive to criticism, he lashed out at his opponents with a vehemence that could be the very opposite of charity. Yet those same hidden springs which gave rise to his weakness were also the sources of his strength. It was they which urged him forward with relentless drive, unquenchable passion, and indefatigable perseverance. They ensured his success and they gave him his place as one of the two most remarkable men in an age of outstanding Welshmen.

Nor was his impact confined to his own lifetime. When he died on 8 April, 1761, Madam Bevan was able to continue his methods with considerable success until her own death in 1779. By the end of the eighteenth century the work was being carried forward by Thomas Charles, the architect of the Methodist denomination in Wales, who readily recognized Griffith Jones as his mentor. As established by Charles, Welsh Sunday Schools were for more than a century the most powerful medium of popular education in Wales, and, following Jones's pioneering lead, were intended as much for adults as children. To Jones more than any man the Welsh owed a massive break-through to literacy. It was this which sealed the success of the Methodist Revival and the triumph of Nonconformity, with all their immense attendant consequences for Welsh life. It did more than anything else to preserve and fortify the Welsh language and literature, of which the Bible was the corner-stone. If the Welsh of the last century and this have had an unusual respect for education and love of learning, credit for the origins of this is in large measure Griffith Jones's. He himself, limited in aims and circumscribed in vision, might be staggered and even appalled at what his handiwork has subsequently wrought. He none the less remains one of the prime makers of modern Wales and one of Britain's most notable educational pioneers.

X.   A Prospect of Paradise?
Wales and the United States of America, 1776–1914*

'Mae eang fyd tu hwnt i'r don,
Paradwys deg y gweithiwr llon.'
('There lies a wide world beyond the wave, a blessed Paradise for the happy worker.')
Thus sang the migrant to his love in a poem by Islwyn. In search of that paradise 35 million people went to the United States during the hundred years or so following 1815. This was easily the biggest movement of people in human history; but when it began there were many who frowned on it. The eminent Methodist, Robert Jones of Rhos-lan, warned, 'If it is clouding over a little at present, it is our sins that have brought this upon us, and it is folly to think that there exists in America any place to hide from the punishment of Him against whom we have sinned.' And the Baptist, Christmas Evans, derided the two objectionable kinds of creature who emigrated – Mr. Gwladaethwr (the politician) and Mr. Go-to-America alias Lover of Wealth. Half a century later, how different was the general verdict as voiced by David Rees, Llanelli, 'God's finger is very plainly to be seen in this amazing movement, and a high responsibility is placed upon us . . . to prepare unto the Lord fit people to go forth, so that Christianity may spread as widely as humanity.' An age so steeped in scripture inevitably saw the hand of divine Providence at the helm. Biblical images came just as naturally in likening America to Paradise, or the Garden of Eden, or the Zion of the Saints, or, most frequently of all, the Land of Promise. America was, for many Welshmen, the Second Canaan, offering a haven of escape from the tyranny of oppressors.

Only a rivulet flowed from Wales into the huge flood of emigrants to the United States. We cannot say for certain just how many went; nor do we know how many came back home, though there is reason to believe that as many as one out of three of the emigrants returned. In the official United States census figures for 1890 it was calculated that 100,079 people born in Wales were then living in America. This was the highest number of Welsh immigrants ever recorded in that source; but it stands to reason that more Welsh people than

*A Welsh version of this essay was broadcast on 15 November 1976 as the Annual Radio Lecture of BBC Wales. It was published in Welsh by the BBC, and also in English, thanks to the generous financial assistance of the Honourable Society of Cymmrodorion.

that had in fact emigrated during the century. The real figure could be twice or three times as high. It represented a serious loss to the population of a small country, especially in upland counties like Cardigan or Merioneth, each of which lost more than 5,000 at least in the years before 1860. Yet even if we assumed that, say, a quarter of a million Welsh went, that still does not compare with the 4½ millions of Irish who emigrated, nor yet with the hundreds of thousands of Welsh who found new homes in the industrial districts of Wales itself or in England. Two reasons chiefly account for this. First, the unparalleled industrial expansion within Britain gave migrants ample opportunity to move inside this country. Second, though the agrarian distress in Wales was real enough, it was nothing like as agonizing as the fate of Ireland.

The thousands who left constituted a cross-section of Welsh people from almost every part of Wales. Inhabitants of the rural areas were some of the first to go. A particular mystique attached to the life of the free American farmer, who was regarded as the only truly independent man, whose occupation was the oldest, healthiest and most honourable known to mankind. Welsh farmers emigrated to seek broader and more fertile acres of which they could be freeholders not having to pay rent. A host of farm labourers dreamed that they, too, could in turn save enough to buy land after working for a time as hired hands. Many of the country craftsmen – carpenters, masons or blacksmiths – shared the same ambition, though several of them never got beyond the big towns in America, where their labour was much in demand to build houses, roads and canals. From the 1830s onwards armies of industrial workers also emigrated. It was easier for them to take the plunge for more than one reason. They had skills and experience which would earn better wages for them in the infant American industries; and they were more mobile since they had already uprooted themselves once by migrating to the realms of industry in the old country. Most of them were miners and iron and steel workers, though there were also a good number of slate quarrymen from North Wales and weavers from Montgomery-shire and Merioneth in their midst; and after the McKinley Tariff of 1890 thousands of tinplate workers emigrated. They also included a minority of merchants and shopkeepers and of professional men – ministers, of course, lawyers, doctors and surveyors; and later many well-known singers and musicians were tempted over. Since America was above all else the land of great opportunity, it was common enough for a man to change his work and his home quite frequently. One example out of thousands must here suffice. Humphrey Jones was born on a farm in Anglesey in 1819. He went to work in the Caernarvonshire slate-quarries and from there to the Monmouthshire coalmines. He emigrated in 1847 and worked in coalmines in Ohio and then West Virginia. In 1855 he went as one of the pioneers of the Welsh settlement in Judson, Minnesota, and worked his own farm there until his death thirty years later.

One striking feature was the difference between men and women as emigrants. It was the men, almost without exception, who were keen to go, while the women were reluctant and, after reaching America, loath to move from one place to another. Such a reaction is portrayed vividly and sensitively in the novel, *Gwen Tomos*. Rheinallt, the husband, is gripped by emigration fever, while his wife, Gwen, cannot bear the prospect of exchanging the close familiar community for the unaccustomed loneliness of the distant land. After years in America her *hiraeth* for Wales was 'not a whit less'. The same plaintive note recurs in one of the rare letters written by a woman emigrant. Elizabeth Williams wrote to her mother in 1850 soon after the birth of her child: 'I have felt the need *for my old country friends* more than ever on this occasion . . . My spirit keeps very low.' Wives knew well that they bore the brunt of the burden of raising families, instructing children, creating a society, sustaining religion, and extending civilized behaviour in the primitive settlements. One such wife, Margaret Davies, lived to be over 90. She settled in Big Woods, Minnesota, when it was a desolate wilderness inhabited only by suspicious Indians and wild beasts. In this unpromising habitat Margaret Davies fashioned a home which became a byword for its hospitality – a welcome, it was said, that was extended as readily to the red man as to the white, to the Jew no less than the Gentile.

All the emigrants were spurred on by much the same kind of motives. It is beyond doubt that the overwhelming majority wanted above all to improve their economic and material circumstances. This one central message dominates the letters of the emigrants themselves, the propaganda of those who sought to attract them,

comments in the press, and contemporary literature like *Farmer
Careful of Cilhaul*. America was the country in which 'to expand and
grow rich more quickly', said Rheinallt Thomas, a character in a
novel; but a real-life emigrant, David Evans, was no less confident:
'in no other part of the world could people prosper so fast'. Even the
Mormons, apparently fleeing from the Babylon of this sinful world
to their holy Zion, were urged on at least as much by hunger for
land and earthly security on the part of the Saints and by the need
for capital and a skilled labour force on the part of their leaders as
they were by piety. Brigham Young had a sharper eye for a plurality
of resources than of wives!

The economic attractions are not difficult to understand. It was a
time of crisis in rural areas when population was increasing faster
than ever before, causing desperate pressure on the resources of the
land and creating a frantic and unhealthy competition for farms.
There were long spells of acute depression in the years following
the 'good times' of 'old Boney's wars', again in the 1840s, and later in
the century. Complaints against the lack of sympathy by landlords
and their agents were loud and frequent, as were protests against
unreasonable rents, heavy taxes and rates, and unjust tithes. In
America, on the contrary, a farmer could confidently hope to own
his farm in more fertile land, where taxes were lower and the tithe
unknown. Even a craftsman or a labourer could at least look
forward to more regular work, better wages and more food. The
constant harping on better-quality and more plentiful food in
America is revealing. 'We get much better food than in Wales',
boasted one farm labourer, 'there is not a house in this district . . .
which keeps two kinds of food, one for themselves and another for
the workers.' But would you expect those who had known the
famine-like shortages of the period, especially those of the 'Hungry
Forties', to feel otherwise?

The attitudes of industrial workers were rather different. Their
particular problem was the familiar pattern of early industry – a
spell of exhilarating prosperity followed by desolating slump. They
soon came to realize that when employment and wages lay under
dark clouds in Wales there might be sunshine and bright prospects
for skilled workers in the United States. Later on in the century,
even when swarms of unskilled workers flocked in from rural

Europe, many a Welshman still managed to make good by being promoted to supervisor. Not all industrial workers intended to stay permanently in America. Many of them were birds of passage coming and going in accordance with the demands for workers and the level of wages.

By and large, it was not the poorest of all in town and country who tended to emigrate but rather those who had a little behind them. They were people who saw their circumstances deteriorating and who feared that prospects for their future were even bleaker. That was precisely the situation of the farmer, John Careful, and the labourer, Billy Active, in the story *Cilhaul* by S.R., an author who knew more about those who emigrated than almost any of his contemporaries. Another key element in the same story is that it was the welfare of their children which motivated Careful and Active more than anything else. This was an attitude prevalent throughout Europe in an age when the tremendous increase in population made it harder with every year that passed for parents to transmit to their children a patrimony similar to that which they themselves had inherited. A Welshman of such standing as John Jones Tal-sarn was in agonies of indecision whether or not to emigrate for his children's sake. Although Roger Edwards's 'Song of the Emigrant' is a rather feeble poem it contains one couplet which sums up neatly one of the deepest and most compelling instincts of emigrants:

'Am fyd gwych fy hunan nid oes ynof chwant,
Ond ceisio yr ydwyf ddaioni fy mhlant.'

('I have no desire for a prosperous world on my own account, but I do seek my children's welfare.')

You may be surprised that I have not put more emphasis on the social and political ideals which might have appealed to emigrants. To be fair, these were not unimportant to them, but they were subsidiary to the economic inducements. A theme constantly reiterated was that the chief reason why a poor emigrant could improve his lot was that American society was more equal and democratic, without a privileged aristocracy or established church. It was hearing his father talk of America as a free and virtuous country, with neither monarchy nor tithe and where poor people could buy farms, claimed the venerable Benjamin Chidlaw, that had made him emigrate there. And another Welsh emigrant, Henry

Davies of Wisconsin, while admitting that there were, of course, rich and poor in America, nevertheless contended that the feeling of equality was stronger than in Wales, and snobbery and servility were far less evident. So democratic was the country that Captain David Evans, formerly of Talsarnau, could find himself sitting next to its president, Ulysses S. Grant, in the Metropolitan Methodist Church in Washington. 'It does one good', mused Captain Evans, 'to see the chief magistrate of a great nation like another human being, not putting on some artificials to endeavour to make him something above human.'

In this respect it was the emigrant-farmer who best succeeded in freeing himself from those whom he saw as oppressors – landowners, stewards, priests, tithe-gatherers, tax-collectors, attorneys and game-keepers. It is no accident that it is the farmers' letters which gave the most rapturous accounts of the superiority of the new country. They were very willing to invite others to join them in filling up the farming settlements. The case of the industrial worker could often be very different; his world had not necessarily been transformed. The condition of industry in the new world frequently bore too close a resemblance to that in the old. The same risks of depression and unemployment existed; employers were just as willing to lower wages and no less stubborn to recognize trade union rights; and 'scabs' and 'tommy shops' were consistently and virulently con-demned. Strikes could break out just as often, and bitterness against the owners be just as raw as it had been in South Wales. A tin-worker in Pittsburg, D. R. Davies, admitted that distance had lent enchantment to America for him and many others before he went there, but now his intention was to 'make plain to my countrymen that America is not all paradise'. Others complained that there were as many sons of Anak among the 'rich oppressors' in America as in Britain. It's fair to remember, of course, that the intention of these workers during periods of slump and lay-offs was to discourage their fellow-Welshmen from emigrating. On the other hand, there were plenty who would have applauded the sentiments of David Morgan, of Minersville, Ohio: 'I like the country and the work famously; I wish I had been wise enough to come here years ago. There is no money to be had without working for it . . . but there are men here working hard and earning big money for doing so.'

The spell cast by the dazzling prospect of emigration could captivate people completely. Time and again in the last century there were references to 'American fever' which could infect almost all the inhabitants of an area. The fever was transmitted most effectually by the letters to their friends and families at home of those who had already emigrated. It is amazing how regularly and for how long the two sides could communicate with one another, especially considering the expense and the difficulties in the early days. There is one set of family correspondence in the National Library, the Plas yn Blaenau collection, which lasted from 1840 to 1965. An almost equally remarkable collection was that of the Hughes family of Anglesey, a selection from which was published by Ms. E. G. Roberts in *Anglesey Family Letters, 1840–1935* (1976). Most of the letter-writers were commendably fluent and articulate, whether writing in Welsh or English. Some of them, though, must have found letter-writing as forbidding a task as did Margaret Jones of Holyhead. Writing to her daughter as late as 1882, she felt obliged to confess, 'I want you to know that write English letter is very hard work for me because I can't speak proper English. I must look in the dictionary for every word so that it take me a long time to write a letter.'

Since the emigrants' letters were private papers, which were not as a rule kept very carefully, most of them have disappeared. The few which have come down to us are very revealing, and letters of that kind exercised the strongest influence on contemporaries. However, there were many other letters which were intended for publication in the press. (Alastair Cooke was by no means the first to think of immortalizing himself by means of a Letter from America!) We owe a great debt to these letters surviving in print, though we have to beware of swallowing their self-conscious testimony too uncritically. As John Evans of Remsen wryly observed, reading some letters might make one suppose that America was a country which destroyed its inhabitants, while reading others gave one the impression that it was a Garden of Eden.

The exiles not only wrote; a number of them also revisited Wales. Estimates suggest that more Welshmen on average crossed and recrossed the Atlantic than any other nation. Some came specifically to sing America's praises. In 1836 B. W. Chidlaw came to preach and lecture; he also seized the opportunity to sell thousands of copies of his emigrant's guide, *Y Teithiwr Americanaidd* ('The American Traveller'). Similarly, Iorthryn Gwynedd (R. D. Thomas) sold 3,000 copies of his guide *Yr Ymfudwr* ('The Emigrant') in six months in 1854. Books, pamphlets, articles in journals and newspapers, diaries, verses and ballads: they all fed the hunger for knowledge. New states and railways in America advertised loudly and importunately for immigrants. Agents and shipping companies proclaimed in bold posters and in newspapers all over the country details of when and how to travel. Speculation and publicity knew no bounds. The one common complaint was that no reliance could could be placed on the truth of much that was so deafeningly trumpeted.

It was one thing to experience an almost overpowering urge to venture to America; it was quite another thing to arrive at an irrevocable decision to go. The obstacles and deterrents were many and powerful. It was no light matter to snap the intense and familiar ties of home, nor yet to sell one's goods and bid farewell, no doubt forever, to kith and kin. If there is one motif that is endlessly repeated in the references to emigration it is the unquenchable nostalgia of the Welshman for his home. Then there was the formidable prospect of a long and dangerous voyage for many who had never previously been near a ship. The majority of Welsh emigrants went from Liverpool since it was from there that ships sailed most frequently and regularly. The city had its boarding-houses for emigrants, though their condition was all too often a disgrace to any civilized society. It was a rarity to find one with a good reputation like that kept by Cymro Gwyllt (N. M. Jones), a man with his finger in every emigrational pie. But posters issued by Welsh companies and shipmasters in glowing terms invited people to sail in local ships from the many little ports all around the coast of Wales. To encourage them to do so an enterprising shipowner like John Davies, a well-known timber merchant of Menai Bridge, underlined in his posters of the 1840s that the commanders of his ships, 'being well-known Welshmen', constituted a guarantee to passengers that their 'comforts will be attended to'.

If John Davies's reassuring promises were fulfilled then the passengers on his ships were a singularly fortunate minority, for in most cases there are awesome accounts of the horrors of a voyage on one of the old sailing-vessels. They were mostly ships intended for carrying merchandise not passengers, and the old ships carrying slates were the worst of all. The voyage lasted weeks if not months in holds shockingly overcrowded with passengers, some of them filthy in person and in habits, and occasionally suffering from infectious diseases. A whole catalogue of other tribulations could be listed: seasickness, villainous crews, appalling dangers of fire, icebergs and tempest, primitive and nauseating sanitary facilities, the ungodliness of fellow-travellers – especially the Irish, and worst of all, possibly, the coarse and inadequate food. During the course of the century there were marked improvements. The advent of steamships and more effective legislation meant bigger and faster ships, shorter and safer journeys, and cleaner and more sanitary arrangements. By 1868 the journey from Liverpool, according to one Welsh emigrant, 'had become very much better as compared to our fathers' days', for 'we in this age can cross the Atlantic in as many days as it took them weeks'.

Having reached the other side, where did the emigrants go? It's difficult to generalize because there were thousands of individuals and over 200 Welsh settlements, great and small. But some characteristics stand out. The Welsh clung to each other more closely than almost any other nation. Each settlement was prone to draw people from the same areas as the original settlers because it was so vital that the newcomers should be sure of getting a welcome and help from friends and relatives. So, for example, people from Llŷn or Llanuwchllyn made for Oneida County; the 'Cardis' went to Jackson and Gallia in Ohio; and the miners of Glamorgan went to Scranton and Wilkesbarre. An upland parish like Cilcennin or Llanuwchllyn or Llanwrtyd might be sorely bereft of its population; it was said that there were more people born in the parish of Llanbrynmair living in Paddy's Run, Ohio, than there were in Llanbrynmair itself. Welsh-American settlements were widely scattered and small in size – the biggest of them all in the Pennsylvania coalfields numbered no more than 20,000 in 1900, and the vast majority less than 2,000. Almost without exception they were located in the northern states; not primarily because the slavery of the South was hateful to the Welsh but because land could not be bought cheaply there, nor was there any significant demand for industrial workers there as in the North. The four favourite northern states were Pennsylvania, New York, Ohio and Wisconsin, and as late as 1880 four out of five of the Welsh lived in these states. In the course of the century, as wave after wave of emigrants rolled westwards, small companies of Welsh went with them to states like Missouri or Kansas, some even venturing as far as Nebraska or Oregon, not to mention the numerous intrepid Welsh Latter-Day Saints who reached their Zion in Mormon Utah. Handfuls of venturesome Welsh speculators went to mine gold in California or silver in Colorado, although most of them found the gold-rush to be 'all a lottery', in which 'there were many more losers than winners', as Richard Hughes of Anglesey described it. But most of the Welsh were reluctant to leave their traditional anchorages. In 1900 one in three still lived in Pennsylvania, and two out of three in the states of Pennsylvania, Ohio, New York, Minnesota and Wisconsin.

The Welsh stuck close to one another, but how much of their Welshness did they preserve in their new home? It has always to be borne in mind first of all that they did not go there with the express intention of maintaining their identity as Welsh people. As one of their number, D. S. Davies, put it, the great question for them before they left Wales was, 'Where can I be sure of finding bread and clothing for my children with less worry than at present? And since America answered that question that was the end of the argument.' In that case why did they retain so many of their old-country ways? Not by virtue of any conscious patriotic decision so much as because these customs softened the painful process of adapting to America. The easiest way for the first generation to adapt was to live as members of a settlement of emigrants amid friends with a familiar life-style. This was far less alien and uncomfortable, especially for monoglot Welsh people, than trying to plunge willy-nilly into the native American life around them. The function served by keeping up old customs amid every national group was to try to create some measure of friendly and customary environment which would help bridge the gap between the old world and the new. It was a timely and consoling standby for the first generation or two, but with every succeeding generation the old was bound to become remote and anachronistic and the new near and natural.

Much would obviously depend on how consciously Welsh the immigrants had been before leaving. A proportion of them had always been distinctly tepid, and in the course of the century as large parts of Wales itself became less Welsh the number of such immigrants increased. It is interesting, nonetheless, to see how others, in common with many exiles, became more conscious of their nationality in a new country. One John Davies, at the ends of the earth in California, insisted that however fine were the advantages of America, 'nothing rouses my temper quicker than hearing men run down the old country'. Crucially important, also, was the kind of community in which the emigrant chose to live. In a huge city like New York it was easy to be swallowed up without trace; it was claimed that 9,000 Welsh lived there in 1872, but that nine out of ten of them did not give a fig for things Welsh. In a rural community like Foreston, Iowa, on the other hand, as much Welsh was said to be spoken there in 1895 as had been a generation earlier. Even in an industrial locality, like some of the coalmining districts of Pennsylvania, if there existed a compact, close-knit community of Welshmen, the Welsh language and Welsh culture could flourish for a long time.

The Welsh life of the United States was a transplant to American soil of the Welsh way of life created in Wales during the last century. It could not be otherwise, for the old Welsh settlers of the seventeenth and eighteenth centuries had long lost their Welshness. Welsh institutions in the United States, therefore, were a mirror image of those existing in Wales and among Welsh colonies in English cities. Their flourishing condition among the Welsh of the *diaspora* bears witness to the remarkable creative energy of nineteenth-century Welsh life. Its central and most cherished institution was the Welsh chapel, with the Welsh language as an indissoluble element of the worship. A typically positive affirmation of the inter-connection was made in the American periodical, *Y Traethodydd yn America*, in 1860: 'The main reason for teaching the Welsh language to our children is the inextricable association between the fostering of the language and the reinforcement of religion.' The same sort of plea was regularly heard among Welsh migrants to England and would, indeed, be repeated with comparable urgency in the industrial areas of Wales late in the nineteenth century as the tide of anglicizing influences rose. To lose the language, it was argued, was virtually to lose religion, for those who left the Welsh congregations nearly always abandoned religion entirely.

The godly took it very much to heart when they saw so many compatriots backsliding. Typical of their reaction was Henry Davies's distress at the sight of thousands of 'our countrymen, after emigrating, . . . losing not only their patriotism but also their religion . . . instead of "cleaving to the fellowship" becoming licentious, thoughtless and careless; giving free rein to their corrupt desires and tendencies'. The gnawing fear was that too many Welshmen were adapting to life in America by yielding to 'earth's vain pleasures'. Strong drink was the cardinal enemy, and those who 'cherished in their bosoms the serpent of intoxicating liquor or some comparable idol' were roundly denounced. Dewi Emlyn's somewhat self-righteous verdict was that 'too many graves in America were filled with the corpse of a drunken Welshman, and we want no repetition of that sort of disaster'. Drunkenness had always been the social evil most regularly and passionately de-nounced by Nonconformists and social reformers in industrial South Wales. So it comes as no surprise to read that the worst offenders in the United States were usually said to be found among the coalminers and ironworkers, whose 'insatiable thirst for intoxi-cating liquor' was deeply deplored, together with their habit of 'drinking whisky in the taverns and boasting how much money they spent'. Their own Welsh taverns existed to slake the thirst of these convivial topers, like the 'Owain Glyndŵr' in New York and the Welsh saloons of Pennsylvania.

In face of these worldly (and expensive!) temptations the pious were conscious of being called upon to exert themselves more strenuously than ever in the cause of religion. There was a popular joke to the effect that the first thing a Frenchman did in America was start a trading-post, an American built a city, a German opened a beer-hall, and a Welshman built a chapel. However libellous that may be of some of the others, it was perfectly true that many a Welshman's priority was to institute the 'advantages of religion', in contemporary parlance. A Sunday school or a prayer-meeting would be arranged in a dwelling-house at the outset, and within a short space a church was founded and a chapel built. The need for such religious activity was the constant refrain of endless letters and articles. It was an aspiration shared by other emigrant nationalities; not only because they belonged to an unusually pious generation that yearned for the consolation of religion in a hard and alien environment, but also because their church was the sheet-anchor of their distinctive language and society. Furthermore, religion was the bulwark of that social morality which was believed to be indispensable for worldly and spiritual well-being. No opportunity to applaud the merits of industriousness, frugality and sobriety was ever missed. A measure of the zeal for religion is the founding of over 600 Welsh chapels in America. In their palmy days each was a social and cultural focus as well as a place of worship. From the chapel sprang a spate of activities that linked the members of all ages and both sexes: the Sunday school, missionary work, the temperance cause, women's and young people's societies, philanthropic and literary meetings, the singing-school and the *gymanfa* (singing-festival). Wider denominational and religious organization provided some of the main connecting-links between the far-flung settlements.

In the United States, as in Wales, a close connexion existed between the Welsh chapels and the other usual media of Welsh culture: the press, the eisteddfod and the patriotic society.

The press was a great boon to every linguistic group; and thousands of publications were printed in a variety of languages. When we remember how few the Welsh were in number it is astonishing how prolific the Welsh-language press was. Some hundreds of books and about 65 magazines and periodicals and newspapers were published, though many of the latter lasted less than five years. The most celebrated of them, *Y Drych*, boasted about 12,000 subscribers in its prime.

The eisteddfod became popular in the United States from about the 1840s onwards. The queen of all the multifarious eisteddfodau held in America was that of the Chicago World Fair of September 1893, when the most famous singers, choirs and poets of Wales and America flocked to compete against one another. The proud assertion of one leading Welsh American, Cynonfardd, was that nothing in the World Fair had made 'so deep an impression of great and uplifted culture' as the Welsh eisteddfod. There's nothing like going the whole hog! Whatever the merits of the Chicago eisteddfod may have been, there is no doubt that it was the eisteddfodau in general which did most to stimulate the literary activity in Welsh, not to mention the proud bardic pseudonyms, which were once so popular.

It was the eisteddfod and the gymanfa which also kindled the fires of the extraordinary enthusiasm for singing and provided the opportunities for musical celebrities like Joseph Parry and Dan Protheroe. It's intriguing to recall that the Welsh were singing Handelian choruses with gusto in the solitudes of Wisconsin as early as the 1840s and that it was for a Scranton eisteddfod that the old favourite 'Ar Don o Flaen Gwyntoedd' was composed.

Much of the singing was rather sentimental, as indeed the patriotic emotion cherished by the Welsh societies tended to be. More than a hundred of these societies, mostly called 'St. David's Society' or the like, have been traced. Their chief purpose was to keep Welsh speakers and non-Welsh-speaking Welshmen together, to help needy immigrants, and to celebrate St. David's Day. Closely akin to them in spirit was the American wing of the Welsh Friendly Society of the Ivorites – the Ivorites of America – which at one time had forty lodges revelling in high-flown historical names like 'Hywel Dda' Lodge.

To all outward appearances, therefore, Welsh-American life seemed to be as effervescent with vigour and creativity as that of Wales. But more than one observer commented that this culture was essentially that of the *first* generation. One of the most percipient and best-informed of them, Iorthryn Gwynedd, wrote: 'The life and strength of Welsh settlements depend on continuing emigration from the old country and the continuity of the Welsh language.' He added somewhat sadly, 'the children of the old settlers are, almost without exception, completely apathetic towards speaking, reading, and writing the Welsh language'. By the third and fourth generation they were wholly americanized. So ardent a patriot as D. S. Davies was sunk in complete despair at the contemplation of it: 'This powerful and varied emigration . . . has become a total loss to our nation and language.'

But what alternative existed? The dynamic of American achievement was this process of assimilation; this capacity to receive people of every land and language and mould them into a single American nation. The Welsh were as much exposed to its influence as the motley band of other peoples, and pressure on them to assimilate was powerful. The government of the country naturally exerted itself to hasten the achievement of one language, one culture and one nation. The official language of law, administration and business was English or, if you prefer, American. It was the inescapable medium of communication with every other individual, except of course fellow-Welshmen – on the street, in the store, the mine, the factory, the trade union and all other social intercourse. Public education was also conducted in English; and the Welsh were among the most enthusiastic in seeking its benefits.

Nevertheless, it would be misleading to conclude that the Welsh were forced to become Americans. On the contrary, it seems undeniable that they were more eager than almost any other national group to be received as naturalized citizens. Statistics show that 73 per cent of them wished to do so, the highest percentage recorded for any nation. How is such striking unanimity to be explained? One reason may well be that because it was so easy to move somewhere else in Wales or England only those most committed to the notion of the superiority of America went there. Moreover, it was easier for British emigrants to assimilate than any others. They were thought to belong to the same racial stock as native Americans and were not reviled with opprobrious nicknames like 'Polacks'. The British had also been reared into much the same sort of legal and constitutional inheritance as the Americans; and the Welsh enjoyed one advantage over the English – they, like the Americans, were not overfond of the government of England nor its aristocratic and ecclesiastical institutions. Another blessing was a respectable economic status. Ordinarily, they did not belong to the poor unacceptable classes who worked in despised occupations and lived in the slums. It was not difficult for them to mix with the Americans on equal terms. Like many Americans, too, the Welsh were earnest evangelical Protestants who shared native prejudices against papist immigrants. Indeed, many of them, like their counterparts in Wales, thought it more essential to perpetuate their religious principles than their language.

Their language! That, certainly, was a trait which made the Welsh seem more like continentals than British. Many were monoglot Welsh, and others were pretty tongue-tied in English. It does seem, however, that the majority had some moderate grasp of English, and it was obviously easier for almost all of them to understand and speak the language than it would be for some poor wretch from the heart of Europe. In general, therefore, adapting to America was a much smoother operation for the Welsh than for most emigrants. For their children and their grandchildren born in the United States it was the easiest thing in the world to grow up as Americans; proud enough of their ancestral origins, but loyal Americans to the hilt.

To weigh and measure the contribution of these Welsh Americans and their descendants to the United States is an impossible task. Some proved to be very eminent figures, a few even of worldwide note. The temptation for the excessively filio-pietistic has been to include among them everyone with a name that looked or sounded remotely Welsh. Without going to such extremes it has been possible to list over 500 with sound claims to Welsh ancestry who were famous enough to be included in reputable works of reference such as the *Biographical Dictionary of America*.

But I have deliberately refrained from concentrating on the famous. Instead, my emphasis throughout has been on those ordinary folk who, in the words of one Welsh American, 'did more for America than all the lawyers, politicians and preachers'. They were the 'pioneers who prepared the way for civilization and progress . . . They and their descendants were the ones who made America' (Henry Blackwell). It is fitting to commemorate the labour and the sacrifice of the thousands of obscure men and women. In their ranks were the farmers who cleared the forests, ploughed the prairie, and made American farming the most productive in the world. There were the miners who ventured into the perilous depths of the earth, the skilled craftsmen who nurtured infant industries, and the brawny labourers who built cities and communications; all these gave America her world supremacy in industry and technology. Nor should we forget the women who shared the trials and tribulations of the new world and who contributed to the full to the men's success. It is the share of Welsh people in all this that represents America's deepest debt to them.

The two particular characteristics of Welsh Americans' life for which they were praised and in which they took pride were their radicalism and their religion. The strongest and most enduring influence of their radicalism was their part in establishing the earliest American trade unions. The Welsh, especially among the miners, were some of the first and most stubborn champions of workers' rights. Nor is it a coincidence that one of the most masterful of American trade unionists, John Ll. Lewis, was a Welshman and a miner. The fruits of their religiosity were the unremitting exhortations to honesty, sobriety, hard work, and the zeal for self-improvement. If these virtues now have an old-fashioned ring, America's indebtedness to them in the last century was profound. Just as deep was the pride which many Welsh people took in them. One of their number claimed that it was these qualities which placed the Welsh, 'whether as preachers, farmers, teachers, labourers, craftsmen, merchants or singers . . . at all times on the top rung of the ladder. We are the leaders . . . and we are recognized as such by other nations.' That brings us perilously near, if not indeed over the edge of, the besetting sin of the historiography of American emigration: excessive praise of the feats and merits of one particular group or nation.

All credit, nonetheless, to those diligent students of Welsh-American history on both sides of the Atlantic. As Welsh historians we should do well to adapt some of their techniques and sources to the study of that urban and industrial society which came into existence in Wales and among Welsh colonies in English cities in the last century. From where did those migrants come? How did they discover where to migrate and to whom did they go? Exactly what kind of people went, and why? How did they adapt from the old life to the new? When and why did Welsh decline amongst some but survive among others – a problem which, by the way, is infinitely more complex and difficult to solve than most of us imagine. But it would be pointless to multiply such questions here without being able to answer them.

Finally, something should be said about America's contribution to Wales over and above receiving thousands of her people and offering them livelihood, homes and hope. We have already seen how close were the relationships between the two countries. The point at which it was realized most clearly how deep was the mutual

sympathy which existed was in 1862 when war between England
and the United States appeared to be imminent. The Welsh Nonconformist press was unanimous in opposing such a conflict and
in its support of the Northern states. *Seren Gomer* summed up majority
opinion in condemning outright any suggestion of war against a
country 'which sustains so close a connexion with us in the matter of
blood, patriotism, trade, constitutional laws and religion. Slavery
excepted, America is more like our country than any other country
under the sun.'

One of the dominant keynotes of Victorian Nonconformists'
religion and sociology was the conviction that the state of the world
was improving. The surest basis of that optimism in Wales was the
success of Nonconformist principles at home and abroad. Nothing
gave the growing confidence greater reassurance than the progress
of these ideals in America. It gave the Welsh rare delight to see their
denominations and the religious press flourishing in America and to
learn that it was the same religious societies – the Foreign Missions
and the Bible Society – which were blossoming there. These societies
were the 'morning star of the Millennium' for John Roberts in
Llanbrynmair and his brother George in Ebensburg, Pennsylvania.
Just as encouraging and powerful was the mutual impact of the
numerous religious revivals in both countries. Two examples only
can here be briefly noted. H. R. Jones came back to Wales bearing
with him sparks from an American revival which were to touch
off the vast conflagration of the revival of 1859 in Cardiganshire;
and secondly, there was the hypnotic effect which Sankey and
Moody exercised in Wales.

Inextricably bound up with the religious convictions was the
moral crusade against the unholy trinity of strong drink, slavery
and war. This broadened out into a demand for an altogether more
liberal and democratic régime in state and church. In consequence,
the first half of the nineteenth century became the seminal era in the
formation of the Nonconformist conscience and the radical tradition.
True it was only an enthusiastic handful of Welshmen who at first
embraced this kind of idealism; men like Morgan John Rhys,
Joseph Tregelles Price, Henry Richard or the Llanbrynmair brothers
in Wales, or B. W. Chidlaw and Robert Everett in the United States.
The portents were gloomy enough in Wales at first, but what gave

these men the encouragement and inspiration to persevere was the close connexion with radicals in England and America. The leaders in Britain and the United States co-operated closely to arrange meetings, publish literature, and create a propitious climate of public opinion. A man like Henry Richard learned an enormous amount about those techniques of organization and propaganda which were later to be invaluable to him in the work of the Liberation Society, which so largely shaped Wales into a Liberal country. By the 1860s it was the most natural thing for Lewis Edwards to assert in *Y Traethodydd* that Britain and America were 'foremost among all nations of the earth in trade, liberty, civilization, Christianity and all virtue'. They were, he claimed, 'the life and strength of all the evangelical missions of the world, whose task it is to send the Word of Life to all nations of the earth'.

The century between 1815 and 1914 constituted a unique chapter in Welsh-American relationships, the like of which can never be repeated. Wales gave America a host of her sons and daughters; America offered them a haven, opportunity and a future. The two countries shared in a religious, political, moral and cultural connexion, which brimmed over with a spirit of confidence and optimism. It seems superfluous to say that the ethos of our own day and generation is very different. Since 1918 the relationship has been revolutionized; the flood of emigration from Wales has dried up and typical Welsh institutions in both countries have declined. Much of that certainty in the present and confidence about the future has evaporated. The deficiencies of the United States are now all too readily criticized. America no doubt has her share of them; yet it would be an injustice to minimize what she has achieved over two centuries in sustaining the cause of liberty. Two hundred years ago, when American independence was proclaimed in 1776, almost nothing exerted more influence on the tone and spirit of the immortal Declaration than the pamphlet by the Welshman, Richard Price, *Observations on Civil Liberty*. Price believed that the American cause had a fateful significance and wrote, 'were I in America I would go barefoot, I would cover myself with skins and endure any inconvenience' in the decisive struggle for 'the sacred blessing of liberty'.

Nothing became more precious to the Americans of the last

century than the concept of their country as the bastion of liberty. This was the kind of impression they made on one ordinary Welsh emigrant, Owen Williams, who went to live in their midst at Olney, Illinois: 'They delight in their freedom, bought by the blood of their forefathers . . . They glory in remembering 1776 when liberty and independence were established in this country.' They won 'freedom for everyone from among all the peoples of the world to enjoy without differentiation' in America. It is worth pausing for a moment to remind ourselves that a free society is still an exception in the long course of human history. Whatever may be said of the shortcomings of the United States it would be an appalling step backward into darkness if anything were to extinguish the lamp of that principle which Richard Price described as the 'sacred blessing of liberty'.

General
The notes which follow should not be seen as anything more than a very
selective introduction to the available reading. A detailed guide to the
literature will be found in *A Bibliography of the History of Wales* (2nd. ed.
Cardiff, 1962), with supplements to it in the *Bulletin of the Board of Celtic
Studies*, XX, XXII, XXIII and XXIV (1963–72). A shorter but helpful
volume is Meic Stephens (ed.), *Reader's Guide to Wales* (London, 1973).
The Dictionary of Welsh Biography down to 1940 (London, 1959) gives
bibliographical notes at the end of each biographical entry.

Valuable general studies of the history of Wales are:
Bowen, E. G. *Wales: a Study in History and Geography* (Cardiff, 1941)
Dodd, A. H. *Life in Wales* (London, 1972)
Evans, Gwynfor. *Land of My Fathers* (Llandybïe, 1973)
Griffith, Ll. W. *The Welsh* (Cardiff, 1964)
Jones, R. Brinley. *Anatomy of Wales* (Cardiff, 1972)
Lloyd, J. E. *A History of Wales from Earliest Times to the Norman Conquest*
  (2 vols. London, 1939)
Morgan, Prys T. J. *Background to Wales* (Llandybïe, 1968)
Roderick, A. J. (ed.) *Wales through the Ages* (2 vols. Llandybïe, 1959–60)
Rees, William. *An Historical Atlas of Wales* (London, 1959)
Williams, A. H. *An Introduction to the History of Wales* (2 vols. Cardiff,
  1941, 1948)
Williams, David. *A History of Modern Wales* (revised ed. London, 1977)

I. *Religion, Language and Nationality* (see also notes to chaps. IV and VI)
   For nationality and nationalism:
Coupland, Reginald. *Welsh and Scottish Nationalism* (London, 1954)
Davies, R. R. 'Owain Glyn Dŵr and the Welsh squirearchy', *Trans.
  Cymmrodorion*, 1970; 'Colonial Wales', *Past and Present*, Nov. 1974
Dodd, A. H. 'Nationalism in Wales: a Historical assessment', *Trans.
  Cymmrodorion, 1970*
Edwards, Owen D. (ed.). *Celtic Nationalism* (London, 1968)
Geoffrey of Monmouth, *The History of the Kings of Britain*, transl. by L.
  Thorpe (Penguin Books, 1966)
Gerald of Wales, *The Description of Wales*, transl. by W. Ll. Williams
  (Everyman Books, 1908)
Hechter, Michael. *Internal Colonization: the Celtic Fringe, 1536–1966* (London,
  1975)
Jenkins, Dafydd. *Cyfraith Hywel* (Llandysul, 1970)
Jenkins, R. T. 'The development of nationalism in Wales', *Sociological
  Review*, 1935
Lloyd, J. E. *Owen Glendower* (Oxford, 1931)
Lloyd, D. M. (ed.) *The Historical Foundations of Welsh Nationalism* (Cardiff,
  1950)

Smith, J. B. 'Gwleidyddiaeth a diwylliant cenedl', *Efrydiau Athronyddol*, 1975
Williams, G. A. 'Twf hanesyddol cenedlaetholdeb Cymru', ibid., 1961
Brief outline histories of the Church are:
Edwards, A. G. *Landmarks in the History of the Welsh Church* (London, 1913)
James, J. W. *A Church History of Wales* (Ilfracombe, 1945)
Walker, D. G. *A History of the Church in Wales* (Cardiff, 1976)
A superb one-volume guide to Welsh literature is
Parry, Thomas. *A History of Welsh Literature*, transl. by H. I. Bell (Oxford, 1955); cf. also
Parry, Thomas (gol.). *Llyfryddiaeth a Llenyddiaeth Gymraeg* (Caerdydd, 1976)
Also lively and interesting are:
Bowen, Geraint (gol.). *Y Traddodiad Rhyddiaith* (3 cyf. Llandysul, 1970, 1974 a 1976)
Conran, A. *The Penguin Book of Welsh Verse* (Penguin, 1967)
Jones, Gwyn. *The Oxford Book of Welsh Verse in English* (Oxford, 1977)
Lewis, Henry. *Datblygiad yr Iaith Gymraeg* (Caerdydd, 1946)
Lewis, Saunders. *Braslun o Hanes Llenyddiaeth Gymraeg* (Caerdydd, 1932)
Parry, Thomas. *The Oxford Book of Welsh Verse* (Oxford, 1962)
Morgan, Gerald. *The Dragon's Tongue* (Cardiff, 1966)
Stephens, Meic (ed.) *The Welsh Language Today* (Llandysul, 1973)
Williams, G. J. *Agweddau ar Hanes Dysg Gymraeg* (Caerdydd, 1969)
Williams, Gwyn. *An Introduction to Welsh Poetry from the Beginnings to the Sixteenth Century* (London, 1953)

II. *Monuments of Conquest*
Useful introductory works are:
Brown, R. A. *English Medieval Castles* (London, 1954)
Colvin, H. M. (ed.). *The History of the King's Works* (2 vols. London, 1963)
Gilyard-Beer, R. *Abbeys in England and Wales* (London, 1958)
Renn, D. F. *Norman Castles in Britain* (London, 1968)
Simpson, W. D. *Castles in England and Wales* (London, 1969)
More specifically on Wales:
Admirable short guides to all the more important monuments in the care of the Department of the Environment are published by HMSO. See also
Cowley, F. G. *The Monastic Houses of South Wales* (Cardiff, 1977)
Hilling, J. B. *The Historical Architecture of Wales* (Cardiff, 1977)
Foster, I. Ll. and Alcock, L. *Culture and Environment: Essays in Honour of Sir Cyril Fox* (London, 1962)
Hogg, A. H. A. and King, D. J. C. 'Early castles in Wales and the Marches' *Archaeologia Cambrensis,* CXII (1963)
Idem. 'Masonry castles in Wales and the Marches', ibid., CXVI (1967)
Royal Commission. *Inventories of Ancient Monuments* (Anglesey, Caernarvonshire, Carmarthenshire, Denbighshire, Flintshire, Glamorgan

239

(in preparation), Merioneth, Montgomeryshire, Pembrokeshire and Radnorshire) published by HMSO.
Taylor, A. J. *The King's Works in Wales, 1277–1330* (London, 1974)
Williams, David H. *The Welsh Cistercians: Aspects of their Economic History* (Pontypool, 1969)
Idem. *White Monks in Gwent and the Border* (Pontypool, 1976)
Williams, Glanmor. *The Welsh Church from Conquest to Reformation* (revised ed. Cardiff, 1976)

III. *Prophecy, Poetry and Politics*
For medieval and early modern prophecy, see:
Cohn, Norman. *The Pursuit of the Millennium* (London, 1957)
Reeves, Marjorie. *Prophecy in the Later Middle Ages* (Oxford, 1969)
Taylor, Richard. *The Political Prophecy in England* (New York, 1967)
Thomas, K. V. *Religion and the Decline of Magic* (London, 1971)
On Wales:
Davies, J. H. *Hen Ddewiniaid Cymru* (Privately printed, 1901)
Griffiths, M. E. *Early Vaticination in Welsh with English Parallels* (Cardiff, 1937)
Hanning, R. W. *The Vision of History from Gildas to Geoffrey of Monmouth* (New York, 1966)
Jones, Thomas. 'Historical writing in medieval Wales', *Scottish Studies*, XII (1968)
Rowlands, Eurys. 'Dilid y broffwydoliaeth', *Trivium*, II (1967)
Williams, Ifor. *Armes Prydein o Lyfr Taliesin* (Caerdydd, 1955)

IV. *Religion and Education in Wales*
On religion see
Bassett, T. M. *Bedyddwyr Cymru* (Abertawe, 1977)
Bell, P. M. H. *Disestablishment in Wales and Ireland* (London, 1969)
Bowen, E. G. *The Settlements of the Celtic Saints in Wales* (Cardiff, 1954)
Idem. *Saints, Seaways and Settlements* (Cardiff, 1969)
Chadwick, N. K. *Studies in the Early British Church* (Cambridge, 1958)
Davies, E. T. *Religion in the Industrial Revolution in South Wales* (Cardiff, 1965)
Jones, I. G. and David Williams (eds.), *The Religious Census of 1851* (Cardiff, 1977).
Jones, R. T. *Hanes Annibynwyr Cymru* (Abertawe, 1966)
Morgan, Kenneth O. *Freedom or Sacrilege? A History of the Campaign for Welsh Disestablishment* (Penarth, 1966)
Rees, Thomas. *A History of Protestant Nonconformity in Wales* (London, 1883)
Richards, Thomas. *The Puritan Movement in Wales, 1639–53* (London, 1920)
Idem. *Religious Developments in Wales, 1654–1662* (London, 1923)
Idem. *Wales under the Penal Code, 1662–87* (London, 1925)
Roberts, G. M. (ed.) *Hanes Methodistiaeth Galfinaidd Cymru. I Y Deffroad Mawr* (Caernarfon, 1973)
(See also I above)

240

On education:
Clement, Mary. *The S.P.C.K. and Wales, 1699–1740* (Cardiff, 1954)
Education in Wales, 1847–1947 (London, 1948)
Ellis, E. I. *The University College of Wales, Aberystwyth, 1872–1972* (Cardiff, 1972)
Ellis, T. I. *Development of Higher Education in Wales* (Wrexham, 1935)
Evans, D. E. *The University of Wales* (Cardiff, 1953)
Evans, L. W. *Education in Industrial Wales* (Cardiff, 1971)
Gittins, C. E. (ed.) *Pioneers of Welsh Education* (Swansea, 1964)
Jones, E. J. *History of Education in Wales* (Wrexham, 1931)
Idem. *Education in Wales during the Middle Ages* (Oxford, 1949)
Jones, M. G. *The Charity School Movement* (Cambridge, 1938)
Price, D. W. T. *A History of St. David's College, Lampeter* (Cardiff, 1977)
Williams, J. L. *Ysgrifau ar Addysg* Cyf. IV (Caerdydd, 1966)
(See also below IX)
Williams, J. L. and Hughes, G. R. *The History of Education in Wales* (Swansea, 1978).

V.   *The Tradition of Saint David in Wales*
Baring-Gould, S. and Fisher, J. *The Lives of the British Saints* (4 vols. London, 1907–13)
Bowen, E. G. and Chadwick, N. K. see p. 239.
Doble, G. H. *The Lives of the Welsh Saints* (ed.) D. S. Evans (Cardiff, 1971)
Evans, D. S. *Buched Dewi* (Caerdydd, 1959)
Harris, S. M. *St. David in the Liturgy* (Cardiff, 1940)
James, J. W. *Rhigyfarch's Life of St. David* (Cardiff, 1967)
Jones, J. Ll. 'Dewi Sant', *Y Geninen*, XLI (1923)
Rees, Rice. *An Essay on the Welsh Saints* (London, 1836)
Richter, Michael. 'The life of St. David by Giraldus Cambrensis', *Welsh History Review*, IV (1968–9)
Williams, Glanmor. *Welsh Reformation Essays* (Cardiff, 1967)
Williams, J. E. C. 'Buchedd Dewi', *Llên Cymru*, V (1959)

VI.   *Language, Literacy and Nationality*
Butt-Philip, Alan. *The Welsh Question* (Cardiff, 1975)
Davies, J. H. (ed.) *The Morris Letters, 1728–65* (2 vols. Aberystwyth 1907–9); cf. also Owen, Hugh. *Additional Letters of the Morrises* (2 vols. London, 1947–9)
Dodd, A. H. *The Industrial Revolution in North Wales* (3rd ed. Cardiff, 1971)
Evans, E. D. *A History of Wales, 1660–1815* (Cardiff, 1976)
Evans, Thomas. *The Background of Modern Welsh Politics, 1789–1846* (Cardiff, 1936)
Jenkins, Geraint H. *Literature, Religion and Society in Wales, 1660–1730* (Cardiff, 1978)

Jenkins, R. T. *Hanes Cymru yn y Ddeunawfed Ganrif* (Caerdydd, 1928)
Idem. *Hanes Cymru yn y Bedwaredd Ganrif ar Bymtheg* (Caerdydd, 1933)
Jenkins, R. T. and Ramage, Helen. *A History of the Honourable Society of Cymmrodorion* (London, 1951)
John, A. H. *The Industrial Development of South Wales* (Cardiff, 1950)
Jones, Ieuan G. 'The election of 1868 in Merthyr Tydfil', *Journal of Modern History*, XXXIII (1961)
Idem. 'The Liberation Society and Welsh Politics', *Welsh History Review*, I (1960–3)
Idem. 'The elections of 1865 and 1868 in Wales', *Trans. Cymmrodorion*, 1964
Jones, R. Brinley. *The Old British Tongue, the Vernacular in Wales, 1540–1640* (Cardiff, 1970)
Minchinton, W. E. (ed.) *Industrial South Wales, 1750–1914* (London, 1969)
Morgan, Kenneth O. *Wales in British Politics, 1868–1922* (Cardiff, 1970)
Idem. 'Welsh nationalism: the historical background', *Journal of Contemporary History*, VI (1971)
Morgan, Prys T. J. 'The Abbé Pezron and the Celts', *Trans. Cymmrodorion*, 1965
Owen, A. L. *The Famous Druids* (Oxford, 1962)
Piggott, Stuart. *The Druids* (Penguin Books, 1974)
Roberts, Peter F. 'The union with England and the identity of "Anglican" Wales', *Trans. Royal Hist. Soc.*, v, XXII (1972)
Thomas, Brinley. *The Welsh Economy* (Cardiff, 1972)
Thomas, J. D. H. *A History of Wales, 1485–1660* (Cardiff, 1972)
Williams, Glanmor. *Welsh Reformation Essays* (Cardiff, 1967)
Williams, G. J. *Agweddau ar Hanes Dysg Gymraeg* (Caerdydd, 1969)
Idem. *Iolo Morganwg* (Caerdydd, 1956)
Williams, W. Ll. *The Making of Modern Wales* (London, 1919)
Williams, W. Ogwen. 'The survival of the Welsh language after the union of England and Wales', *Welsh Hist. Rev.*, II (1960)

VII. *The Gentry of Wales*
Bebb, W. Ambrose. *Cyfnod y Tuduriaid* (Wrecsam, 1939)
Carr, A. D. 'Sir Lewis John – a medieval London Welshman', *Bulletin Board of Celtic Studies*, XXII (1966–8)
Idem. 'Welshmen and the Hundred Years' War', *Welsh History Rev.*, IV (1968)
Davies, R. R. and Smith, J. B. 'The social structure of medieval Glamorgan', in T. B. Pugh (ed.) *Glamorgan County History: III. The Middle Ages* (Cardiff, 1971)
Dodd, A. H. *Studies in Stuart Wales* (Cardiff, 1971)
Idem. 'The pattern of politics in Stuart Wales', *Trans. Cymmrodorion*, 1948
Idem. *A History of Caernarvonshire* (Denbigh, 1968)
Evans, G. Nesta. *Social Life in Mid-Eighteenth Century Anglesey* (Cardiff, 1936)

Idem. *Religion and Politics in Mid-Eighteenth Century Anglesey* (Cardiff, 1953)
Howell, David W. *Land and People in Nineteenth-Century Wales* (London, 1978)
Howells, Brian E. 'The Elizabethan squirearchy in Pembrokeshire', *The Pembrokeshire Historian*, I (1959)
Jones, Emyr G. 'Notes on the principal county families of Anglesey', *Trans. Anglesey Antiq. Soc.*, 1939, 1940
Jones, Francis. 'The old families of Wales' in D. Moore (ed.), *Wales in the Eighteenth Century* (Swansea, 1976)
Jones, Gareth E. *The Gentry and the Elizabethan State* (Swansea, 1977)
Jones, R. W. *Bywyd Cymdeithasol Cymru yn y Ddeunawfed Ganrif* (Caerdydd, 1931)
Lloyd, Howell A. *The Gentry of South-west Wales, 1540–1640* (Cardiff, 1968)
Mathew, David. *The Celtic Peoples and Renaissance Europe* (London, 1933)
Owen, Geraint D. *Elizabethan Wales: the Social Scene* (Cardiff, 1962)
Pierce, T. Jones. *Medieval Welsh Society* (Cardiff, 1972)
Roberts, Glyn. *Aspects of Welsh History* (Cardiff, 1969)
Roberts, P. F. 'The social history of the Merioneth gentry, 1660–1840', *Journal Merioneth Hist. Soc.*, IV (1961–4)
Idem. 'The decline of the Welsh gentry in the eighteenth century', *National Library Wales Journal*, XIII (1963–4)
Thirsk, Joan (ed.) *The Agrarian History of England and Wales, 1540–1640* (Cambridge, 1967)
Vaughan, H. M. *The South Wales Squires* (London, 1926)
Williams, Glanmor. 'The Social Order' in *Glamorgan County History: IV Early Modern Glamorgan* (Cardiff, 1974)
Williams, W. Ogwen. *Tudor Gwynedd* (Caernarvon, 1958)
Idem. 'The social order in Wales', *Trans. Cymmrodorion*, 1967

VIII. *The Welsh in Tudor England*

N.B. *The Dictionary of Welsh Biography down to 1940* (London, 1959) is particularly helpful on individuals.
Bartley, J. O. *Teague, Shenkin and Sawney* (Cork, 1954)
Chrimes, S. B. *Henry VII* (London, 1972)
Donaldson, G. S. 'The foundations of Anglo-Scottish union' in S. T. Bindoff *et. al.* (ed.), *Elizabethan Government and Society* (London, 1961)
Dodd, A. H. 'North Wales in the Essex revolt of 1601', *English Hist. Rev.*, LIX (1944)
French, Peter. *John Dee* (London, 1972)
Ellis, T. P. *The Catholic Martyrs of Wales* (London, 1933)
Idem. *Welsh Benedictines of the Terror* (Newtown, 1936)
Gwyndaf, Robin. 'Sir Richard Clough of Denbigh', *Trans. Denbighshire Hist. Soc.*, XIX (1970), XX (1971)
Harries, F. J. *The Welsh Elizabethans* (Pontypridd, 1924)
Idem. *Shakespeare and the Welsh* (London, 1919)

Hughes, W. J. *Wales and the Welsh in English Literature* (Wrexham, 1924)
Jordan, W. K. *Philanthropy in England, 1480–1660* (London, 1959)
Kendrick, T. D. *British Antiquity* (London, 1950)
Knight, L. S. *Welsh Independent Grammar Schools to 1600* (Newton, 1926)
McKisack, May. *Medieval History in the Tudor Age* (London, 1970)
Miller, E. J. 'Wales and Tudor drama', *Trans. Cymmrodorion*, 1948
Pierce, William. *John Penry; His Life, Times and Writings* (London, 1923)
Quinn, David B. *The Elizabethans and the Irish* (Cornell, 1967)
Rowse, A. L. *The Elizabethan Renaissance* (London, 1971)
Thomas, D. A. *The Welsh Elizabethan Catholic Martyrs* (Cardiff, 1971)
Thomas, D. Ll. 'Welsh lawyers of the Tudor and Stuart period', *Trans. Liverpool Welsh Nationalist Society*, 1899–1900.
Williams, E. R. *Some Studies in Elizabethan Wales* (Newtown, 1924)
Williams, Ieuan M. 'Ysgolheictod Hanesyddol yr unfed ganrif ar bymtheg', *Llên Cymru*, II (1952)
Williams, Penry. *The Council in the Marches of Wales under Elizabeth I* (Cardiff, 1958)

IX. *Religion, Language and the Circulating Schools*
Much the most important source of information is Griffith Jones's own report on his schools, *The Welch Piety*, published annually after 1737. Useful extracts were published in W. Moses Williams (ed.), *Selections from the Welch Piety* (Cardiff, 1938). See also:
Cavenagh, F. A. *Griffith Jones* (Cardiff, 1930)
Clement, Mary. *The S.P.C.K. and Wales, 1699–1740* (Cardiff, 1954)
Jenkins, R. T. *Gruffydd Jones, Llanddowror* (Cardiff, 1930)
Jones, David A. *Griffith Jones, Llanddowror* (Wrecsam, 1923)
Kelly, Thomas. *Griffith Jones, Pioneer in Adult Education* (Cardiff, 1950)
Shankland, Thomas. 'Sir John Philipps and the charity schools movement', *Trans. Cymmrodorion*, 1904–5
Williams, W. Moses. *The Friends of Griffith Jones* (London, 1939)
(See also above, IV)

X. *Prospect of Paradise? Wales and the United States, 1776–1914*
There is a huge literature on emigration to the U.S. I have found the following particularly helpful:
Hansen, M. L. *The Atlantic Migration, 1607–1860* (London, 1961)
Jones, Maldwyn A. *American Immigration* (London, 1960)
Idem. *Destination America* (London, 1976)
Wittke, C. *We who Built America* (Cleveland, Ohio, 1964)
    On the specifically British aspects:
Berthoff, R. T. *British Immigrants in Industrial America, 1790–1850* (Cambridge, Mass., 1953)
Erickson, Charlotte. *Invisible Immigrants . . .* (London, 1972)
Taylor, P. A. M. *Expectations Westward . . .* (London, 1965)
Thomas, Brinley. *Migration and Economic Growth* (Cambridge, 1954)

On emigration from Wales:

Browning, C. H. *The Welsh Settlement of Pennsylvania* (Philadelphia, 1912)

Conway, Alan. *The Welsh in America* (Cardiff, 1961)

Dodd, A. H. *The Character of Early Welsh Emigration to the United States* (Cardiff, 1953)

Eames, Aled *et. al.* (ed.) *Letters from America* (Gwynedd Archive Service, 1976)

Harries, F. J. *Welshmen in the United States* (Pontypridd, 1927)

Hartmann, E. G. *Americans from Wales* (Boston, 1967)

Hughes, Thomas. *The History of the Welsh in Minnesota* (Mankato, 1895)

Lewis, T. H. *Y Mormoniaid yng Nghymru* (Caerdydd, 1956)

Owen, Bob. 'Yr ymfudo o Sir Gaernarfon i'r Unol Daleithiau', *Trans. Caerns. Hist. Soc.*, 1952–3–4

Idem. 'Ymfudo o Sir Aberteifi i Unol Daleithiau America', *Ceredigion*, II (1954)

Idem. 'Ymfudo o Sir Frycheiniog, 1785–1860', *Brycheiniog*, VII (1961)

Roberts, E. G. (ed.) *Anglesey Family Letters* (Liverpool, 1976)

Shepperson, W. C. *Samuel Roberts* (Knoxville, Tenn. 1961)

Thomas, R. D. *The History of the Welsh in America* (Utica, N.Y., 1872)

Williams, Daniel J. *The Welsh of Columbus, Ohio* (Oshkosh, Wisc., 1913)

Williams, David. *Cymru ac America: Wales and America* (Cardiff, 1946)

A

Aberconway, abbey, 69, 70
   Treaty of, 44
Abergavenny, 38, 39, 194
Aberystwyth, 44, 48, 56, 57, 60
Acts of Parliament, see Act(s) of Union,
   Propagation Act
Act(s) of Union (England and Wales), 3,
   16, 49, 60, 130, 132, 156, 161, 162
Ambrosius Aurelianus, 2
Ancient Britons, Society of, 120–1
Aneirin, 2
Anglesey, 22, 35, 44, 46, 48, 138, 150,
   219, 226
Anglican Church, Anglicans, 99–107,
   123–4, 140, 159, 164, 167, 209, 212
Anglo-Saxons, Saxons, 1, 3, 4, 5, 6, 7,
   11, 17, 18, 19, 34, 36, 73, 76, 78, 82,
   91, 112, 129, 171
Annales Cambriae, 3
Armes Prydein, 72, 77, 111, 125
Arthur, 3, 7, 17, 23, 29, 73, 74, 124, 150
Asser, 87, 92, 111
Aubrey, William, 176, 181, 193
Augustinian Canons, 40, 42, 70

B

Bangor, 27, 40, 70
Bardsey, 42
Basingwerk, 40, 64, 66–7, 69, 70
Beaumaris, 45, 56, 58, 59, 148
Beddgelert, 42
Bede, 3, 76
Benedictine monks, 40, 42, 67, 69, 70
Berain, Catherine of, 197–8
Bere, Castell y, 43, 45, 56
Beuno, St., 2
Bevan, Aneurin, 147
Bevan, Madam Bridget, 203, 208, 215
Blackwell, Henry, 232
Blaenau Ffestiniog, 141
Bleddyn Fardd, 10
Bosworth, battle of, 48, 84, 129, 171–2,
   177
Brad y Llyfrau Gleision, 105
Brecknock, Breconshire, 36, 53, 180, 191,
   193
Brecon, 37, 38, 39, 59, 70
Brenhinedd y Saesson, 6
Bristol, 50, 173, 186
Britain, 'matter of', 84, 85; see also
   Geoffrey of Monmouth
British and Foreign Schools Society, 105
Britons, 1, 2, 3, 4, 7, 18, 24, 102, 171, 213
Brittany, Bretons, 7, 73, 111, 132, 137
Bronllys, 53

Brutus (of Troy), 4, 24, 128, 150; see also
   Trojans
Brut, Walter, 24, 95
Brut y Tywysogyon, 10, 93
Builth, 44, 45, 56, 57, 58
Bulkeley, family, 148, 150
Burgess, Bishop Thomas, 87, 122
Button, Sir Thomas, 184

C

Cadog, St., 2, 113
Cadwaladr, 8, 73, 82, 84
Caerleon, 112, 186
Caernarvon, 35, 42, 45–6, 48, 56, 58–9,
   61–2, 70, 95
Caernarvonshire, 46, 183, 219
Caerphilly, 55, 56
Caldicot, 53
California, 226, 227
Calixtus II, Pope, 115
Cambridge University, 172, 176, 187
Camden, William, 172, 173, 189
Canterbury, Archbishop, -ric, of, 9, 12,
   40, 114–6, 117
Cardiff, 37, 38, 50, 53, 69, 70
Cardigan, 37, 44, 46, 148
Cardiganshire, 218, 234; see also Cere-
   digion
Carew Castle, 61, 155
Carmarthen, 36, 37, 43, 44, 46, 118,
   200
      castle, 53, 59
      priory, 40, 67
Carmarthenshire, 200, 201
Carne, Sir Edward, 179
Carreg Cennen, 44, 59, 60
Castles, 50–62
      concentric, 55–6
      Edwardian, 45, 51, 56–9
      motte-and-bailey, 37, 50–1, 52
Catalogue of Irish Saints, 111
Cecil, Sir William, Lord Burghley, 18,
   178, 182, 186, 190, 198
      Sir Robert, 81, 82, 85, 182
Celtic Church, 9, 15, 18, 23, 39, 76,
   90–2, 110, 119
      Saints, 2, 110, 126
Celts, 24, 25, 29, 138
      religion of, 71–2, 77
Ceredigion, 36, 110
Charles I, 61, 100, 153, 157
Charles, Thomas, 102, 215
Chepstow, 35, 37, 38, 39
      castle, 51, 54, 59, 61
Chester, 35, 37, 43, 46, 50, 56, 57, 173,
   186

Chidlaw, Benjamin W., 221, 223, 234
Chirk Castle, 56, 58, 153, 193
Christianity, Christians, 1, 2, 3, 8, 18, 71, 76, 87, 88, 91, 95, 124, 202, 204, 212, 217, 235
Church of England, see Anglican Church
Cilcennin, 225
Cilgerran Castle, 51, 54, 59
Cistercian monks, 9, 11, 12, 40, 42, 43, 63, 64, 66, 67, 70
Cîteaux, 40, 68
Civil Wars, seventeenth-century, 49, 61, 62, 80, 100–1, 157, 159, 160, 212, 214
Clergy, 19, 21, 41, 88–90, 93–5, 97–8, 134, 158, 168, 208, 210
higher, 11, 93, 127, 135
Clough, Sir Richard, 175, 193, 197, 198
Clwyd, river, 35, 57
Coety Castle, 52
Commonwealth, 100, 136, 202
Conwy Castle, 45, 56, 58, 59, 61
Cornwall, 6, 132
Cox, Leonard, 186
Crawshay, William II, 154
Crécy, 46, 172
Cricieth Castle, 55, 56, 59
Cromwell, Oliver, 62, 82
Cromwell, Thomas, 19, 50, 179
Cundell, Henry, 189
Cwmhir Abbey, 69
Cwndidau, 99
Cyfarthfa Castle, 154
Cymer Abbey, 62, 63, 67
Cymmrodorion, Society of, 120, 138
Cymreigyddion, Society of, 121, 138

D

Dafydd ap Gruffydd, Prince, 44, 45
Dafydd ap Gwilym, 139
Dafydd Llwyd o Fathafarn, 71, 72, 77, 84
David, Dewi, St., 2, 9, 77–8, 87, 109–26
St. David's Day, 109, 117, 119, 120–2, 123, 126, 230
Societies, 122, 230
Davies, David, coalowner, 169
D.S., 226, 230
Dr. John of Mallwyd, 134
Bishop Richard, 98, 119, 182
Dee, Dr. John, 17, 187–8, 189
De Excidio Britanniae, 1
Degannwy, 35, 44
Deheubarth, 8, 37, 42
Denbigh Castle, 56, 58
Denbighshire, 151, 193
Disestablishment, 28, 29, 107
Dissenters, 100–3, 107; see also Non-conformists

Dolbadarn Castle, 43, 45, 53
Dolforwyn Castle, 43
Dolwyddelan Castle, 45, 52, 56
Drayton, Michael, 17, 189
Druids, 23, 29, 71, 138, 139
Dyfed, 1, 110
Dyfrig, St., 21, 91, 110, 112
Dynevor family, 73, 81; see also Rhys ap Gruffydd, Rhys ap Thomas

E

Edward I, 9, 15, 20, 43–7, 55, 57, 58, 80, 150
conquest of Wales by, 43–7, 59, 72, 172
Edward III, 15, 59, 172
IV, 172
VI, 179
the Black Prince, 46, 59
Edwards, Charles, 19, 24, 120
Edwards, Dr, Lewis, 235
Edwards, Roger, 221
Eisteddfod, -au, 25, 27, 29, 30, 139, 140–1, 211
Elizabeth I, 19, 81, 99, 151, 154, 174, 176, 178, 181, 183, 184, 187, 189, 190, 191, 196–8
Ellis, Thomas E., 28
Emrys ap Iwan (Robert Ambrose Jones), 30
England, English people, 11, 12, 16, 17, 19, 21, 37, 47, 49, 53, 58, 71, 80, 82, 127, 140, 147, 160, 161, 165, 171–99, 202, 231, 234, 235
English language, 26, 30, 49, 130–2, 144–6, 161–2, 164, 169, 180, 184, 194, 204–5, 207, 210, 231–2
Enoc Huws, 165
Essex, Robert Devereux, 2nd Earl of, 81, 82, 175, 178, 179, 183, 194
Evans, Christmas, 217
Evans, Capt. David, 220, 222
Evans, Evan (Ieuan Brydydd Hir), 22, 138
Evans, Sir Geraint, 195
Evans, Dr. Gwynfor, 126, 166
Evans, Sir Hugh, 186
Evans, John, of Eglwys Gymun, 209
Evans, Theophilus, 23, 25, 120
Ewenni, 39, 63, 66, 68, 70
Ewloe Castle, 53

F

Farmer Careful of Cilhaul, 220, 221
Ferrar, Bishop Robert, 81, 85, 118
Fitzosbern, William, 34, 38, 39, 41, 51

Flint Castle, 44, 56, 57, 62
Flintshire, 46, 53, 148, 150
Foreston, Iowa, 227
France, 42, 47, 48, 53, 57, 58, 59, 167, 183
Franciscan friars, 12, 70
Freemen, 15, 16, 20, 79, 150
Friars in Wales, 9, 43, 211
Friars' School, Bangor, 193

G

Gaelic, 140, 146
Gamage, Barbara, 198–9
Garmon, St., 3
Gee, Thomas, 142
Genealogies, 4, 7, 128, 150, 151
Gentry, 3, 16, 19, 20, 21, 22, 28, 86, 127, 133, 135, 140, 148–70
Geoffrey of Monmouth, 6–8, 18, 23, 71–2, 81–2, 135, 150, 188
George, David Lloyd, 28, 195
Gerald of Wales (Giraldus Cambrensis), 6–8, 18, 20, 24, 34, 113, 115, 116
Gildas, 1–3, 7, 8, 18, 76, 92
Glamorgan, 22, 36, 39, 40, 91, 99, 139, 150, 151, 152, 186, 225
Gloucester, 36, 50, 186
Glyn, Geoffrey, 193
Glyn, Bishop William, 176
Goch, Mathew, 172
Gogynfeirdd, 72
Goldcliff, 39
Gomer, son of Japhet, 24, 29, 137
Goodman, Gabriel, 182, 193
Gospels of St. Chad, 92
Gouge, Thomas, 202
Gough, Richard, 189
Gower, 37
Grant, President Ulysses S., 222
Greek, Greeks, 96, 134
Griffith, John, 176
Grosmont Castle, 54
Gruffydd ab yr Ynad Goch, 12
Gruffydd ap Llywelyn, 5, 34
Guttun Owain, 70
Gwen Tomos, 165, 219
Gwent, Richard, 179
Gwynedd, 8, 9, 12, 35, 36, 40, 42, 44, 45, 46, 47, 53, 58, 72, 92, 115
Gwyneddigion, Society of, 120, 138
Gwynne, Richard, 183

H

Hanmer family, 151
Hanmer, Sir David, 172
Halsingod, 99

Harlech Castle, 45, 48, 56, 58, 60, 61
Haverfordwest, 38, 40
Hawarden Castle, 56
Hebrews, 1, 24, 25, 88, 134
Hebrew language, 96, 187
Henry I, 36, 37, 40, 151
    II, 15, 24, 41
    III, 43, 55
    IV, 15, 177
    V, 117, 172, 173
    VI, 172
Henry VII, Henry Tudor, 48, 49, 73, 74, 84, 85, 86, 117, 129, 171, 172, 173, 177, 178, 179, 182, 192; see also Tudor family
Henry VIII, 15, 49, 50, 69, 80, 86, 131, 132, 153, 166, 171, 176, 179, 185, 190
Hen Fynyw, 110
Herbert family, 70, 189; see also Pembroke, Earls of
Herbert, Sir John, 153
Hereford, 34, 37, 38, 186
Herefordshire, 53, 197
Historia Brittonum, 3, 7, 18
History of the Kings of Britain, 7
Holt Castle, 56
Home Rule (Welsh), 12, 28
Hopcyn ap Thomas, 76
Hope Castle, 56
Howell, Thomas (Seville), 185
Hugh of Avranches, 35
Hywel Dda, 5, 34, 112

I

Ieuan ap Rhydderch, 116
Iestyn ap Gwrgant, 151, 152
Illtud, St., 2, 91, 92, 110
Industrial Revolution, 103, 135, 140–1, 157, 163
Inns of Court, 95, 174, 177
Iolo Morganwg (Edward Williams), 22, 136, 139, 144
Iorthryn Gwynedd (R. D. Thomas), 224, 230
Ireland, 28, 48, 58, 70, 73, 92, 111, 143, 153, 159, 166, 183, 218
Irish, 18, 19, 91, 111, 140, 146, 147, 192, 193, 195, 218, 225
Islwyn (William Thomas), 217
Ivorites, Society of, 230

J

Jacobite Rising, 1745, 212
James I, 99, 173, 180, 192
James II, 157
James ap Gruffydd ap Howell, 81

James, Thomas (Bristol), 186
James, Thomas (librarian), 189
Japhet, 4, 29, 137
Jenkins, Prof. R. T., 26, 27, 185
Jenkins, Dean T. E., 126
Jenkins, Thomas, 186
Jesus College, Oxford, 177
John, Augustus, 195
John, Lewis, 173
John of Tynemouth, 113
Johnes, A. J., 168
Jones, Edward ('Bardd y Brenin'), 23
Jones, Edward (Plas Cadwgan), 191
Jones, Griffith, 24, 102, 103, 136, 137, 200–16
Jones, Henry, 181
Jones, Prof. Ieuan G., 26, 143, 169
Jones, John (Catholic martyr), 190
Jones, John (Talsarn), 221
Jones, Michael D., 30
Jones, N. M., 224
Jones, Richard (printer), 189
Jones, Rhys, 22
Jones, Robert (musician), 187
Jones, Robert (Rhos-lan), 217
Jones, William (London merchant), 175, 185, 194
Jonson, Ben, 173, 189, 199
Jordan, Prof. W. K., 185, 202
Joseph of Arimathea, 18

K

Kelton, Arthur, 17, 24
Kidwelly, 37, 38, 39, 55, 56, 59
Kyffin, Edward, 24

L

Labour party, 31, 147
Lancastrians, 48, 60
Latin, 2, 6, 89, 92–4, 95, 116, 187, 194
Laugharne, 49, 201
Lay brothers, 64, 68
Leicester, Robert Dudley, Earl of, 182, 183
Leland, John, 17, 70, 152, 188
Lewis, Judge David, 181
Lewis, Griffith, 182
Lewis, John (Llywene), 17, 24
Lewis, John Ll., 233
Lewis, Bishop Owen, 176
Lewis, Saunders, 32
Lhuyd, Edward, 22, 27, 137–8
Liberal Party, 28, 31, 144, 147, 165, 166
Liberation Society, 143, 235
Lincoln's Inn, 177

Literacy, 89–90, 96, 102–3, 104–5, 121, 127–8, 129–30, 136–7, 141, 144, 146, 160, 210, 211, 215–6
Llancarfan, 92
Llandaff, 40, 92, 113, 182
Llanddewibrefi, 109, 110, 111, 112, 114, 116
    anchorite of, 113, 116
Llanddowror, 201, 203, 205
Llandovery, 37
Llanelli, 141
Llangennydd, 39
Llanilltud Fawr (Llantwit Major), 92
Llanthony Priory, 40, 65, 66, 67, 68
Llantriddyd, 181
Llanuwchllyn, 225
Llanwrtyd, 225
Lloyd, Hugh (Plas Du), 181
Lloyd, Sir John E., 13
Lloyd, Lewis (banker), 169
Lloyd, Lodovic, 81
Llwyd, Humphrey, 17, 175, 188
Llŷn, 225
Llywelyn ab Iorwerth, Prince, 9, 42, 53, 55
Llywelyn ap Gruffydd, Prince, 9, 10, 42–5, 46, 53, 55, 72, 125
Londres, William de, 52
London Welshmen, 119, 120, 125, 138, 139, 141, 175, 180, 184–5, 189
Loughor, Judge Robert, 181
Lucius son of Coel, 8, 18

M

Madog ap Llywelyn, 47, 58
Madryn, Thomas, 194
Mansel, Sir Rhys, 61
Mansel, Sir Robert, 184
Manuscript copying, 132, 135
Marcher lords, 9, 16, 41, 43, 47, 53, 55, 56, 152, 156
March, Marches, of Wales, 11, 37, 38, 48, 49, 60
Margam Abbey, 40, 62, 66, 68, 70
Martyrology of Oengus, 111
Marshall, William, 53, 54
Mary I, 19, 176, 179, 183
Mary Queen of Scots, 181, 191
'Massacre of the Long Knives', 3, 23, 105
Merioneth, 46, 148, 218
Merlin, 7, 11, 81, 82, 85, 118
Merrick, Rhys, 156
Merthyr Tydfil, 141, 154
Methodism, Methodist Revival, 103, 104, 136, 139, 209, 215

Meyrick, Sir Gelly, 175
Middleton, Sir Hugh, 185, 195
Middleton, Sir Thomas, 153, 185, 193
Middleton, William, 184
Milford Haven, 171
Minnesota, 219, 226
Monasteries, 9, 49, 68–70
Monastic buildings, 62–8
Monmouth, 35, 38, 39, 60
Monmouthshire, 53, 148, 185, 186
Montgomery, 35, 143
    castle, 49, 55, 56
    family, 41
    Roger of, 35, 36
    Treaty of, 43
Montgomeryshire, 218
Morgan, Bishop John, 179
Morgan, Dr. Kenneth O., 147
Morgan, Bishop Philip, 172
Morgan, Thomas (conspirator), 191
Morgan, Bishop William, 134, 161
Mormons, 220, 226
Morris brothers, 22, 138
Morris, Lewis, 22, 144
Morris, Richard, 22
Morris, William, 22
Myrddin, 71
Myvyrian Archaiology, 139

N
Nannau, 148
Nationality, Welsh sense of,
  in early Wales, 1–6; in Middle Ages,
  6–14, 16, 20–1, 36–7, 41–3, 47–8,
  71–80, 114–7, 127–9; in Tudor and
  Stuart era, 14–20, 20–1, 48–9, 81–6,
  119–20, 131–4, 160–3,193–5; revival in
  eighteenth century, 21–5, 135–40, 209;
  nineteenth-century nationalism, 25–9,
  121–3, 140–6, 168–9; contemporary
  nationalism, 29–33, 146–7; in the
  U.S.A., 226–31
  see also Plaid Cymru
National Library of Wales, 27
National Museum of Wales, 27
National Schools Society, 105
Neath, 38, 152
    Abbey, 40, 50, 62, 64, 65, 66, 67,
  68, 69, 70, 154
Nennius, 3
Newcastle (Bridgend), 52
New York, 226, 227, 228
Nonconformists, Nonconformity, 26,
  103–7, 123, 125, 140–1, 143, 158,
  164–7, 215, 228, 234; see also Dissenters
Normans in Wales, 6, 34–42, 50, 72, 76,
  90, 92, 93, 112, 113, 125, 152

O
Offa's Dyke, 4, 17, 173
Ogmore Castle, 52, 59
Ohio, 219, 222, 225, 226
Oneida County, 225
Ortelius, Abraham, 180, 188
Oswestry, 56, 173, 186
Owain Glyn Dŵr, 12–4, 20, 48, 59–60,
  68–9, 72, 74, 94, 117, 125, 148, 172
Owain Gwynedd, 42
Owain Lawgoch, 12, 47, 72, 73, 81
Owen, Bob (Croesor), 185, 189
Owen, Daniel, 165
Owen, George (Henllys), 48, 86, 156,
  171–2, 173, 174
Owen, Goronwy, 22, 138
Owen, Hugh (Plas Du), 190
Owen, John (epigrammatist), 189
Owen, William (Henllys), 193
Owen-Pughe, William, 22, 139
Oxford University, 94, 95, 172, 187, 190
Oxwich Castle, 49, 61

P
Padarn, St., 2, 110
Paris University, 93, 94
Parker, Archbishop Matthew, 18, 181,
  189
Parry, Blanche, 189, 196–7
Parry, Dr. Joseph, 230
Parry, Robert (author), 189
Parry, Sir Thomas, Controller of the
  Household, 178, 193
Parry, William (conspirator), 191
Patrick, St., 3, 124
Patriotic societies, 25, 29, 120–1, 123,
  139–40, 141, 229, 230
  in U.S.A., 120, 229–30; see also
  Ancient Britons, Cymmrodorion,
  Cymreigyddion, Gwyneddigion
Peckham, Archbishop John, 20, 80
Pembroke, 36, 37, 38, 39
    castle, 48, 49, 53, 54, 59, 62
Pembrokeshire, 37, 53, 61, 148, 193, 200,
  205, 206
Pembroke, William Herbert, 1st Earl of
  (1st creation), 60, 72, 74, 172
Pembroke, William Herbert, 1st Earl of
  (2nd creation), 151, 178, 183, 189
    Henry Herbert, 2nd Earl of,
  178, 189; see also Herbert
  family
Penboyr, 200
Penmon Priory, 42, 65, 66
Pennsylvania, 225, 226, 227, 228
Penry, John, 189, 191–2

Penshurst, 198–9
Perrott, Sir John, 61, 179
Peter, David (Carmarthen), 123
Pezron, Abbé, 24, 137–8
Philipps, Sir Grismond, 154
Philipps, Sir John, 201, 203, 208
Phillips, Sir Thomas, 168
Picton, 148, 201
Pilgrimages, pilgrims, 116–8, 125
Plaid Cymru, 26–8, 30–2, 145–7
Poitiers, 46, 172
Polydore Vergil, 82, 180
Powel, David, 13, 17, 197
Powell, Edward (Catholic martyr), 190
Powell, Thomas (antiquary), 188
Powys, 8, 36–7, 42, 82
Price, Sir John (Brecon), 17, 132, 162
Price, Joseph Tregelles, 234
Price, Dr. Richard, 235–6
Price, Thomas (Carnhuanawc), 122
Prichard, Vicar Rhys, 99
Principality, 11, 47
Printing, printing-press, 96–7, 98, 130, 132, 142–3, 161, 162–3; see also Welsh books
Propagation Act (1650), 100, 202
Prophecies, prophetic themes, 7, 8, 11, 12, 47, 48, 71–86, 117–8, 129, 134, 171
Protheroe, Dan (musician), 230
Prys, Tomos, 175, 184–5
Pugh, Thomas (author), 82
Pura Wallia, 9, 153
Puritanism, Puritans, 100–1, 212–4
Pwllheli, 42

R

Radnor, 36
Raglan Castle, 49, 52, 60, 61, 62, 155
Rebecca Riots, 167
Recorde, Robert, 187
Red Dragon, 171
Rees, David (Llanelli), 26, 217
Rees, Rice, 123
Reformation, Protestant, 18, 78, 83–4, 91, 95, 96–7, 99, 117–9, 129–31, 132–4, 153, 158–9, 160, 181
Religion in Wales, 87–108
pagan religion, 3, 71–2, 77; conversion to Christianity, 1–2, 3, 7, 8, 18; Celtic Church, 1–3, 9, 15, 18, 23–4, 76–8, 87, 90–2, 109–11; medieval religion, 11–3, 39–41, 42, 62–70, 93–6, 111–7; impact of Reformation, 14, 15, 17–20, 49–50, 83–4, 96–100, 117–20, 130–1, 133–5, 158–9; religion in 17th and 18th centuries, 23–5, 100–3, 135–7, 159–60, 200–16; 19th-century

religion, 25–6, 103–7, 121–3, 140–1, 142–4, 164–5, 167–9, 227–9, 234–5; decline in 20th century, 29, 107–8, 146
Renaissance, 14, 17, 83–4, 90, 95–7, 129–33, 160, 162, 177
Rhigyfarch, 87, 111, 112–4, 116, 125, 126
Rhuddlan, 35, 38
castle, 44, 51, 52, 56, 57, 58, 59, 62
Rhys, the Lord, 42
Rhys ap Gruffydd, of Dynevor, 73, 81
Rhys ap Maredudd, 47
Rhys ap Tewdwr, 35, 36
Rhys ap Thomas, of Dynevor, 74, 182
Rhys, Sir John, 27
Rhys, Morgan John, 234
Rhys, Siôn Dafydd, 132
Richard I, 41
III, 171
Richard, Henry, 234, 235
Richards, Robert, M.P., 147
Richards, Rev. Thomas, 24
Robert, Gruffydd (Milan), 193
Robert of Rhuddlan, 35
Roberts, Prof. Glyn, 74
Roberts, James (printer), 189
Roberts, John, Llanbrynmair, 234
Roberts, Samuel (S.R.), 221
Romans, 2, 4, 91, 134, 213
Rome, Roman Church, 14, 19, 77, 80, 97, 119, 116–7, 122, 124, 157, 159, 179, 181, 190
Rowlands, Henry, 138
Ruthin, 56, 194

S

St. David's, bishop of, 40, 81, 112, 114, 115, 181
church and diocese of, 12, 92, 110, 113, 117–8
St. David's College, Lampeter, 87
St. Dogmael's Abbey, 40, 63, 66, 67, 70, 116
Salisbury, Salusbury, family, 151
Salesbury, William, 98, 131, 132, 161, 188
Salusbury, Sir John, 189, 197
Thomas, 189, 191
Samwell, David, 120
Saunders, Dr. Erasmus, 136
Schools, 91–2, 98, 100, 102–3, 105–6, 136–7, 145–6, 160, 200–16
circulating, 102, 103, 136, 200–16
grammar, 93, 98, 160, 176
Sunday, 102, 136, 141, 144, 215, 219

Scotland, 6, 47, 48, 59, 71, 73, 81, 155, 166
Scots, 14, 147, 160, 192, 193, 195, 196
Scranton, Pa., 225, 230
Shakespeare, William, 117, 186, 189
Shrewsbury, 35, 173, 186, 193
    castle, 50, 56
    guild, 174
    school, 176
Sidney, Robert, 198–9
Singleton Abbey, Swansea, 154
Skenfrith Castle, 51, 53, 54
Smith, Peter, 155
Smith, Sir Thomas, 151
Somerset family, Earls of Worcester, 61, 70, 178
S.P.C.K., 102, 136, 201, 202, 203, 206, 208, 210
Spenser, Edmund, 17, 189
Strata Florida Abbey, 50, 64, 65, 66, 68, 70
Stradling family, 150
    Sir Edward, 198
Stratford-on-Avon, 186, 189
Sulien, Bishop, 87, 92, 93, 112
Swansea, 27, 38, 153, 154

T

Taffy, 119
Taliesin, 2, 71, 81, 127, 137
Talley Abbey, 63, 68, 70
Talsarnau, 222
Teilo, St., 2, 110
Tenby, 187
Thelwall, Edward, 198
Thomas, William (Clerk to Privy Council), 179, 180, 191, 195
Tintern Abbey, 40, 62, 63, 64, 65, 66, 67, 68, 69, 70
Tithe War (N. Wales), 167
Tredegar, 148
Tretower Castle, 51, 53
Trojans, myth of Welsh descent from, 4, 8, 12, 17, 29, 128, 149–50
Tudor family, 14, 17, 18, 49, 81, 85, 86, 190, 192
    Jasper, 72, 74, 172, 177
    Owain, 84, 172; see also Henry VII, Henry VIII

U

University of Wales, 27
United States of America, 25, 165
    Welsh in, 122, 141, 217–36
Urdd Gobaith Cymru, 30

V

Valle Crucis Abbey, 63, 64, 65, 66, 67, 69, 70
Vaughan, H. M., 154
Vaughan, Bishop Richard, 182
Vivian, John Henry, 155
Vortepor, ruler of Dyfed, 1, 2
Vortigern, 3

W

Waleys, Thomas, 94
Wallensis, John, 94
Wallop, Sir Henry, 18–19
Welch Piety, The, 200, 208, 210, 211, 214
Welsh bards, 2–3, 7, 9, 10–11, 17, 20–1, 47, 83, 89, 134, 138, 151, 161, 162, 171, 211; see also Welsh poetry
Welsh Bible and New Testament, 98, 102, 133, 134, 141, 188, 203, 206
Welsh Book of Common Prayer, 98, 132, 188
Welsh books, 20, 25, 121, 132–4, 135–6, 137, 141–2, 143, 146–7, 162–3, 164, 206, 208, 229
Welsh language, 4, 6, 7, 18, 24–6, 30–3, 47, 49, 89, 105–6, 116, 121, 122, 126, 127–9, 130–5, 137–9, 141, 144–7, 159–62, 164–5, 168–9, 180, 187, 193, 194, 197, 201, 204–5, 206, 209–11, 215, 227–31, 233
Welsh Language Society, 32
Welsh laws, 5–6, 10–11, 38–9, 42, 79, 89, 128
Welsh literature, 6, 9, 15, 17, 20–1, 23, 27–8, 83–4, 89, 94–5, 98, 127–9, 134–5, 137–9, 144–5, 147, 161–3; see also Welsh poetry
Welsh periodical press, 25, 121, 142–3, 146–7, 164, 229
Welsh poetry, poets, 5, 6, 7, 10, 11, 14, 21–3, 69, 71–86, 94–5, 116–7, 118, 127–9, 133, 139, 142, 150–1, 161–3, 175, 184–5; see also Welsh bards
Welsh Trust, the, 102, 136, 202, 203
Westminster School, 176
White Castle, 55
Whitford, Richard, 189
Whitland Abbey, 50, 63
Wilkesbarré, 225
William I, 34, 35, 114, 151
    II, 36
    IV, 121
Williams, Judge David (Gwernyfed), 180
Williams, Prof. Gwyn A., 13
Williams, Sir Ifor, 72
Williams, Archbishop John, 61

252

Williams, Moses (scholar), 22
Williams, Sir Roger, 183, 192, 195
Winchester College, 176
Wisconsin, 222, 226, 230
Wolfe, Morgan (royal jeweller), 185
Worcester, 186
Wynn, Sir John of Gwydir, 95, 149
Wynn, Maurice, 198

Y

Y Drych, 229
Yorkists, 48, 60, 172
Young, Archbishop Thomas, 181, 191
Young Wales, 13, 28